Sociocultural Psychology

CW01522182

PA

Series Editor
Tania Zittoun
Institute of Psychology and Education
University of Neuchâtel
Neuchâtel, Switzerland

The Sociocultural Psychology of the Lifecourse book series seeks to further our knowledge of the development of people in their complex sociocultural worlds, both empirically and theoretically. Its sociocultural psychological perspective proposes to account for the development of people as unique persons, with their perspective and subjectivity, within the social and cultural environments that guide them and yet which they can themselves transform. The book series showcases works that provide a complex understanding of development in the lifecourse, contribute to the theorization of the lifecourse and present original data – based on case studies, segments of lives, or trajectories of living. It will also include books which present synthetic theoretical, epistemological or methodological contributions. By documenting the richness of lives and developing the relevant theoretical tools, books in this series will make a unique contribution to sociocultural, developmental psychology, and to the study of the courses of lives.

*   *   *

Series Advisory Editors:
Alex Gillespie
Department of Psychological and Behavioural Science
London School of Economics and Political Science
United Kingdom

Pernille Hviid
Department of Psychology
University of Copenhagen
Denmark

Jaan Valsiner
Department of Communication and Psychology
Aalborg University
Denmark

More information about this series at
http://www.palgrave.com/gp/series/15435

Mariann Märtsin

Identity Development in the Lifecourse

A Semiotic Cultural Approach to
Transitions in Early Adulthood

Mariann Märtsin
School of Natural Sciences and Health
Tallinn University
Estonia

Sociocultural Psychology of the Lifecourse
ISBN 978-3-030-27755-0   ISBN 978-3-030-27753-6   (eBook)
https://doi.org/10.1007/978-3-030-27753-6

Cover illustration: © Maram_shutterstock.com

This Palgrave Macmillan imprint is published by the registered company Springer Nature Switzerland AG.
The registered company address is: Gewerbestrasse 11, 6330 Cham, Switzerland

The original version of this book has been revised, An error in the production process caused the author's affiliation to be corrected into the series editor's affiliation by mistake. This has been corrected in the copyright page and the cover.

To Pille and Ülo
who taught me how to dream and how to work hard to catch my dreams

Series Editor's Preface

Identity Development in the Lifecourse

This book explores the development of young people over time, as they leave their home country, go abroad and define their own goals and interests. It is about people's lives as they unfold, and as such, it narrates stories that could be that of many of us; it is also is a theoretical book, asking fundamental questions about human development. For these two reasons, I am very happy to inaugurate this new series of book on the lifecourse with Mariann Märtsin's monograph.

The aim of this series is to investigate, in depth, the course of lives of people in their sociocultural environment. Although that is not a new question, researchers rarely take the time to fully focus on one person, or a small group of persons, to understand the specificities of the lives they are engaged in, in the times and places in which they live, which present them with specific challenges. Only such focus can enable us to identify the process by which people deal with life: how they understand themselves, their relation to others, how they imagine their future, and how they think that their past led them to their present. Indeed, not only do then people have to solve these issues once, but through time, they change, and their understanding of what is going also does; in the meantime, the environment in which they made their past choices, and the one they will have to face, are themselves in transformation. Therein lies the challenge of a sociocultural psychology of the lifecourse: to rethink psychological theorising in light of the course of a situated life.

In *Identity development in the lifecourse: A semiotic cultural approach to transitions in early adulthood*, Mariann Märtsin gives herself the task of accounting for the lives of eight young people, born in Estonia, who decided to move the UK for their studies. Although this little adventure in people's lives may seem at first sight, anecdotic, it actually enables to reveal the richness and complexity of unfolding young lives in the twenty-first century. This is the strength of this monograph in lifecourse research: to turn a common fact into the site of acute and deep observations and render visible what is not. Mariann Märtsin proposes to consider the changes experienced by these young people as a double movement: a mobility, in geographical space, and a transition—a process of change initiated by ruptures—in the timespan of their lives. This double change engages people's beliefs about themselves, transforms their relationships to their families and friends, brings them to discover their strengths and vulnerabilities, to confront with other's representation of what life should be, and to re-examine their values and goals. The strength of the book is that this enables to build an original theory of identity: rather than being a structure, or a category, or a statement, identity is shown to be a semiotic process, a future-oriented guidance constantly renegotiated in the light of past, current and future experiences. In what follows, I wish to highlight some of the key contributions of this elegant monograph.

Forever, Young

First, topic wise, youth and the extended adulthood has been a preferred topic of psychologists and identity researchers for a long time; a landmark in that field is, of course, the work of Erik Erikson (Erikson, 1968). Since then, societal transformation has led to a double dissolution of the thresholds traditionally bordering adolescence—in it, with the lowering of age of puberty, and the increase of a 'youth' fashion for children—and out of it, with 'youth' conduct admitted now in people all along the lifecourse as lifestyle, family arrangement, professional careers and body-care have been deeply transformed. Whether youth has been simply extended into 'late adolescence' or 'emerging adulthood' or whether adulthood still exists at all or not (Arnett, 2006; Hendry & Kloep, 2007), there is still an effect of 'first time' for many people engaged in their youth—and foremost, this is the time during which, for the first time, they have to engage their symbolic responsibility and define a system of orientation that functions as a moral or personal compass (Schwartz, 2016; Zittoun, 2006, 2007). Over the past ten years, the field of 'youth studies' and 'emerging adulthood' has considerably expanded in social sciences and psychology, with a more clear recognition of the tensions that young people are facing, now coined by authors as specificity to that period in life. Hence, Threadgold conceives young people

> as figures of struggle (Threadgold, 2017), reflexively positioned between the doxic governmental promises—study hard, work hard, the meritocracy will see you prevail—and the everyday reality of precarious labour markets, political upheaval lead by conservative and reactionary forces, and global risks such as climate change. (Threadgold, 2019, p. 5)

Comparably, Schwartz identifies the 'two-faced' nature of the period (which he calls a stage), "a time of great optimism but also great uncertainty, a time of increasing well-being but also characterised by the onset of anxiety and depressive disorders in many people" (Schwartz, 2016, p. 307). In his review, he also notes that predictors of outcomes of that period are parents, peers and identity and that these factors must be related. But how to articulate the demands of the socio-economic environment and people's own need to explore their world, how to take in account the sets of tensions and relations in which people are located and their unique ways of handling with them? How to be a psychologist, studying the psyche, without being blind to the sociocultural environment? This is precisely where the qualitative, processual approach proposed by Märtsin can make her unique contribution, approaching young adults without the preconceptions of current studies (e.g., Côté, 2014), from a more distant, developmental and theoretical stance. From such a perspective, indeed, young adults are people engaged in liminal transitions in the courses of their lives—these have specificities, notably socioculturally defined, yet their development depends on much more general psychological processes.

Student Mobility

The socio-historico-cultural context of the study is the early twenty-first century, a decade after the opening of former 'Eastern' countries to the UK job and study market (Estonia joined the UE in 2004). It is also a period where it became increasingly clear, for young people who want to make a 'career', that a stay abroad is an implicit demand of a certain range of professions, and for longer academic involvement. Of course, these demands apply to a selective part of the population and a certain range of socio-economical domains (Cairns, 2014; Cairns, Cuzzocrea, Briggs, & Veloso, 2017). Also, these demands do not have the same meaning for residents from various European countries; the 'freedom' of moving abroad may have been for many a 'forced push' (Salamońska & Czeranowska, 2019). And these socio-economic factors may still be independent of, or accompanied by, personal life projects and an imagination of places or of oneself in the future (Salazar, 2011). Academic mobility is thus, again, a double-sided experience: if it is, mostly, constructive in terms of experience, training, acquisition of diploma, and so on, it can also be financially grieving (as in student loan), relationally demanding (Schaer, Dahinden, & Toader, 2017), and, as the cases here reveal, affectively difficult. If there is a growing literature examining such mobility from a sociological, geographical, educational or anthropological and clinical perspectives (Saravanan, Alias, & Mohamad, 2017), little is known on how people experience this tension—again, between social guidance and personal needs and aspiration—and deal with it, and little is done to describe and analyse such tension in psychological, theoretical terms—there lies this book's second contribution.

Studying Development

To study development, one has to capture change (Valsiner, 1988, 2007); with a particular care for being consistent with her theoretical approach, Mariann Märtsin can achieve this thanks to a third remarkable feature of her work: her longitudinal, mobile fieldwork. Märtsin, indeed, has followed up with the young adults that became part of her study during one year, interviewing them three times each; she thus could capture, at the scale of a year, how people experienced change: how they anticipated what was about to come on the basis of their past experience, how they experienced these new situations, how they revised their past imagination of the future and how they could now develop new ones. Only such real-time, developmental techniques enable capturing the extreme change-ability of experiences of change (Gillespie & Zittoun, 2010)—especially when people are fully within a transition or, precisely, experiencing the 'zone' of liminality (Stenner, 2017a). In addition, Märtsin displays here methodological creativity—adjusting this longitudinal methodology to the need of a mobile group, thus turning it into a 'mobile method' and including an interesting invitation to draw—which didn't work with all. Case studies, located in the environment of people's real lives, differs from the reassuring, controlled environment of the lab or even the standardised interviews—here, the researcher's flexibility and empathy for these persons were key in co-constructing a narrative of their lives.

A Semiotic Theory of Identity: Meta-Signs and Borders

The fourth, and main, contribution of Mariann Märtsin's book is theoretical: she proposes a new conceptualisation of identity as a semiotic process. Instead of seeing identity as categories (I am an X) or a series of fluctuating positions (I as-an-Y, I as-as-Z), she starts from the fundamental fluidity of our being, conceived from a semiotic perspective, in time. She thus writes (emphasis added):

> I conceptualise identity as a semiotic field, because it includes a wide range of interrelated meanings tied to different aspects of our way of being. I consider it to be a fuzzy field, because we cannot clearly define its perimeter and boundaries, we don't quite know where it starts and where it ends, what belongs to it and what does not. *Importantly, identity as a field of hyper-generalised metasigns regulates our movement into the future, that is our process of becoming.* (Märtsin, p. 38)

Doing so, Märtsin proposes a reconciliation between semiotic approaches to development, which emphasise meaning-making, and identity approaches, which, even in their more performative versions, tend to be more static or to entify processes (Valsiner, 1988). Even more, taking very seriously Vygotsky's idea of higher semiotic—cultural mediation (Zavershneva & van der Veer, 2018), as worked out over the recent years by Valsiner (Valsiner, 2019) and Salvatore (Salvatore, 2016), she conceives of identity as meta-signs—generalisation from experience, which can, ahead of us, guide our conduct towards an imagined future. Yet, these are constantly readjusted, in a dialectical movement, through what is and what could be—which can only ever be guessed, or wished for, again and again. This is beautifully expressed:

> The way I see it human meaning making is thus an ongoing process in which relative stability is created from permanent impermanence, just like the maintenance of the upright body posture and balance is achieved through continuous correction of instantaneous imbalanced moments. (Märtsin, p. 39)

The second part of this proposition is that, within these semiotic processes, the identity dynamics may produce 'border' effects. Such idea is necessary to account for the moments in which people facing change or diversity are drawn to reassess that they are still the same—and nor something else, typically when experiencing ruptures, facing change or otherness (Erikson, 1968; Hviid, 2012). For, after all, feeling 'the same' is as important as changing. Mariann Märtsin understands borders in a semiotic way, as something which can be constantly redrawn: "identity can be conceptualized as a semiotic border-making process, where borders between various others, between self and others and between past, present and future self are constantly drawn and redrawn" (Märtsin, p. 18).

The concept of border is a complex one, imported in cultural psychology through mathematics and conceived in extremely abstract terms (Valsiner, 2014). By doing so, it enables to include phenomena otherwise identified under parent concepts (e.g., boundary, category, limit, etc.), addressing slightly different issues. In this book, Märtsin defines two main types of border: spatial and temporal ones.

In terms of space, she notes that a geographical movement—an actual mobility, or a real (national) border being crossed, may correspond to a variety of more psychological, semiotic work. She identifies what appears to be three subtypes. One, typical for social sciences, is the border brought about when people are confronted with what they perceive as difference, in others: I become part of a 'we' and these people then become part of 'they'. Here, 'border' has a meaning very close to that conceptualised as 'boundary dynamic', or boundary-work, in current social anthropology (Eade, 2013; Lamont & Molnár, 2002; Lamont, Pendergrass, & Pachucki, 2015). In their synthesis of existing work, Lamont and Molnár thus, for instance, distinguish between symbolic and social boundaries:

> Symbolic boundaries are conceptual distinctions made by social actors to categorize objects, people, practices, and even time and space. They are tools by which individuals and groups struggle over and come to agree upon definitions of reality. (…) Social boundaries are objectified forms of social differences manifested in unequal access to and unequal distribution of resources (material and nonmaterial) and social opportunities. (Lamont & Molnár, 2002, p. 168)

Hence, when the young people interviewed by Märtsin suddenly feel that they are 'more' Estonian now in the UK, and 'we' are so different from them, their border-meaning work corresponds to such boundary dynamics. However, being at a higher level of abstraction, the concept of border also affords other, more evanescent uses. Hence, a second modality of border is that taking place between competing meaning fields, for a given person at a specific moment, such as one occurring when a person hesitates to interpret others as 'real' or 'fake' friends; such border zone, Märtsin suggests, is liminal enough to be the zone of potential emergences of new meaning. A third type is the border between the person and her environment; here "border making process [are] a temporary stabilization of the mutually transformative flow between person and environment" (Märtsin, p. 171).

The main temporal border identified by Märtsin is then that constantly taking place "between past and future": "as humans we always make meanings, including meanings about the persons we want to be or become, ahead of time in order to pre-adapt to the unpredictable but anticipated future" (Märtsin, p. 173). Here, border takes a meaning closer to work on phenomena of the proximal zones of development, whether triggered by others or self-generated via inner dialogue and through imagination (Josephs, Valsiner, & Surgan, 1999; Valsiner & van der Veer, 2014; Zittoun & Valsiner, 2016).

Put together, these propositions thus allow Märtsin to see identity as a fluid process, in the making, constantly engaged in defining temporary goals for itself, which act as meta-signs, a form of self-promoter signs. This sense-crunching advance that is life then hits obstacles—the border, when sense-making gets interrupted (as in semantic barriers (Gillespie, 2008)) or suspended, confronting people with ambivalence and uncertainty, which may also trigger the emergence of newness.

In some sense, this intuition of the conceptual potential of 'border' joins the concept of liminality, which has also been analysed as operating in time, space, as well as between facts and fiction, and eventually become disquietingly expanded (Stenner, 2017b). In addition, Märtsin suggests, in a poetic conclusion, these semiotic border work leave traces—knots in the threaded carpet that is one's life, thus creating a unique pattern. Living, one engages these semiotic dynamics that participate in creating the unique melody of one's life (Zittoun et al., 2013).

Towards a General Sociocultural Theory of Development

Thanks to her theoretical propositions, Märtsin makes a series of interesting observations which find echoes in recent and past work, on other case studies, at times addressed with other conceptual tools. In order to indicate possible roads for generalisation across case studies, I wish to pick on two of these facts.

First, Märtsin observes the importance of friends in young people's transitions: there are the friends that support change and transformation towards the new life one is living, and these that block us because they retain us towards what we used to be, or what some think we should be.

One of the interviewees, Mari, thus finds new friends in the UK: "I felt that we think in the same way, that we have similar goals in life, exactly these girls also felt that they want to travel and see the world and experience different things and so on". As Märtsin comments, such friends "represent a voice that strengthens and supports Mari's new self-understandings" (p.114). This, in some ways, goes in the same direction as her observation that these young people's need of social recognition through university success: former good students, they are now exposed to the most demanding programme, in a foreign language, and sometimes to challenging teachers. Here as well, support through peer groups is important; hence, Säde can make the experience of being competent and supported in one of her reading groups (p.132). Altogether, this suggests something not only about the importance of friendship during youth, which is well documented, but something about the importance of peers, or significant others, in order to make sense of new experience. It is perhaps precisely within these safe and trusting relationships that some part of the affective load of the new experiences can be absorbed, named, discussed, and thus, distanced, semioticed: peer groups or reading groups may, in such way, work as 'semiotic chambers', supporting that hard work of thinking and developing.

The importance of such groups to 'detoxicate' difficult and challenging experiences has been documented in very different contexts—inner-youth groups (Heath, 2004), minority students (Walker, 2014), youth at war (Daiute, 2013), refugee experience (Womersley, 2019)—where the importance of affective support, narration and symbolisation has been shown. What seems new here is to connect such observation with a *semiotic* understanding of identity. For if identity is semiotic, and semiotic work is the foremost elaboration of affect that grows in social and cultural interactions (Zavershneva & van der Veer, 2018), then the role of positive social relationships in semiotic identity work is to be underlined. This is a point not to be forgotten in a sociocultural psychology of development: one needs both signs and culture, and significant human relationships, to develop.

Second, Märtsin describes Tania as a young woman who used to go to church every Sunday and was raised in a conservative environment; now in the UK, she is much more freely experimenting what life has to offer. She reports Tania's words:

> All these people that surround you, they take things very easily … If there is a party, then it is a party, if we drink, then we drink, that kind of thing … And I feel I've started to take things more easily as well. I'm not sure yet, if it is right or wrong. Sometimes I feel guilty. How come? Before I would've never had parties like this or something. But now it's like … Sometimes I don't know what's happening to me. (p. 97)

Tania has moved geographically and is brought to new environments and settings, where the cultural subsystem and the social implicit rules are different from the one she is used to and has internalised. She is learning (or socialised) into these social frames; yet these new conducts, in her current proximal spheres of experience, trigger distal experiences, and within them, the voices of distant others—her mother, perhaps, her past values or meta-signs—creating tensions. This intense inner dialogue is thus expressed by her language, with interrogations ('How come?') and contradictions ('But'). More interestingly, she finally states: "I don't know what's happening of me". This kind of utterance expresses this moment of self-realisation: if I am not whom I used to think I was becoming, then what am I? If my fundamental notions of good and bad are shaken—the core of one's system of orientation, where does it go?

Interestingly, we observed almost the same sentence expressed by another young woman ("I don't know what is becoming of me"), far from home, for the first time dating young man although she came from a conservative family—but this time, in the UK during WWII (Zittoun, Aveling, Gillespie, & Cornish, 2012; Zittoun & Gillespie, in press). Whether this says something about young womanhood, or perhaps—and still needs to be documented—about moments of self-realisation during development, needs to be clarified; but the movement, marked by such utterances, is definitely worth mentioning. Indeed, development in the lifecourse, and especially during youth, may especially demand, in some cases, the radical transformation of people's core values, basis of their system of orientation–called the meta-meta-signs. This can be for the best, bringing people to progressive freedom from semiotic constraints internalised along their educational trajectory; it can also be for the worst, when people are brought to extreme actions which force them to change these core values, yet alienate them from their sense of themselves (as, for instance, in children soldiers). Yet even there, from a sociocultural developmental perspective, and with a semiotic approach to identity, one can conceive that development is never final and that there is always a possibility to transform even these core values. In some ways, ethics are at the core of our being—they can be our moral compass, and as such, sometimes, they can be readjusted.

Opening

In the following pages, thus, the reader will accompany young people in their life adventure. With her gentle listening, Mariann Märtsin does not only present us with the ups and downs of their experience, but she also builds a challenging and promising semiotic theory of identity. On the way, youth, mobility and methodology are questioned, but more importantly, a real processual understanding of identity development is proposed. Based on carefully documented case studies, this book thus triggers and nourishes dialogues with other cases of courses of lives. Thanks to both its theoretical propositions and its rich case studies, it thus becomes an important voice in the joint venture of a better understanding of development in the lifecourse.

Rip (Czech Republic)   Tania Zittoun
August 2019

References

Arnett, J. J. (2006). Emerging adulthood in Europe: A response to Bynner. *Journal of Youth Studies, 9*(1), 111–123. https://doi.org/10.1080/13676260500523671

Cairns, D. (2014). *Youth transitions, international student mobility and spatial reflexivity. Being mobile?* London: Palgrave Macmillan.

Cairns, D., Cuzzocrea, V., Briggs, D., & Veloso, L. (2017). *The consequences of mobility: Reflexivity, social inequality and the reproduction of precariousness in highly qualified migration*. Cham: Palgrave Macmillan.

Côté, J. E. (2014). The dangerous myth of emerging adulthood: An evidence-based critique of a flawed developmental theory. *Applied Developmental Science, 18*(4), 177–188. https://doi.org/10.1080/10888691.2014.954451

Daiute, C. (2013). Living history by youth in post-war situations. In K. Hanson & O. Nieuwenhuys (Eds.), *Reconceptualizing children's rights in international development living rights, social justice, translations* (pp. 175–198). Cambridge: Cambridge University Press.

Eade, J. (2013). Crossing boundaries and identification processes. *Integrative Psychological and Behavioral Science, 47*(4), 509–515. https://doi.org/10.1007/s12124-013-9244-0

Erikson, E. H. (1968). *Identity: Youth and crisis*. London: Faber & Faber.

Gillespie, A. (2008). Social representations, alternative representations and semantic barriers. *Journal for the Theory of Social Behaviour, 38*(4), 375–391. https://doi.org/10.1111/j.1468-5914.2008.00376.x

Gillespie, A., & Zittoun, T. (2010). Studying the movement of thought. In A. Toomela & J. Valsiner (Eds.), *Methodological thinking in psychology: 60 years gone astray?* (pp. 69–88). Charlotte, NC: Information Age Publisher.

Heath, S. B. (2004). Risks, rules, and roles: Youth perspectives on the work of learning for community development. In A.-N. Perret-Clermont, C. Pontecorvo, L. Resnick, T. Zittoun, & B. Burge (Eds.), *Joining society: Social interaction and learning in adolescence and youth* (pp. 41–70). Cambridge/New York: Cambridge University Press.

Hendry, L. B., & Kloep, M. (2007). Conceptualizing emerging adulthood: Inspecting the emperor's new clothes? *Child Development Perspectives, 1*(2), 74–79. https://doi.org/10.1111/j.1750-8606.2007.00017.x

Hviid, P. (2012). 'Remaining the same' and children's experience of development. In M. Hedegaard, K. Aronsson, C. Hojholt, & O. Ulvik (Eds.), *Children, childhood, and everyday life: Children's perspectives* (pp. 37–52). Charlotte, NC: Information Age Publishing, Inc.

Josephs, I. E., Valsiner, J., & Surgan, S. E. (1999). The process of meaning construction. Dissecting the flow of semiotic activity. In J. Brandstädter & R. M. Lerner (Eds.), *Action & self-development. Theory and research through the lifespan* (pp. 257–282). Thousand Oaks, CA: Sage.

Lamont, M., & Molnár, V. (2002). The study of boundaries in the social sciences. *Annual Review of Sociology, 28*(1), 167–195. https://doi.org/10.1146/annurev.soc.28.110601.141107

Lamont, M., Pendergrass, S., & Pachucki, M. (2015). Symbolic boundaries. In J. D. Wright (Ed.), *International encyclopedia of the social & behavioral sciences* (2nd ed., pp. 850–855). https://doi.org/10.1016/B978-0-08-097086-8.10416-7

Salamońska, J., & Czeranowska, O. (2019). Janus-faced mobilities: Motivations for migration among European youth in times of crisis. *Journal of Youth Studies*, *0*(0), 1–17. https://doi.org/10.1080/13676261.2019.1569215

Salazar, N. B. (2011). The power of imagination in transnational mobilities. *Identities*, *18*(6), 576–598. https://doi.org/10.1080/1070289X.2011.672859

Salvatore, S. (2016). *Psychology in black and white. The project of a theory driven science.* Charlotte, NC: Information Age Publishing, Incorporated.

Saravanan, C., Alias, A., & Mohamad, M. (2017). The effects of brief individual cognitive behavioural therapy for depression and homesickness among international students in Malaysia. *Journal of Affective Disorders*, *220*, 108–116. https://doi.org/10.1016/j.jad.2017.05.037

Schaer, M., Dahinden, J., & Toader, A. (2017). Transnational mobility among early-career academics: Gendered aspects of negotiations and arrangements within heterosexual couples. *Journal of Ethnic and Migration Studies*, *43*(8), 1292–1307. https://doi.org/10.1080/1369183X.2017.1300254

Schwartz, S. J. (2016). Turning point for a turning point: Advancing emerging adulthood theory and research. *Emerging Adulthood*, *4*(5), 307–317. https://doi.org/10.1177/2167696815624640

Stenner, P. (2017a). Being in the zone and vital subjectivity: On the liminal sources of sport and art. In T. Jordan, K. Woodward, & B. McLure (Eds.), *Culture, identity and intense performativity: Being in the zone* (pp. 10–31). Abingdon, UK: Routledge.

Stenner, P. (2017b). *Liminality and experience. A transdisciplinary approach to the psychosocial.* London: Palgrave Macmillan.

Threadgold, S. (2017). *Youth, class and everyday struggles.* https://doi.org/10.4324/9781317532859

Threadgold, S. (2019). Figures of youth: On the very object of youth studies. *Journal of Youth Studies*, *0*(0), 1–16. https://doi.org/10.1080/13676261.2019.1636014

Valsiner, J. (1988). *Developmental psychology in the Soviet Union* (1st ed.). Bloomington: Indiana University Press.

Valsiner, J. (2007). Developmental epistemology and implications for methodology. In W. Damon & R. M. Lerner (Eds.), *Handbook of child psychology*

(Vol. 1, pp. 166–209). Retrieved from http://onlinelibrary.wiley.com/doi/10.1002/9780470147658.chpsy0104/abstract

Valsiner, J. (2014). *An invitation to cultural psychology.* London: Sage.

Valsiner, J. (2019). *Ornamented lives.* Charlotte, NC: Information Age Publishing.

Valsiner, J., & van der Veer, R. (2014). Encountering the border. In A. Yasnitsky, M. Ferrari, & R. van der Veer (Eds.), *The Cambridge handbook of cultural-historical psychology* (pp. 148–174). https://doi.org/10.1017/CBO9781139028097.009

Walker, D. (2014). *A pedagogy of powerful communication: Youth radio and radio arts in the multilingual classroom* (1st ed.). New York: Peter Lang Publishing Inc.

Womersley, G. (2019). A sociocultural exploration of shame and trauma among refugee victims of torture. In C.-H. Mayer & E. Vanderheiden (Eds.), *The bright side of shame: Transforming and growing through practical applications in cultural contexts* (pp. 103–116). https://doi.org/10.1007/978-3-030-13,409-9_8

Zavershneva, E., & van der Veer, R. (2018). *Vygotsky's notebooks. A selection.* Singapore: Springer.

Zittoun, T. (2006). *Transitions. Development through symbolic resources.* Greenwich, CT: Information Age Publishing.

Zittoun, T. (2007). Symbolic resources and responsibility in transitions. *Young. Nordic Journal of Youth Research, 15*(2), 193–211.

Zittoun, T., Aveling, E.-L., Gillespie, A., & Cornish, F. (2012). People in transitions in worlds in transition: Ambivalence in the transition to womanhood during World War II. In A. C. Bastos, K. Uriko, & J. Valsiner (Eds.), *Cultural dynamics of women's lives* (pp. 59–78). Charlotte, NC: Information Age Publisher.

Zittoun, T., & Gillespie, A. (in press). A sociocultural approach to identity through diary studies. In M. Bamberg, C. Demuth, & M. Watzlawik (Eds.), *Cambridge handbook of identity.* Cambridge: Cambridge University Press.

Zittoun, T., & Gillespie, A. (2015). Integrating experiences: Body and mind moving between contexts. In B. Wagoner, N. Chaudhary, & P. Hviid (Eds.), *Integrating experiences: Body and mind moving between contexts* (pp. 3–49). Charlotte, NC: Information Age Publishing.

Zittoun, T., & Valsiner, J. (2016). Imagining the past and remembering the future: How the unreal defines the real. In T. Sato, N. Mori, & J. Valsiner

(Eds.), *Making of the future: The trajectory equifinality approach in cultural psychology* (pp. 3–19). Charlotte, NC: Information Age Publishing.

Zittoun, T., Valsiner, J., Vedeler, D., Salgado, J., Gonçalves, M., & Ferring, D. (2013). *Human development in the lifecourse. Melodies of living.* Cambridge: Cambridge University Press.

Acknowledgements

This book has been a long time in the making. The research that forms the core of it was conducted more than 10 years ago, in the years 2006–2008. The idea to write this work-up in a book format emerged straight after it was completed. However, life had other plans for me. In the years that followed the completion of this research, I myself experienced repeated mobility that brought me away from Europe and to Australia. My years in Australia taught me a lot about myself, about home and about being away; they taught me about academia and, in many ways, made me the kind of researcher I am today. In addition to that, while living in Australia, I also had the fortune to welcome two brand new members to my family. So for many years, this book was taking shape only in my head. And then in 2018, after 13 years abroad, I moved back home to Estonia with my family. I returned to undertake a research project at Tallinn University, supported by a grant from European Regional Development Fund, and thanks to this I was able to focus only on research for one year and, finally, turn the thoughts about this book into reality.

Many people have helped me to conduct the research and write this book. While their contributions have been invaluable, the failings of this work are only mine. I would not have been able to undertake this work without the wisdom, energy, encouragement and kindness of my PhD supervisor Harry Daniels. I will always be thankful to Harry for not only introducing me to the world of sociocultural research but, in important ways, to the academic world in general. I have also had the fortune to collaborate with Jaan Valsiner whose work has deeply inspired the research presented in this book. But it is Jaan's generosity and support beyond this conceptual influence that I hold so very dear. In addition to this, the thoughts presented in this book have grown out of my participation in the activities of the network of sociocultural researchers across Europe. The discussions in Cambridge and London, in Braga, Toronto and Nanjing, in Athens, Copenhagen, Aalborg and Neuchâtel with Alex Gillespie and Tania Zittoun, Pernille Hviid and Brady Wagoner, Sergio Salvatore, Hala Mahmoud, Lisa Whittaker, Emmilie Aveling and Irini Kadianaki have offered me opportunities to test my ideas with some of the most brilliant minds in cultural psychology. I am also thankful to Katrin Kullasepp for our discussions in Worcester, Cardiff and Tallinn that have helped me to clarify and solidify some of the core ideas presented in this book. I also thank my Queensland University of Technology colleagues, in particular, Melanie White, Erin O'Connor, Areana Eivers, Brooke Andrews, Colette Roos and Trish Obst for welcoming me into their midst and always supporting my work and ideas even if they were sometimes drastically different from theirs. I thank Grace Jackson and Joanna O'Neill and the rest of the team at Palgrave Macmillan for being patient but firm with me during the many years of writing this book.

In many ways, this book is a story of eight amazing young people from Estonia. The current project would not exist without their enormous effort. I hope my analytical lens has not ruined the fascinating richness of their voices and experiences. My own life is richer now that I have known them.

This book would not have become a reality without the emotional and moral support of my family and friends. Riina and Rika have been fantastic in asking the right kinds of questions in the right kinds of moments and simply always being there. The days spent in the home of Giovanna and Renzo, surrounded by their love and care, have been essential in times when I lost focus or hope or when there were simply too many things to worry about. I also owe the experience of completing this book to the endless care, love and support of my parents and sister. I am especially thankful to my mum for looking after my kids when I needed to work. And although my father did not live to see the publication of this book, its publication is, in many ways, a testimony to the wisdom, passion for knowledge, strength and care that he has given to me. And last, I want to thank my closest family, Luca, Sofia and Daniel, for supporting me during the years of conducting the research, thinking about this book and finally writing it. Luca has been with me through it all and, together, we have experienced multiple transitions between home and away and moved into adulthood. I am grateful for his love and patience and for gently pushing me to challenge myself in ways I never would have imagined being able to. And finally, my deepest gratitude goes to Sofia and Daniel who have sometimes generously, sometimes unwillingly donated me the time to write this book. I hope I have made good use of your precious gift.

Contents

1 Introduction: Identity Development, Mobility and Transition to Adulthood   1

2 Identity Development in a Semiotic Cultural Key   23

3 Studying Identity Development: Merging Theory and Phenomenon in the Methods   53

4 Home, Adventure and Belonging   83

5 Reconstructing Relationships   105

6 Competence, Self-confidence and Recognition   125

7 Making Plans   145

8 Conclusion: Moving Forward   167

Correction to: Identity Development in the Lifecourse   C1

References   177

Index   191

List of Figures

Fig. 2.1   Laminal model of sign construction (Modified from Lawrence
& Valsiner, 2003, p. 731)   34
Fig. 3.1   Lisa's timeline drawing   68
Fig. 3.2   Andres's timeline drawing   68

1

Introduction: Identity Development, Mobility and Transition to Adulthood

Identity Development and Meaning-Making

In recent decades identity has become a widely theorised and researched subject in social sciences. It is a complex notion that encompasses a variety of views and ideas all centred around a question "Who am I?" (Brinkmann, 2010). Identity has something to do with identifying with, being the same with something or someone. But as Brinkmann (2010) suggests in our postmodern times, this sameness has become problematic and is difficult to achieve, as the person who is seeking to be someone is always changing, always being on the move. From this follows that identity has also something to do with the sameness within the self across time and space. Questions about changing and remaining are relevant to this meaning of identity. Yet the notion of identity is also closely connected with the notion of agency. Questions about being and becoming, as well as issues of marginalisation and giving voice to those who previously were unseen, unheard or unrecognised, are essential here (Kompridis, 2007).

Many theoretical perspectives to describe and explain the emergence and functioning of identity have been proposed over the years. When

© The Author(s) 2019
M. Märtsin, *Identity Development in the Lifecourse*, Sociocultural Psychology of the Lifecourse, https://doi.org/10.1007/978-3-030-27753-6_1

considering the underlying assumptions of different models in this diverse theoretical landscape, two general perspectives emerge: an individualistic and essentialist view of identity and a constructionist view of identity. In broad terms, the former considers person and context as related, yet onto-logically separated, realms and sees identity as a pregiven entity that exists in the world, therefore, neglecting the need of showing how that entity emerges in the process of human functioning (see, for example, Hogg, Terry, & White, 1995; Phinney, Horenczyk, Liebkind, & Vedder, 2001; Phinney & Ong, 2007; Rudmin, 2009; Stets & Burke, 2000; Stryker & Burke, 2000). In contrast, the constructionist approaches deny the pre-given existence of identity and, instead, direct the attention to the pro-cesses by way of which identity is produced by collective discourses that individuals engage with in their everyday functioning within the society (see, for example, Shi-xu, 2006; Shotter, 2008; Shotter & Gergen, 1989). In fact, these approaches emphasise the many ways in which persons cre-ate identifications, therefore referring to the plurality of identities that are constantly constructed and reconstructed in our everyday functioning in the social world. Dialogical perspectives on self and identity are also close to this view, being interested in the ways how identities become con-structed and reconstructed through our dialogues with real and imagined self and others (Hermans, 2001; Hermans, Kempen, & van Loon, 1992; Hermans, Konopka, Oosterwegel, & Zomer, 2016; Marková, 2003). In general terms then, identity research, as many other topics in social sci-ences, has also been impacted by the shift towards process-oriented approaches in recent years. In accordance with this shift, the conceptuali-sation of identity has increasingly moved from an entity-centred to a process-centred perspective. That is to say, the conceptualisation of iden-tity has moved from understanding identity as a fixed and relatively stable entity that people create based on their interactions with the environment and thereafter carry with them from one context to another, to under-standing identity as a fluid, multiple, fragmented, dialogical, constantly constructed, reconstructed and negotiated process. Hence, the main-stream individualistic and essentialist theories of identity have given space to studies that seek to unpack the processes of identity development while also opening up many new questions about how this process of construc-tion could and should be conceptualised (Brinkmann, 2010).

It is within this plethora of works and conceptual debates on identity that this book is situated. Being motivated by the goal of moving beyond those debates, I go back to the basics and ask what do we actually do when we construct identities and make claims about who we are? In this book, I propose a simple answer to this question: when making claims about our identities, when stating who we are, we construct signs and make meanings. According to the view I put forward in this book, identity is not a special kind of entity, nor is identity development a special kind of psychological process. Rather, I suggest, identity development can be understood as part of a person's ongoing meaning-making process. Identity is, according to this view, a personally significant and highly generalised sign that people construct in order to create a sense of sameness and continuity across time and space and that guides their movement from past through present towards an unpredictable, yet anticipated, future.

In developing this conceptualisation of identity development in this book, I build on recent advances in semiotic cultural psychology and sociocultural studies of the lifecourse and examine the meaning-making processes in relation to the complex interplay between two potentially challenging experiences—mobility and transition to adulthood. I do this by assuming that these situations can create a break—a rupture, in one's normal way of being and thus open up opportunities for exploring how existing meaning structures—hierarchically organised meanings about self, others and the world (see Chap. 2)—are dismantled, abandoned, maintained or modified and new ones created. In other words, I think that the situation of losing one's known and solid grounding and having to rebuild a sense of sameness and continuity is well-suited for examining identity processes in the developmental key.

Studying Developmental Processes

As can be gathered from the above opening, this book focuses on young people's experiences of change as these lead to the creation of new self-understandings. Developmental psychology has traditionally connected the processes of change with the processes of maturation, viewing change as organised, sequential, chronological and universal, and this has led to the creation of many normative, stage-theories of development (see, for example, Erikson, 1968; Levinson, 1986; Marcia, 2002; Piaget & Inhelder, 1969). In this kind of developmental psychology, time is seen in a linear, sequential and causal manner as a unit that measures the intervals and degrees of difference between events and states (Valsiner, 2001). In contrast to this, Kloep and Hendry (2011) suggest it does not make sense to describe human development by referring to "'stages' because in our 'movement' through the life course we are advancing, regressing, developing in some domains and not others; in a sense ever-becoming and never arriving!" (p. 54). They argue that instead of creating normative labels based on chronological age, developmental psychology should focus on analysing mechanisms and processes that underlie human development in general. In a similar vein, Valsiner (2001) points out that using chronological and sequential time in the exploration of development makes human experience seem stable and static and allows describing entities and forms of the past as these have already emerged, while offering little for understanding the dynamic and future-oriented nature of human development. Instead, he suggests that recognising the irreversible nature of time and taking into account the ever-present novelty in human experience might be a better starting point for developmental psychology.

This future-oriented process view of development is adopted in this book too. When examining identity processes as part of general meaning-making processes, the focus is on the ways in which these processes emerge and unfold—the dilemmas that keep the development going and the dialogues between different meanings that are fuelling the change. The signs about self, others and the world that are created in this process are seen as products of this ongoing meaning-making. They are seen as a temporarily created and fixed meaning that emerges in order to be re-interpreted and re-created in the next moment in the never-ending cycle of unfolding meaning-making (Salvatore, 2018). This focus on the process of meaning-making thus allows asking questions about the ways in which the change unfolds and about the kinds of intermediate forms or patterns of feeling, thinking and acting that are created as a result of this, instead of fixing these forms and patterns as essential and final products or endpoints in a stage of development. In short, the focus of this book is not on describing stages of development but rather on explaining how transitions from one way of being to another occur in the human lifecourse.

Conceptualising Transitions

The concept of 'transitions' is another widely used term in social sciences. In developmental psychology, it usually signifies the movement from one developmental stage to another, being linked to the chronological age and referring to the time it takes to pass through life stages (see, for example, Levinson, 1986). In sociology and especially in youth research it is often used specifically in relation to the timing and duration of the passage into adulthood (Heinz, 2009). In relation to the latter, it is argued that while the timing of transitions used to be defined by age, these markers have lost their value in the last few decades, as the borders between all phases of life have become fuzzy, less age-dependent and more related to individual choices and decisions. In line with these macro-level shifts, Heinz (2009) suggests viewing transitions not as self-contained phases of life but rather as components of people's lifecourses that connect "social time and space with individual biographies and the sequence of life events" (p. 4). In other words, he sees transitions as "time-dependent passages of individuals between life spheres" (p. 4) that are embedded in historical times, influenced by social circumstances and events and shaped by social relationships and networks. This focus allows viewing transitions as emerging through the complex interplay between individual agency and social structures, resulting in multiple, heterogeneous and non-linear pathways into adulthood (see also below).

In semiotic cultural psychology and sociocultural studies of the lifecourse that have informed the work presented in this book (Zittoun et al., 2013), the concept of transitions also captures the complex and dynamic interplay between person and environment, with the specific focus on how this intertwinement occurs as people move physically and in their imagination between various environments and as a result of this movement experience change and development in their life. In this conceptualisation, it is not only the person that changes and develops through the interaction with the (new) environment; the environment too undergoes transformations, and person and environment are seen as mutually transformative. Importantly though, the focus is not on the moment of change or the result of this change but rather on the experiences of simultaneously changing and remaining the same (Crafter, Maunder, & Soulsby, 2019). For, as Kloep and Hendry (2011) argue, it is impossible to determine when a transition starts and when it ends and what exactly are its results.

In using the term 'transition' in this book, I thus build on Zittoun's (2012) work, who suggests that our everyday functioning is punctured by moments when a normal flow of being becomes temporarily interrupted by a significant life-event. We can call this moment a rupture, a critical moment or a turning point, but effectively, it is a break from existing ways of being that pushes us to question who we are, how we got there and how can we move forward from it. Rupture and transition thus emerge as twin concepts, where transition follows the rupture and signifies the processes of transformation through which the change is made sense of and new ways of being are established (Zittoun, 2012). There is no one way how transitions can be experienced but rather the individual experiences are varied and complex, sometimes being sudden and intense, other times emerging as elongated, multiphasic or even stalled (Crafter et al., 2019). Furthermore, transitional experiences are not unique to a specific period in the lifecourse; rather, transitions are linked to everyday events that are experienced as having an impact and being influential to the ways we conduct our lives and make sense of our experiences. It is argued that transitional experiences typically challenge our sense of self and identity, for they trouble our lives and make us question who we are, how we are situated in relation to others, and make us wonder where we are heading. In short, transitions in this book are understood as "shifts in identity as a response to periods of uncertainty" (Maunder, Cunliffe, Galvin, Mjali, & Rogers, 2013, p. 139).

Transition to Adulthood

While the conceptualisation of transition used in this book does not link it directly to a specific period in the human lifecourse, some transitions are nevertheless related to certain life stages and events or normative and quasi-normative shifts in life (Crafter et al., 2019; Kloep & Hendry, 2011). In this book, the focus will be on those transitional experiences that occur during the journey towards adulthood.

The transition from adolescence to adulthood is a critical period of life where many decisions about future trajectories in areas of education, work and family are made and independence from one's family of origin is established (Benson, 2014). In the past few decades, the landscape of transition to adulthood has drastically changed as the key contexts of education, labour market experiences and patterns of dependency have gone through significant transformations, impacting ways in which young people conduct their lives (Furlong, 2009). As a result of these changes, the number of young people who follow the traditional normative pathway from school completion to stable career, offering economic independence and enabling the move into marriage and parenthood, is rapidly decreasing. Instead, young people spend a greater proportion of their lives on education and take up employment opportunities that are very different from those experienced by their parents and grandparents. Benson (2014) suggests that the reasons for these shifts are manyfold but globalisation and economic restructuring, gender revolution and the increasing availability of educational opportunities together with higher educational aspirations and expectations are among the many factors that have destabilised and disrupted the compressed and rapid transition to adulthood that was characteristic of the mid-twentieth century. He contends that due to these and other structural, economic and cultural changes transition to adulthood today is characterised by four major trends: (1) the transition has lengthened as it takes longer for young people to pass through school and further education and to secure a job that can support a family; (2) choices and opportunities are increasingly dependent on family background, creating increased economic inequality among young adults; (3) marriage and parenthood are postponed and for less advantaged young people are increasingly decoupled; and (4) traditional work-family gender roles have begun to unravel creating new opportunities and challenges for families.

As the social norms and cultural scripts about 'proper adulthood' have loosened, institutionalised pathways have eroded and opportunities to establish economic independence through stable and well-paid job have become less available, the transition to adulthood has become destandardised, heterogeneous and non-linear (Thomson et al., 2002). It is suggested that there is no one proper way of becoming an 'adult' anymore but many idiosyncratic ways of establishing independence in some areas or for certain periods of life, while remaining dependent in some other areas or for other periods. Research evidence points to the 'yo-yo biographies' of young people who switch between life stages and phases and feel young and adult simultaneously (du Bois-Reymond, 2009). As Heinz (2009) contends: "Today, becoming adult requires the coordination of multiple transitions and the construction of biographical continuity in view of discontinuities, reversals and detours" (p. 7).

Some have argued that the situation where the pathway into adulthood is less socially and culturally structured and destandardised has created increased choice and flexibility for young people to construct their lives (Beck & Beck-Gernsheim, 2002; du Bois-Reymond, 2009). Individual agency and ability to make 'good choices' has thus become paramount. As Heinz (2009) suggests: "Young generations are expected to self-direct their decisions regarding education, training and employment in order to become flexible participants in volatile labour markets. They must identify the most promising pathways to adult independence and navigate multiple transitions with uncertain outcomes" (p. 5). The possibility to choose thus comes with the pressure to make the 'right decision' at the 'right time', a pressure that not all young adults are equipped to handle.

In the area of developmental psychology, Jeffrey Jensen Arnett (2000) has argued that the lack of institutional structure for the transition to adulthood has created a new developmental stage in human lifespan between adolescence and young adulthood that extends from late teens through the twenties. He suggests that this new developmental stage—emerging adulthood—is demographically and psychologically distinct

(Tanner & Arnett, 2011). Its demographic distinctness stems from the delayed school-to-work transitions and postponed entries into marriage and parenthood. Its subjective and psychological distinctness is related to the differences between emerging adults and younger or older individuals in terms of personality, cognitive and neurological development, physical and mental health, emotional development and relationships with significant others. Changes in social relationships are particularly important in emerging adulthood when shift towards accelerated independence occur and individuals recentre, "shifting their primary involvements away from contexts that supported dependence (e.g., families, schools) to contexts of adulthood, which nourish adult interdependence (e.g., peer and intimate relationships, careers, community)" (Tanner & Arnett, 2011, p. 22). Arnett further suggests that this stage is characterised by five features: "(1) seeking identity, (2) experiencing instability, (3) focusing on self-development, (4) feeling in-between adolescence and adulthood, and (5) optimistically believing in many possible life pathways" (Tanner & Arnett, 2011, p. 15). It is thus seen as a moratorium from adult roles and responsibilities and entails extensive exploration and experimenting in the areas of education, work and partnership. Arnett suggests that as young people are freed from normative pressures to move into adulthood in a particular manner, they have more agency over choosing the pathway that is most suitable and rewarding for them (Arnett, Kloep, Hendry, & Tanner, 2011; Tanner & Arnett, 2009).

While widely referred to in developmental psychology, Arnett's conceptualisation of emerging adulthood has also received significant criticism in terms of its conceptual and methodological basis (Côté, 2014; Kloep & Hendry, 2011) and its empirical evidence base (Bynner, 2005; Hendry & Kloep, 2010). Overall, his approach has been criticised for failing to consider the familial, social and cultural constraints that shape young people's abilities to choose and construct their lives, for the opportunities and options to delay adult roles and responsibilities may not be available for all young people, but a viable option only for those who come from most advantaged backgrounds. These are the young people who have the social support and economic resources to extend their transition to adulthood by investing in education and exploring their career options before moving into partnership and parenthood. However, these opportunities are significantly more restricted for young people from disadvantaged backgrounds, who postpone partnership and parenthood because of insufficient educational preparation, instable employment prospects and economic instability. For them, emerging into adulthood is stressful not because there is too much choice but because they lack choice in terms of their social, relational, and/or occupational opportunities and skills (Hendry & Kloep, 2011). It is thus suggested that the choices in early adulthood are still largely dependent on structural social factors together with family and community bonds and making generalisations about this 'new' developmental stage and considering it to be a universal phenomenon misses the variations that exist within individuals, groups and across cultural contexts (Bynner, 2005).

In the current book, the concept of emerging adulthood is used simply as a descriptive term referring to the transition period between adolescence and early adulthood (Côté, 2014). It is used interchangeably with other terms referring to the same period, such as 'early adulthood' and 'young adulthood', and the group of individuals experiencing it, such as 'young adults' and 'young people'. The participants in the study discussed in this book are all postponing entry into partnership and parenthood due to the investments they are making into their education. They are all experimenting with various roles and exploring different career and employment options. Yet, at the same time, a number of them are also making serious commitments and taking on significant responsibilities in terms of independent living away from home in another country. As will be discussed later in the book, many of them are thus making sense of themselves as being an adult and not-yet-an-adult at the same time. And while their experiences may resemble the ways in which Arnett has characterised the stage of emerging adulthood, conceptually, this stage-approach is inconsistent with the perspective developed in this book, that is first and foremost interested in exploring the processes and mechanisms of meaning-making, including identity development, that underlie human development. While the transition into adulthood may bring up many significant experiences and turning points in one's developmental pathway that offer unique opportunities to explore these processes, they are nevertheless seen as universal, describing human development in general terms and not being specifically related to the period between adolescence and early adulthood.

Being on the Move

In addition to the developmental context of transitioning into adulthood, the case studies described in this book are also situated within the context of mobility. It has been suggested that the mobility of people, things and ideas has become the central fact of our contemporary lives (Büscher, Urry, & Witchger, 2010; Cresswell, 2010; Urry & Grieco, 2012). And this is not only because the physical travel has become considerably easier and significantly intensified in recent decades. For as Elliott and Urry (2010), propose mobility does not only entail the corporeal travel of people for work, leisure, family life, pleasure, migration or escape, but it also involves physical movement of objects to producers, consumers and retailers, imaginative travel, virtual travel and communicative travel via various technologies. Tim Cresswell (2010) too suggests that mobility is not only about the physical movement of people or objects but is intertwined with various ways of experiencing and making sense of this movement. He suggests that mobility should be understood as an entanglement of physical movement (i.e., travel from point A to point B), the representations of movement that gives it shared meaning (e.g., travel understood as adventure or as a burden) and the experienced and embodied practice of movement (e.g., travel experienced as a thrilling or nerve-wrecking). Cresswell suggests that these meaningful entanglements have personal and collective histories and are not separated from broader social and societal practices, being instead produced by social relations that involve the distribution and production of power while also producing these social relations. Seen in this way, mobility is clearly not something that characterises only societal mobility systems, that involve travel, tourism, transport and communications, but affects also the ways in which lives are lived, experienced and understood and the ways personhood and identities are constructed (Elliott & Urry, 2010).

These ideas have influenced the ways in which mobility and its impact on identity development is understood in this book. Following this line of thinking, I turn away from looking at the study participants' migration to the UK as a unique, once-in-a-lifetime settlement into a new cultural context and rather seek to describe what it means for individuals to move between imagined, virtual or real places, institutions and relationships. I aim to unpack what it means for the young adults to move in these complex ways, what they gain and what they lose through that movement, what kind of constraints and boundaries these movements create for their meaning-making and what kind of affordances and opportunities these movements offer for them.

In exploring these movements of human minds between imagined and real societies, cultural systems, institutions and relationships, I build on semiotic cultural psychology that sees human meaning-making as working through its connections and interdependency with other meaning-making systems—other minds—and available cultural resources (Valsiner, 2007). Human meaning-making is fundamentally hooked into the meaning-making of others and the world around us and mobility creates a unique situation for its functioning. For mobility can be seen as an experience that ruptures one's ordinary flow of being and opens up a period of transition where old structures of meaning are re-examined and new ones established in order to respond more effectively to the callings of new environments (Aveling & Gillespie, 2008; de Abreu & Hale, 2011; Kadianaki, 2009; Märtsin & Mahmoud, 2012). In this sense, moving between societies and cultural systems entails both physical and semiotic encounters with others and othernesses and requires repositioning oneself in relation to this alterity (Gillespie, Kadianaki, & O'Sullivan-Lago, 2012). It is assumed that these ruptures and transitions occur irrespective of the kind of mobility (or immobility) experienced: imagined or real, temporary or permanent, short- or long-term, repeated or uni-directional, blocked or encouraged, forced or voluntary (Levitan, 2019; Zittoun, Levitan, & Cangiá, 2018). The case studies discussed in this book allow exploring several of these forms of mobility. While all the students where making study visits to the UK with the aim of returning to Estonia in the future, some of them did this after experiencing several previous moves across countries (i.e., repeated mobility), some moved for a relatively short period of time (e.g., six months or one year), and some moved for a longer period (e.g., three or four years). None of them thought about their move to the UK as a permanent migration at the time of arrival and all of them moved back and forth between home and away during the study period, with one participant moving permanently back home after six months of living in the UK but planning to move away again in the near future. These differences in mobility patterns—as will become evident in the book—impacted the ways in which they experienced and made sense of their experiences and themselves in relation to these. However, for all of them, moving away from home and, at the same time, also moving towards adulthood, brought up questions about the future and, for many, the experience of being on the move complicated the attempt to make plans and imagine their way forward into the future. This seemed to be particularly challenging for the older participants in this study who experienced repeated mobility while also starting to make plans about settling down, for they had to settle down while maintaining the readiness to move again in the anticipated future (see also Levitan, 2019). Building on this empirical basis, the future-orientedness of human conduct and meaning-making and the human propensity to make plans for the unpredictable but anticipated future will emerge as a critical theme throughout the book as life-goal construction is seen to go hand in hand with identity development.

Reconstructing Complex Life-Trajectories

The conceptual model of identity development introduced in the book is brought to life by discussing the experiences of a group of young adults, striving to make sense of their lives and construct a sense of sameness and continuity beyond the ruptures of travelling through different sociocultural worlds and institutions and simultaneously moving towards adulthood. The book provides an opportunity to journey with eight young adults as they embark on their developmental journeys into adulthood, dealing with issues that matter most to them: home, adventure and belonging, social relationships, recognition and future planning. Although the semi-longitudinal study that underpins the book and provides its empirical basis was conducted more than a decade ago, the issues that the young people grapple with and the experiences they seek to make sense of continue to be relevant also today. Furthermore, as the aim of this book is first and foremost to make theoretical generalisations about the processes of identity development, then the analytic tools that are illustrated and advanced through the case studies are meant to go beyond this specific empirical context of time and space and instead explain how the processes of meaning-making occur in general terms as part of our development across the lifecourse.

The lives of the eight young adults who will be discussed in this book are obviously complex and multifaceted and in line with the conceptual underpinnings of this work, capturing this complexity is one of the aims of this book. Nevertheless, in order to develop some of the key theoretical ideas the case studies will be discussed through various broad themes that inevitably loses some of that complexity. At the same time, it allows exploring some commonalities and differences across the eight cases and highlights ideas that can be generalised beyond the specifics of these.

In this book, I have chosen to focus on themes that were most commonly discussed by the young people. And while each theme is unpacked by referring to two case studies, they were picked up and referred to also by others. There are some predictable topics, such as intimate relationships or employment that the reader will not find in a separate chapter. This is not to mean that these topics were not relevant for the group of young people participating in this study. On the contrary, many of them experienced the beginning and ending of significant romantic relationships during the study period and many of them were discussing their previous, current or anticipated future employment opportunities. These topics will, therefore, emerge throughout the chapters, in relation to the past relationships or employment opportunities that were left behind when moving away from home or as future relationships or careers that are imagined and longed for in relation to the future home and sense of belonging. The theme of intimate relationships also emerges in the chapter about reconstructed relationships as social ties that simultaneously trigger and support transitions, while the topic of employment emerges strongly in the chapter about planning, as a future signpost in relation to which many tensions and worries in the present are experienced. As such, these themes illustrate the complexity of young people's life experiences and the difficulties in holding these apart and neatly dividing them into discreet themes to be discussed in separate chapters.

In unpacking these various themes in this book, I have tried to bring examples from all the eight case studies. However, there is one case—Lisa—that has not been discussed in length in any of the chapters. This is not because her case was somehow different and did not provide insights about any of the themes covered in the book. On the contrary, her case provided fruitful input for developing many of the themes, especially those related to the reconstruction of relationships and regaining self-confidence after the rupture of moving into a new educational environment. Furthermore, Lisa's case was unique amongst the eight in terms of the opportunities it provided for me to reflect on and think through some of the methodological challenges encountered in this study (see also Märtsin, 2017). Although her case is not explicitly discussed, Lisa is very much part of this book, as her journey has shaped my analytic lens and has thus been woven into the thematic and conceptual threads developed in this book.

Structure of the Book

This book is divided into eight chapters. This opening chapter has introduced some of the key concepts used in this book, such as identity, development and transitions, and started to explain how these concepts can be viewed from semiotic cultural perspective. It has also placed the research study discussed in the book in relation to two interlinked contexts—transition to adulthood and mobility. By discussing the complexities of transitioning into adulthood in contemporary societies and considering the notion of 'emerging adulthood', the chapter has placed the case studies in relation to contemporary debates in sociology and youth studies and in mainstream developmental psychology. The chapter has also explained how mobility is conceptualised in this book and briefly considered the different forms of mobility that were experienced by the eight young people whose lives form the core of this book.

Chapter 2 is dedicated to conceptual matters as I provide an overview of the most important conceptual tools that have been used to develop this study and have also been refined and advanced through the empirical material collected. By introducing the various concepts and ideas, I move towards the central idea put forward in this book. Namely, that identity development can be understood as part of our ongoing meaning-making process through which signs about who we are, have been and are becoming, get created. I introduce the idea that identity can be conceptualised as a field of hyper-generalised meta-signs that become activated in moments of rupture. In moving towards those central ideas, I discuss several underlying conceptual assumptions, including the inseparability of person and environment, process-orientation, semiotic mediation, irreversibility of time and future-orientation of human meaning-making, building on the contemporary frameworks of semiotic cultural psychology.

These underlying assumptions will be briefly revisited in Chap. 3, where the methodological approach used in the study will be introduced. It builds on Valsiner's (2017) notion of methodology cycle that is seen as a dynamic intertwinement between the theoretical assumptions of the researcher, the way the phenomenon is understood and the manner in which data collection methods are constructed. I explain how methods cannot be seen as stand-alone tools of data collection, but rather should be understood as a purposefully constructed sub-part of methodology that works as a cycle. I will describe the oscillations between theoretical assumptions and the conceptualisation of the phenomenon that have led to the creation of the methods used in this study. In this chapter, I also describe the main steps of the data analysis and give a brief overview of all the study participants and their recruitment and consider the unique position of myself as a researcher and the ways it has impacted the research process.

Chapters 4, 5, 6, and 7 will focus on the four themes that are unpacked in this book through the eight case studies. In Chap. 4, the focus will be on the theme of mobility as I discuss how the dialectics of home and away are activated by the movement away from home that pushes us to reconsider our various ways of being and belonging to home and homeland. These themes are unpacked in this chapter by drawing upon examples from two case studies—Säde and Tania. The case of Säde allows examining the ways in which meanings about belonging to a specific ethnic group are challenged, suspended and reconstructed in relation to the experience of moving away from home and being away from the home community. The case of Tania allows exploring how the adventure away from home and the journey into adulthood can become intertwined and create the simultaneous identities of a child and of an adult. With the help of these case studies, I start to unpack the idea that identity development can be conceptualised as a semiotic border-making process that involves different ways of drawing and redrawing borders between different others, between self and others, and within the self.

Chapter 5 focuses on the theme of relationships, with a particular focus on friendships. The chapter builds on two case studies—Mari and Eva—that together show how the movement between sociocultural environments creates challenges for identity development that are both supported and challenged by the relationships with peers. Mari's case suggests that, sometimes, this leads to initial distancing from or even abandoning of the existing relationships in favour of the newly acquired social networks, while Eva's experiences suggest that it can lead to the strengthening of existing relationships as well as the creation of new ones in light of new experiences and related self-understandings. The micro-level analysis of the dynamics of meaning-making related to the two case studies enables exploring how young adults' relationships with their friends simultaneously trigger self-explorations and provide semiotic resources for managing these in the context of mobility.

In Chap. 6, I turn to the theme of educational transitions, as I consider how self-confidence and sense of competence become ruptured in the process of transitioning into a new educational environment. The chapter builds on two case studies—Säde and Kersti—whose experiences suggest that students do not enter universities in isolation from their social and cultural backgrounds and personal histories but instead come being embedded in a complex web of connections with real and imaginary others, from who they expect to receive recognition to their chosen ways of seeing themselves and creating pathways into the future. Both case studies point to the importance of real and imagined others in providing recognition for one's experiences from the past, present and for the future and through that supporting or challenging the development of the sense of identity in a new educational environment.

In Chap. 7, I conclude the exploration of the themes developed in this book by focusing on the issue of planning. In many ways, the idea that human conduct is always oriented towards the future runs through all the chapters and all the case studies in this book. However, in this last chapter, I consider the unique challenges that are presented for planning and movement into the future by the experience of being on the move and not knowing where and with whom one will be. I will discuss two case studies—Andres and Nora—who both have experienced repeated mobility and for whom the issue of making plans is thus most pronounced. Furthermore, the case of Andres, who is the oldest and the only male participant in this study, offers a unique opportunity to examine the tensions related to the pairing of transition to adulthood with repeated mobility in terms of settling down and imaging one's own family.

The concluding chapter brings together the main ideas discussed in the book and articulates the contributions to the sociocultural study of human development in the lifecourse and to the field of identity research this book has made. It returns to the idea that identity development can be seen as part of the ongoing meaning-making process. In particular, it comes back to the idea that identity can be conceptualised as a semiotic border-making process, where borders between various others, between self and others and between past, present and future self are constantly drawn and redrawn. In this chapter, it is argued that identity development involves crossing and maintaining, creating and dismantling borders across two dimensions: spatial borders between self and others and temporal borders between past and future. The chapter discusses how these ideas could be advanced in future theorising and research.

References

Arnett, J. J. (2000). Emerging adulthood: A theory of development from late teens through the twenties. *American Psychologist, 55*(5), 469–480.

Arnett, J. J., Kloep, M., Hendry, L. B., & Tanner, J. L. (2011). *Debating emerging adulthood: Stage or process.* New York: Oxford University Press.

Aveling, E. L., & Gillespie, A. (2008). Negotiating multiplicity: Adaptive asymmetries within second-generation Turks' 'society of mind'. *Journal of Constructivist Psychology, 21*(3), 200–222.

Beck, U., & Beck-Gernsheim, E. (2002). *Individualization: Institutionalized individualism and its social and political consequences.* London: Sage.

Benson, J. (2014). Transition to adulthood. In A. Ben-Arieh, F. Casas, I. Frønes, & J. Korbin (Eds.), *Handbook of child well-being* (pp. 1763–1783). Dordrecht: Springer.

Brinkmann, S. (2010). Character, personality, and identity: On historical aspects of human subjectivity. *Nordic Psychology, 62*(1), 65–85.

Büscher, M., Urry, J., & Witchger, K. (Eds.). (2010). *Mobile methods*. London: Routledge.

Bynner, J. (2005). Rethinking the youth phase of the life-course: The case for emerging adulthood? *Journal of Youth Studies, 8*(4), 367–384. https://doi.org/10.1080/13676260500431628

Côté, J. E. (2014). The dangerous myth of emerging adulthood: An evidence-based critique of a flawed developmental theory. *Applied Developmental Science, 18*(4), 177–188. https://doi.org/10.1080/10888691.2014.954451

Crafter, S., Maunder, R., & Soulsby, L. (2019). *Developmental transitions: Exploring stability and change through the lifespan*. London and New York: Routledge.

Cresswell, T. (2010). Towards a politics of mobility. *Environment and Planning D: Society and Space, 28*, 17–31. https://doi.org/10.1068/d11407

de Abreu, G., & Hale, H. (2011). Trajectories of cultural identity development of young immigrant people: The impact of family practices. *Psychological Studies, 56*(1), 53–61. https://doi.org/10.1007/s12646-011-0061-6

du Bois-Reymond, M. (2009). Models of navigation and life management. In A. Furlong (Ed.), *Handbook of youth and young adulthood. New perspectives and agendas* (pp. 31–38). New York: Routledge.

Elliott, A., & Urry, J. (2010). *Mobile lives*. New York: Routledge.

Erikson, E. H. (1968). *Identity. Youth and crisis*. New York: W.W. Norton & Co.

Furlong, A. (Ed.). (2009). *Handbook of youth and young adulthood. New perspectives and agendas*. New York: Routledge.

Gillespie, A., Kadianaki, I., & O'Sullivan-Lago, R. (2012). Encountering alterity: Geographic and semantic movements. In J. Valsiner (Ed.), *The Oxford handbook of culture and psychology* (pp. 695–709). Oxford: Oxford University Press.

Heinz, W. A. (2009). Youth transitions in an age of uncertainty. In A. Furlong (Ed.), *Handbook of youth and young adulthood. New perspectives and agendas* (pp. 3–13). New York: Routledge.

Hendry, L. B., & Kloep, M. (2010). How universal is emerging adulthood? An empirical example. *Journal of Youth Studies, 13*(2), 169–179. https://doi.org/10.1080/13676260903295067

Hendry, L. B., & Kloep, M. (2011). Lifestyles in emerging adulthood: Who needs stages anyway? In J. J. Arnett, M. Kloep, L. B. Hendry, & J. L. Tanner (Eds.), *Debating emerging adulthood: Stage or process?* (pp. 77–104). Oxford: Oxford University Press.

Hermans, H. J. M. (2001). The dialogical self: Toward a theory of personal and cultural positioning. *Culture & Psychology, 7*(3), 243.

Hermans, H. J. M., Kempen, H. J., & van Loon, R. (1992). The dialogical self: Beyond individualism and rationalism. *American Psychologist, 47*(1), 23–33. https://doi.org/10.1037/0003-066X.47.1.23

Hermans, H. J. M., Konopka, A., Oosterwegel, A., & Zomer, P. (2016). Fields of tension in a boundary-crossing world: Towards a democratic organization of the self. *Integrative Psychological and Behavioral Science*, 1–31. https://doi.org/10.1007/s12124-016-9370-6

Hogg, M. A., Terry, D. J., & White, K. M. (1995). A tale of two stories: A critical comparison of identity theory with social identity theory. *Social Psychology Quarterly, 58*(4), 255–269.

Kadianaki, I. (2009). Dramatic life courses: Migrants in the making. In *Dynamic process methodology in the social and developmental sciences* (pp. 477–492). Retrieved from https://doi.org/10.1007/978-0-387-95922-1_21

Kloep, M., & Hendry, L. B. (2011). A systemic approach to the transitions to adulthood. In J. J. Arnett, M. Kloep, L. B. Hendry, & J. L. Tanner (Eds.), *Debating emerging adulthood: Stage or process?* (pp. 53–76). Oxford: Oxford University Press.

Kompridis, N. (2007). Struggling over the meaning of recognition: A matter of identity, justice, or freedom? *European Journal of Political Theory, 6*(3), 277–289. https://doi.org/10.1177/1474885107077311

Levinson, D. J. (1986). A conception of adult development. *American Psychologist, 41*, 3–13. https://doi.org/10.1037/0003-066X.41.1.3

Levitan, D. (2019). The art of living in transitoriness: Strategies of families in repeated geographical mobility. *Integrative Psychological & Behavioral Science, 53*, 258–282. https://doi.org/10.1007/s12124-018-9448-4

Marcia, J. E. (2002). Identity and psychosocial development in adulthood. *Identity: An International Journal of Theory and Research, 2*(1), 7–28.

Marková, I. (2003). Constitution of the self: Intersubjectivity and dialogicality. *Culture & Psychology, 9*(3), 249–259.

Märtsin, M. (2017). Beyond verbal narratives: Using timeline images in the semiotic cultural study of meaning making. *Integrative Psychological and Behavioral Science*. https://doi.org/10.1007/s12124-017-9409-3

Märtsin, M., & Mahmoud, H. (2012). Never at home? Migrants between societies. In J. Valsiner (Ed.), *The Oxford handbook of culture and psychology* (pp. 730–745). Oxford: Oxford University Press.

Maunder, R. E., Cunliffe, M., Galvin, J., Mjali, S., & Rogers, J. (2013). Listening to student voices: Student researchers exploring undergraduate experiences of university transition. *Higher Education, 66*(2), 139–152. https://doi.org/10.1007/s10734-012-9595-3

Phinney, J. S., Horenczyk, G., Liebkind, K., & Vedder, P. (2001). Ethnic identity, immigration, and well-being: An interactional perspective. *Journal of Social Issues, 57*(3), 493–510.

Phinney, J. S., & Ong, A. D. (2007). Conceptualization and measurement of ethnic identity: Current status and future directions. *Journal of Counseling Psychology, 54*(3), 271.

Piaget, J., & Inhelder, B. (1969). *The psychology of the child*. New York: Basic Books.

Rudmin, F. (2009). Constructs, measurements and models of acculturation and acculturative stress. *International Journal of Intercultural Relations, 33*(2), 106–123.

Salvatore, S. (2018). Culture as dynamics of sense-making. A semiotic and embodied framework for socio-cultural psychology. In J. Valsiner (Ed.), *Cambridge handbook of culture and psychology* (pp. 35–48). Cambridge: Cambridge University Press.

Shi-xu. (2006). Mind, self and consciousness as discourse. *New Ideas in Psychology, 24*(1), 63–81.

Shotter, J. (2008). *Conversational realities revisited: Life, language, body and world*. Chagrin Falls, OH: Taos Institute.

Shotter, J., & Gergen, K. J. (1989). *Texts of identity*. London: Sage Publications.

Stets, J. E., & Burke, P. J. (2000). Identity theory and social identity theory. *Social Psychology Quarterly, 63*(3), 224–237.

Stryker, S., & Burke, P. J. (2000). The past, present, and future of an identity theory. *Social Psychology Quarterly, 63*(4), 284–297.

Tanner, J. L., & Arnett, J. J. (2009). The emergence of 'emerging adulthood'. The new life stage between adolescence and young adulthood. In A. Furlong (Ed.), *Handbook of youth and young adulthood. New perspectives and agendas* (pp. 39–45). London and New York: Routledge.

Tanner, J. L., & Arnett, J. J. (2011). Presenting 'emerging adulthood': What makes it developmentally distinctive? In J. J. Arnett, M. Kloep, L. B. Hendry, & J. L. Tanner (Eds.), *Debating emerging adulthood: Stage or process?* (pp. 13–30). Oxford: Oxford University Press.

Thomson, R., Bell, R., Holland, J., Henderson, S., McGrellis, S., & Sharpe, S. (2002). Critical moments: Choice, chance and opportunity in young people's narratives of transition. *Sociology, 36*(2), 335–354.

Urry, J., & Grieco, M. (Eds.). (2012). *Mobilities: New perspectives on transport and society*. London: Routledge.

Valsiner, J. (2001). Process structure of semiotic mediation in human development. *Human Development, 44*, 84–97.

Valsiner, J. (2007). *Culture in minds and societies: Foundations of cultural psychology*. New Delhi: Sage Publications.

Valsiner, J. (2017). *From methodology to methods in human psychology*. Cham: Springer.

Zittoun, T. (2012). Life-course: A socio-cultural perspective. In J. Valsiner (Ed.), *The Oxford handbook of culture and psychology* (pp. 513–535). New York: Oxford University Press.

Zittoun, T., Levitan, D., & Cangiá, F. (2018). A sociocultural approach to mobile families: A case study. *Peace and Conflict: Journal of Peace Psychology, 24*(4), 424–432. https://doi.org/10.1037/pac0000313

Zittoun, T., Valsiner, J., Vedeler, D., Salgado, J., Gonçalves, M. M., & Ferring, D. (2013). *Human development in the life course. Melodies of living*. Cambridge: Cambridge University Press.

2

Identity Development in a Semiotic Cultural Key

How is it possible to conceptualise identity as multiple and context-bound, while at the same time also providing a person with a sense of sameness and continuity? How can it be thought of as a process that is always moving and changing, being experienced somewhat differently in every new situation, yet also providing a sense of connection and stability across time and space? This chapter is guided by these questions as it provides an overview of the key theoretical ideas that informed the research presented in this book and were used as conceptual tools in the analysis of the eight case studies.

Socio-Genetic Nature of the Human Psyche: A Rediscovered Old Idea

My aim in this book is to present a novel way of conceptualising identity processes. Central to this conceptualisation is the idea that higher-order psychological processes, including human meaning-making, are social and cultural in nature. Yet, in many ways, the ideas put forward in this book are not new at all but can be traced back to the thoughts of some

© The Author(s) 2019
M. Märtsin, *Identity Development in the Lifecourse*, Sociocultural Psychology of the Lifecourse, https://doi.org/10.1007/978-3-030-27753-6_2

seminal thinkers of the turn of the nineteenth century—both in Europe and in the United States. For example, James Mark Baldwin's theory of development that is built around the notion of persistent imitation, which transforms individual's experiences in and of the external world into novel intra-personal constructions, proposes the socio-genetic world-view (Valsiner, 2007a; Valsiner & Van der Veer, 2000). The idea that the origin and nature of the human mind is essentially social was clearly present also in the works of French psychiatrist Pierre Janet, a close friend of Baldwin. His theory of conduct is based on the ideas that all private mental acts, such as language or thought, are originally social; that all higher mental functions are the result of a long and complex development; and that higher mental processes are tied to the actions a subject performs (Van der Veer, 1994).

George Herbert Mead (1934), another influential figure from the turn of the century, explains the emergence of individual consciousness through social communication using the concept of social act, in which a vocal gesture (or a significant symbol) from an individual evokes an appropriate response from others that completes the social act by giving meaning to person's initial action. The social act thus always includes a divergent, yet complementary, perspective, internalisation of which allows the person to take the perspective of the other and turn it towards oneself, becoming the observer of one's own actions, a self-reflective subject with a distinct sense of self (Dodds, Lawrence, & Valsiner, 1997; Gillespie, 2005).

The complex theoretical framework of Lev Vygotsky that is built around the notion of semiotic mediation of higher psychological functions is also socio-genetic in nature, as it integrates and develops further many ideas of other influential thinkers of his period. For example, Baldwin's ideas about the double nature of imitation, where the imitated copy carries certain social suggestions, but also transcends these in a personally unique way, have found their way into Vygotsky's notion of internalisation as the basis of the social-personal interaction and developed further in his method of double stimulation (Daniels, 2001; Van der Veer, 1994; Van der Veer & Valsiner, 1991). Vygotsky has also used and made well-known Janet's fundamental assertion that higher psychological functions emerge through the social interaction and appear first at the interpersonal, external level and only then intra-psychologically (Valsiner & Van der Veer, 2000). Even if Mead and Vygotsky never met, the similarity between their ideas about significant symbols and signs is noteworthy too (Gillespie, 2005).

The ideas of these theorists, as well as the thoughts of William James, John Dewey and Josiah Royce, have formed the basis of the contemporary sociocultural perspective that has emerged since the 1980s and 1990s. The more recent developments in that tradition that focus on the semiotic aspects of meaning-making, building on Charles Sanders Peirce's work, form the general conceptual background of the work presented in this book (Salvatore, 2015, 2018; Valsiner, 2014).

Person and Environment: A Dynamic and Interwoven Whole

One of the key conceptual assumptions of the semiotic cultural perspective that is used in this book is that a person and his/her environment are inseparable and mutually transformative (Sawyer, 2002). Instead of treating collective and individual as separate elements that somehow influence each other (Costall, 2007), this approach seeks to conceptualise the two as a single, dialogically interrelated system (Marková, 2003), where the individual can be understood as "a higher form of sociality" (Vygotsky, 1989, p. 59). The person and his/her environment are seen as intertwined, open systems, which depend for their existence upon mutual exchanges (Kloep & Hendry, 2011; Valsiner & Diriwächter, 2008) and they are separated only analytically in order to "distinguish the organism (person) from its environment (social world) while remaining their dynamic interdependence" (Valsiner, 1998, p. 352).

In addition to assuming person-environment inseparability, the semiotic cultural perspective takes a process ontological approach to psychological phenomena (Sawyer, 2002). It acknowledges the "need to concentrate not on the product of development, but on the very process by which higher forms [of psychological functioning] are established" (Vygotsky, 1978, p. 64). Hence, psychological phenomena are conceptualised as processes, occurring at the border between person and environment, linking the two together into a dynamic whole, and the focus is on understanding how this linking together emerges and unfolds.

In conceptualising the dynamic interrelatedness of person and environment, I build on Valsiner' (1998) ideas about personal and collective cultures:

> The collective culture entails communally shared meanings, social norms, and everyday life practices, all united in a heterogeneous complex. On the basis of this complex, individual persons construct their personally idiosyncratic semiotic systems of symbols, practices, and personal objects, all of which constitute the personal culture. The relation between the collective and personal cultures is conceptualised as persons' active and constructive internalization-externalization process. (Valsiner, 1998, p. 30)

Collective and personal cultures are thus seen as interconnected semiotic systems. Both of these systems have mental and material aspects. We can think of collective culture as consisting of cultural artefacts as described by Cole (1996): "an artefact is an aspect of the material world that has been modified over the history of its incorporation into goal-directed human action" (p. 117). Cole's view builds on Wartofsky's (1979), who understands artefacts as "objectifications of human needs and intentions already invested with cognitive and affective content" (p. 204). His three-level classification is useful in pointing out the variety of cultural artefacts available for people to engage with. Primary artefacts consist of material objects that can be used in a specific (practical) context for specific purposes (e.g., axe or blackboard). Secondary artefacts include the 'recipes' for using these material objects (e.g., norms, rules, traditions). Tertiary artefacts consist of 'imagined worlds' that are not closely related to the practical activity but allow people to go beyond their immediate life context (e.g., artworks). Hence, historically developed collective culture in its variety of forms is a set of social suggestions or cultural messages that individuals as active agents exploit to create their own personal meaning spaces (i.e., personal cultures).

Personal culture thus emerges within the guidance of collective culture. For Valsiner (1998), personal culture refers to everything that has a meaning to a person, everything that one considers to be related to or belonging to. Personal culture too is both mental and material. The latter is understood as the physical extension of the person into the surrounding environment through tangible objects that carry certain subjective meanings. Referring to the idea that the border between the person and the surrounding world does not run along the body contours of the person, William James uses the concept of 'material self' (Fuhrer, 2004). Hence, my favourite novel is an object out in the collective world, but through the meaning I attach to it, it becomes part of my self, giving me comfort and support when I need it. Similarly, my child is very much an independent person with a mind of her own, but she is also part of me, so much so, that when she is sick, I feel hurt and vulnerable too.

In addition to this partially material, partially semiotic spatial extension of the self, the purely mental aspect of personal culture consists of all the ideas that the individual holds, the emotions, motives, interests and opinions one has and the plans for actions one creates. This is the imaginary space between internalisation and externalisation, that Zittoun (2004) calls 'interiority'. This semiotic sphere consists of subjective signs that person has created in order to capture in abstract and generalised form the ever-changing experience and to create a bridge from the past into the present and forward to the future (Valsiner, 2001).

Although Valsiner and others draw these conceptual distinctions between personal and collective cultures, the two are nevertheless seen as interrelated and dynamic open systems that are separated from each other by a border. The structures of these open systems are fluid and can be transformed through mutual exchanges across the border (Diriwächter & Valsiner, 2005). The processes at the border intertwine the two systems by bringing the semiotic material from the one system to another and back again. And although the border crossing is most of the time automatic, it nevertheless transforms the semiotic material as it moves from one system to another. The person and environment, as parts of a larger whole, become, therefore, simultaneously connected and separated, as their interrelatedness is continuously renewed in a never-ending cycle. In understanding how these movements across the border occur, the semiotic cultural perspective draws on the concept of semiotic mediation.

Semiotic Mediation

A fundamental assumption of the semiotic cultural perspective is the idea that humans do not have direct access to their environment, but their relationship with the world is always mediated by the culture in which they are embedded. As Valsiner explains:

> Human beings are active subjects who relate to their surrounding world by way of constant construction of semiotically mediated intrapsychological […] and extrapsychological […] devices. (Valsiner, 1998, p. 115)

Personal culture, including our ways of seeing ourselves in relation to others and the world, thus emerge through guidance or mediation provided by collective culture. Culture is thus not conceptualised as a container of a homogeneous class that stands outside of the person and somehow makes him or her similar to others in that class and different from others in another class (Valsiner, 2014). Rather, culture is seen as a fundamental part of the person, a tool in a person's mind—a lens between person and environment through which one sees the world and one's position in relation to the world. The use of the word 'culture' to describe both the personal and the collective is thus not accidental but intentional, suggesting that the personal is not separate from collective but instead created and maintained through interactions with the collective.

In explaining how culture and the resources it provides become tools for conducting one's life, Valsiner (1998) refers to the twin concepts of internalisation and externalisation:

> Internalization is the process by which meanings that relate to phenomena, and that are suggested to the individual by 'social others' who pursue their personal goals while assuming social roles, are brought over into individual's intrapsychological system. This 'bringing-over' process involves constructive modification of the 'brought-over' material by the person. The reciprocal process of externalization connotes activities by which the once-social—but now personal—set of meanings is constructively moved into novel contexts within the social environment. (Valsiner, 1998, p. 115)

According to this line of reasoning, the individual is constrained by the collective culture, that is, the sociocultural context influences the development of an individual's psychological functions. However, culture is simultaneously constraining and enabling. It constrains the individual's development to a set of possible pathways but not to a single one (Fuhrer, 2004). Collective meanings are offered as starting points for individuals that allow them to engage with the culture dialogically. The person-environment relationship is understood as an 'independent dependence' (Valsiner, 1998). Thus, a person is an active agent in the internalisation that is essentially a transformative process (Lawrence & Valsiner, 1993). Bringing the external semiotic material over to the internal plane requires innovation and novelty; it requires co-ordination of the new with the old that brings along the restructuring of both. Hence, it is often accompanied by tension and resistance. Internalisation is, therefore, best understood as co-construction (Stetsenko & Arievitch, 2004). The individuals do not simply 'take over' or 'take in' the suggestions offered to them by the social other. The social suggestions are not ready-made and fixed but, rather, they are meaning potentials that become actualised in a specific way in a person's engagement with the world. Vygotsky has differentiated between the relatively stable and unified 'collective meaning' and dynamic and fluid 'personal sense' that changes with the context (Vygotsky, 1987). Similarly, Bakhtin (1986) has illustrated the dynamics between social and personal by pointing out that the word (or utterance) is always half alien, carrying the meanings, intentions and expressions of the others that are unified with one's 'ownness'. Falmagne's (2004) differentiation between active and non-deliberate agency adds another layer to this discussion: while the active agency constitutes person's active and purposeful internalisation, rejection and negotiation efforts, the non-deliberate agency refers to the affective and motivational 'baggage' that influences the personal sense-making, often without individual's awareness. Thus, the personal sense of the individual is "a concrete realization of a cultural possibility that transcends their singularity" (Roth, 2007, p. 89). Personal sense is not an exact reflection of collective meaning space, but the person always "constructs an understanding of the world that goes beyond the collective culture in idiosyncratic ways" (Valsiner, 1998 p. 32).

Internalisation goes hand in hand with externalization. Being brought over and integrated into the internal meaning space, cultural messages are also reflected back to the collective culture, creating novelty and change also in the social sphere. Internalisation and externalisation are interrelated processes that cannot exist without one another. Both, the personal and the collective, become altered in continuous internalisation-externalisation cycles through which new semiotic and material realities are created (Zittoun, Duveen, Gillespie, Ivinson, & Psaltis, 2003). The graffiti artists' creative self-expressions, which Fuhrer (2004) describes, are visible traces of an individuals' meaning-making, that others can engage with. Similarly, the ideas expressed by a young scientist that are taken up and used by his colleagues create new collective meaning spaces. Hence, the collective sphere changes the person and becomes changed as a result of the individual's actions. The object that person engages with changes, while also working back on the individual (Stetsenko, 2005). As Edwards (2005) claims: "In this transactional relationship between subject and object we transform the object through, for example, contesting its meaning and understanding it better and we also transform ourselves" (p. 174). Hence, collective history becomes part of individuals', while individuals simultaneously make history in both their personal as well as in their collective sense (Holland & Lave, 2001).

Georg Simmel's ideas about the intrinsic self-fulfilling nature of human beings who become cultivated, that is, raised to a higher level of development through the use of cultural objects (Levine, 1971), further unpack these ideas about creative externalisation. Fuhrer, who further develops Simmel's ideas about cultivation, suggests that the intertwinement of personal and cultural through semiotic mediation provides the basis for their personal growth and development (Fuhrer, 2004). Persons as active agents do not only use the affordances (Gibson, 1986) offered to them by collective culture, but they actively create possibilities for themselves. Humans can choose which social suggestions to internalise and which ones to reject, as well as being able to choose and create their own sociocultural environment in order to find a more rewarding or allowing situation. In other words, people are actively negotiating their developmental situations; they participate purposefully in the creation of sociocultural contexts that allow them to develop and become what they want to become. A child, who is doing well in school, and is supported in her learning journey by parents and teachers, participates in this context willingly, while another child who gets positive feedback to her performance only in football training prefers the latter context over the one of school where she is seen as a naughty kid who always gets into trouble. By acting upon the collective culture, people are influencing or constraining the shared meaning spaces and that can again be accompanied by tension and resistance. Thus, the person-environment relations are mutually and bi-directionally constraining (Lawrence & Valsiner, 2003).

What follows from this discussion is that semiotic mediation is always social in nature. However, this does not necessarily mean that semiotic mediation is restricted to social interactions between individuals. Instead, it is assumed that the social other is always present in the cultural tool (Bertau, 2007). In making personal sense, the person is in dialogue with the cultural tool in order to grasp the collective meaning potential that is embedded in it. That is, the engagement with the cultural tools is social also when social others are not physically present. As Vygotsky, borrowing Janet's idea (Valsiner & Van der Veer, 2000) has suggested, every psychological function is created first interpersonally, by the person in dialogue with the social other, and only thereafter intra-personally—it then becomes integrated into their intra-psychological system (Vygotsky, 1978). Thus, the basic Vygotskian triangle of semiotic mediation that depicts the subject working on the object using cultural tools (see Vygotsky, 1978, p. 47) could be expanded to include also the social other. Zittoun's (2007c) semiotic prism, which stresses the presence of the social other in the creation and usage of symbolic resources, seems to be useful in this respect. In her account, the other has to be present to give an initial semiotic input for the personal sense-making (for instance, to explain the shared collective meaning or a personal sense for the other) and to acknowledge one's usage of the symbolic tool. But, importantly, the other is present also within the cultural element, that is, "full of the echoes of other voices and discourses" (Zittoun, 2007b, p. 366).

Human Meaning-Making

As I have explained so far, the connection between person and environment is semiotic in nature. That is, it is possible at the level of meanings. Understanding the functioning of psychological processes thus requires understanding how human meaning-making unfolds. It is this focus on the specifics of meaning-making that distinguishes the semiotic cultural perspective used in this book from some of the other sociocultural and dialogical approaches, despite their shared underlying assumptions.

Conceptualising human meaning-making requires explaining the interrelationship between two aspects: sign and meaning. A typical view distinguishes between two elements of the sign: form—the way a concept or idea is expressed, and meaning—the concept or idea that is denoted (Sonesson, 2010). Kress (2010), however, proposes a more dynamic view of signs:

> Signs are always newly *made* in social interaction; signs are *motivated* not *arbitrary* relations of meaning and form; the motivated relation of a *form* and a *meaning* is based on and arises out of the *interest* of makers of signs; the forms/signifiers which are used in the making of signs are *made* in social interaction and become part of the semiotic resources of a culture. (pp. 54–55, original emphasis)

For Kress then, a sign is a dynamic assemblage that is always in the process of transformation. It is by assembling our interests with the expected responses from others, who in turn create their own interpretations of our messages that are guided by their interests and their interpretations of our expected responses that the transformation of signs unfolds in a never-ending cycle. Building on Peirce's (1932) work, Salvatore (2018) also suggests that we should not look at signs as having an inherent content, but rather their content—meaning—emerges, as the signs are interpreted:

> A sign is something that stands for something else, with such a relation having to be interpreted by a further sign (Pierce, 1897/1932). Thus, a sign does not have an inherent content; rather it acquires its value owing to the

transition of which it is a part, that is, the capacity to refer to "something else" as *defined by another sign*—and so on, in an infinite chain. [...] *the meaning is the sign that follows*. (Salvatore, 2018, p. 42, original emphasis)

For Kress and Salvatore meanings are not seen as entities that are held or contained in signs, but rather viewed as products of the ongoing process of interpretation of previous signs in an infinite chain. In other words, meanings are not 'things' that we need to describe, map or uncover, rather they are created by the process of meaning-making as local and temporary states of the whole semiotic dynamic.

In explaining how human meaning-making is guided by culture, Salvatore (2018) uses the notion of cultural scenarios. Culture, he says, "is the field distribution of probabilities of transition among signs. [...] culture is the matrix of asymmetrical preferences that each sign has of combining with other signs" (p. 44). Salvatore refers to the metaphor of a footpath that gets created in the forest when people use it repeatedly. Just like a footpath that emerges through its repeated use, culture offers scenarios as somewhat stable but nevertheless dynamic networks of co-occurring signs. Through these scenarios, Salvatore argues, culture guides the process of meaning-making, for it sets boundaries for sign interpretation. The scenarios are continuously activated and, through that, reproduced over time as the most meaningful and culturally favoured ways of interpreting signs amongst the many possible options. And while this constraining sets limits to possible interpretations, it leaves the final call to interpreters who construct their unique interpretations based on their current motives and purposes. In this way, culture does not determine but simultaneously constrains and enables the meaning-making process.

In conceptualising how signs become constructed in the process of relating to the world through culture, I build again on Valsiner's work. Valsiner's laminal model (Lawrence & Valsiner, 2003; Valsiner, 2007a) is built around the idea that internalisation-externalisation processes involve both resistance and acceptance. According to his model, people's intra-psychological system can be understood as consisting of three layers that proceed gradually from the peripheral zones to the innermost core (see Fig. 2.1). Each layer is separated from the next one by a border that functions as a buffer and needs to be traversed by an incoming social message.

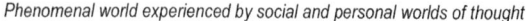

Phenomenal world experienced by social and personal worlds of thought

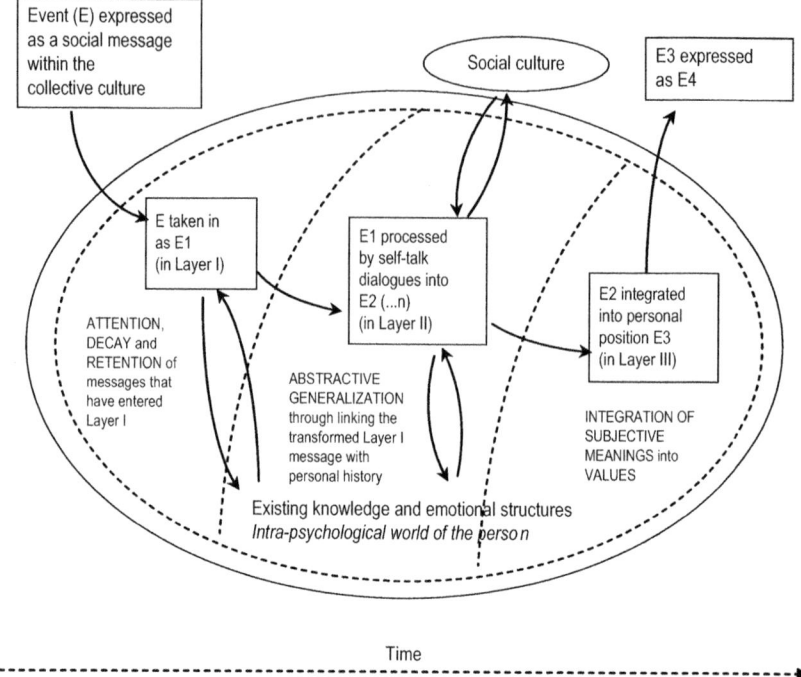

Fig. 2.1 Laminal model of sign construction (Modified from Lawrence & Valsiner, 2003, p. 731)

This border can be conceived as a hierarchically organised complex of signs, where more abstract and general meta-signs regulate the functioning of less generalised signs (Abbey, 2007a). In order for the message to move from the outer layers to the innermost layer, it has to be transformed through inner dialogue between the new message and pre-existing signs. As regulators of the inward movement of new messages, the existing signs can enter into dialogue or block the movement of an incoming message at the border between layers (Abbey, 2007a). The dialogue between different meanings can be resolved by rejection of the message (meta-sign blocks the entrance to the next layer), in which case, it fades away, or by transformation of the message, which creates a congruence between different meanings and allows the message to move on to the next layer, until it becomes integrated into the existing emotional and knowledge structures (i.e., a new sign becomes created). In the innermost layer of the self-system, the message becomes part of the critical dialogue a person has with oneself, that a sign functions as an internal message that is used to 'assess' other incoming social messages. Also, once in this core of a person's interiority, the sign is ready to be transferred into the outer world by externalisation (Lawrence & Valsiner, 2003). Thus, the already existing signs regulate the construction of new signs automatically, without our conscious effort. This semiotic auto-regulation explains simultaneously the continuity and novelty of the self-system.

Valsiner (2001) refers to the process by way of which a social message moves from the periphery to the core as abstractive generalisation and suggests to conceptualise it as a transformation of the concrete response to a given situation into a generalised and abstract subjective sign. This transformation is brought about by inner dialogue between different meanings at every layer, making the message gradually more and more abstract until it reaches the core in the form of a highly generalised metasign. Two parallel processes are at work in abstractive generalisation: schematisation and pleromatisation, where schematisation shrinks the meaning field into a point-like sign, while pleromatisation instantaneously expands it into a field-like sign where the interior of the field is differentiated and affords connections with other signs outside the field (Valsiner, 2007c, p. 1, original emphasis). A generalised sign that is formed through dialogue between various meanings thus retains these meanings or traces of them. These meanings or voices can constitute the perspective of another person or institution, but they can also be the 'AS-IF' perspective of the person, that is, a view about and from an anticipated future situation. According to Abbey (2007b), the presence of different voices creates a tension, an ambivalence that needs to be resolved in the sign construction. She uses the notion 'meaning-as-motion' to highlight "an ever-present ambiguity in meaning, on account of the blending of one literal sense into the next through notions of what could be" (Abbey, 2007b, p. 367). By combining different perspectives, the sign takes a generalised form in which it can be distanced from a particular here-and-now situation and used in meaning-making under new circumstances (Abbey & Valsiner, 2004). According to Valsiner: "Generalizability is the propensity of a sign to create an abstracted reflection upon that initial context" (Valsiner, 2001, p. 90). He distinguishes between four levels of distancing in sign construction: (1) embodied undifferentiated feeling and experience (i.e., fuzzy feeling that cannot be named); (2) labelling a situation (i.e., being able to name and articulate one's thoughts and feelings, e.g., "I miss my family"); (3) creating categories to understand the self and the world (e.g., "I am a person for who close relationships are important"); and (4) creation of orienting values that may not be easy to articulate (i.e., hyper-generalisation) but are guiding one's everyday functioning (e.g., "it is important to be honest" (Valsiner, 2007b). A person's intra-psychological field is thus hierarchically organised, with highly abstract and generalised meta-signs auto-regulating (in the sense of spontaneous and automatic guiding) the functioning of less abstract signs and the ongoing creation of new signs. Valsiner (2001) suggests that at this highest level of abstraction, reflection and articulation become subordinated to speechless affect:

> 'Speechlessness'—the propensity of human being not to say anything (to oneself or to another) can occur at *both* the lowest […] and the highest […] levels of semiotic mediation structure. […] The person has *over*generalised the sign used in the mediational hierarchy to the level where speech turns into speechlessness. (Valsiner, 2001, p. 94, original emphasis)

I will return to the conceptualisation of these hyper-generalised meta-signs later in this chapter. But to finish the discussion about the processes of sign construction, it is important to underline that the auto-dialogue between already existing internal perspectives and new incoming social suggestions that leads to the construction of a generalised sign may not be fast and straightforward but can be a prolonged and complicated process. The person, being in the constant flow of life experiences, can be distracted from one dialogue in order to enter into another, more urgent one. Thus, inner dialogues become interrupted, fade to the background, linger there and are later brought back to the active state by another triggering event until they are finally resolved by a rejection of the message or by incorporating it in a transformed mode into the semiotic architecture of the self-system (Abbey, 2007a). The ambivalence and uncertainty, that is, the perceived difference between perspectives, may thus be a lasting state, as I explain below in relation to the concept of liminality. Each layer of a person's intra-psychological system is, therefore, described by the multiplicity of inner dialogues, some active and some in a temporary passive state (Abbey, 2004). Abbey (2007a) describes this movement of the message through peripheral layers into the subjective core eloquently:

> The other is constantly in the process of flowing into us and ebbing out, and reaching different tide lines in every cycle. At some moments, you are there, entering into the realm of my awareness [...], and moments later, you may be gone, as my attention is called elsewhere. You come in, though not too far, and you recede. You may also linger in my awareness, even as I attend to other things. You are there, maybe even annoyingly so, and at some moment, concrete meanings may come [...]. You may then recede. Or you may extend into generality [...]. And at this point, you may go, again moving onto something else. You come in, reaching higher, and you recede. [...] But if you do not go [...] you can come into my subjective core. [...] You become a being, integrated with me, and any meanings that otherwise form dimensions of difference between us, are, at least temporally, neutralised. [...] You come in, reaching as high as you can, and after moments of lifetimes, you recede. (Abbey, 2007a, pp. 73–74)

Identity as a Field of Hyper-Generalised Meta-Signs

As already explained, signs are constructed based on a person's active participation in different sociocultural environments. They originate from person-environment dynamic intertwining, where a person's reactions to specific situations send a message to others and receive feedback from them, while also creating a feed-forward loop for the self and allowing the person to see themselves from another perspective (Valsiner, 2007a). Hence, the reaction to specific life-events always says something about the person (e.g., "I liked/didn't like this", "I was good/not so good at it" etc.). The person him/herself and others interpret it into several new signs as the recursive semiosis is initiated (Rosa, 2007). As these signs enter the outer-most layer of the person's intra-psychological system, they become re-interpreted in the light of existing signs. The cascade of multi-stranded recursive semiosis is set in motion and, through that, an image of the self emerges. In this process, some constructed signs become rejected, while others become transformed through dialogues with other signs into more abstract and generalised meta-signs until they reach the inner-most layer of the self-system. In this way, the semiotic architecture of the self-system becomes created—the hierarchically organised system of signs about who one is.

I find Valsiner's (2001, 2007a) ideas about generalisation and the hierarchical organisation of signs particularly useful for thinking about identity processes.

Especially interesting for me is his description of the signs at the highest level of the sign hierarchy, the hyper-generalised meta-signs that are hard to articulate but nevertheless, guide the human conduct in the world in a powerful manner. Valsiner has mostly used the ideas about hyper-generalisation in order to not only explain how values guide our functioning in the world (Valsiner, 2002, 2005, 2007a) but also to explain how self could be understood (Valsiner, 2017). I suggest viewing identity in this manner—as a fuzzy field of hyper-generalised meta-signs about who we are, have been and are becoming. As a hyper-generalised meta-sign, it usually functions as an implicit and unspeakable background of our everyday functioning. As a background, it is constantly present, being that aspect of our self that remains and feels the same, despite us continuously living through and making sense of ever-new experiences. Identity understood in this way functions as a regulator of our ongoing meaning-making, for it channels the way we make sense of our experiences into a range of possible interpretations that are congruent with the way we see ourselves. We cannot and usually do not need to talk about this invisible and taken-for-granted background, yet it constantly regulates our way of being as our new encounters with the world are made sense of in relation to it. I conceptualise identity as a semiotic field because it includes a wide range of interrelated meanings tied to different aspects of our way of being. I consider it to be a fuzzy field because we cannot clearly define its perimeter and boundaries, we don't quite know where it starts and where it ends, what belongs to it and what does not. Importantly, identity as a field of hyper-generalised meta-signs regulates our movement into the future, that is, our process of becoming.

The Process of Becoming: Sign Construction in the Irreversible Flow of Time

Sign construction in the flow of human conduct is always oriented towards the future. According to Valsiner (2007c): "All semiotic processes that the person brings into one's life are oriented toward regulating and directing that flow into some selected future direction" (p. 351). Signs prepare individuals for the immediate future based on their previous experiences, by capturing in an abstract and generalised form the ever-changing experience. They go beyond creating a fit with the present state and, instead, build a basis for facing new, unpredictable, but anticipated, experiences in the future as in Bergson's (1907) creative adaptation. The signs that are created in the past are used and altered in the present to respond to the new experience and, therefore, create a bridge from the past through the present into the future. Yet, they are created ahead of time, setting up a range of possible personal meaning potentials for the anticipated future and, in this way, they have a feed-forward function (Valsiner, 2005).

Marsico and Tateo (2017) use the notion of tensegrity to explain how this feed-forward function creates a dynamic stability for the self-system. They write:

> The psyche should be understood in terms of a tensegrity system: that is, a system in which the organizing principle is not equilibrium and homeostasis, but rather dynamic tension. In this kind of system, endogenous and exogenous forces, tension and compression are at work to create a state of tensegrity (Tateo & Marsico, 2013) in which the organism's integrity is based on a state of constant dynamic pre-tension that ensures both flexibility and stability over time. What becomes relevant is then the future state that the system is striving for. Identity is conceived as movement, thus change cannot affect its integrity. Such a kind of system can perfectly deal with ambivalence and tension. (p. 538)

The way I see it, human meaning-making is thus an ongoing process in which relative stability is created from permanent impermanence, just like the maintenance of the upright body posture and balance is achieved through continuous correction of instantaneous imbalanced moments.

In this kind of system tension and dialogue between various meanings are seen as a defining feature of the system, instead of a state to be avoided. I will come back to this idea soon.

The fact that human conduct takes place in the irreversible flow of time makes it impossible for people to predict the future with certainty based on their past experiences. Yet, the resources that culture provides us, and the signs that we have ourselves created based on our experiences in the past, enable us to imagine and anticipate possible future scenarios and trajectories. It is in this sense that our meaning-making is future-oriented. As Valsiner (2014) writes: "The function of signs is always future-oriented, both in their immediate impact (turning the next immediate future into a new present) and in their general orientation towards encountering similar situations in some indeterminate future moment" (pp. 117–118). Culture thus frees us from the immediacy of our everyday life, from our AS-IS life, and gives us tools for creating AS-IF scenarios that enable us to imagine that what is not yet but could be or that what is not real but could be. In fact, we spend a significant amount of time thinking about the AS-IS world and revisiting the past in order to imagine how it could have been different (Märtsin, 2018). As Valsiner (2014) writes:

> What looks as if it entails 'looking back' at the given moment is actually 'looking forward', thanks to the accessibility of different traces of signs from the past. Within irreversible time one cannot reference 'what was' without making it to be in the service of 'what might come'. (p. 118)

As explained above, Valsiner conceptualises the cultural guidance of meaning-making in terms of the creation of sign hierarchies where the creation of new signs is regulated by highly generalised field-like signs at the highest level of the sign hierarchy. He suggests that there is a particular group of these meta-signs—promoter signs, which are highly generalised and function as value-orientations that guide our movement towards the future. He writes:

> The promoter role of these signs is a feed-forward function: they set up the range of possible meaning boundaries for the unforeseeable, yet anticipated,

future experiences with the world. The person is constantly creating meaning ahead of time when it might be needed: Orienting oneself towards one
or another side of the anticipated experience, and thus preparing oneself for
it. (Valsiner, 2007a, p. 58)

In my reading, promoter signs or value-orientations thus capture the
idea of the future goal-orientedness of human conduct, for they point us
towards certain ways of thinking, feeling and acting in our world and
push us away from some other ways of moving forward. They are highly
abstract and generalised meta-signs, providing not a rational and articulated reason for our conduct but rather an affective orientation about
how we should or could act, feel or think. In my interpretation, they echo
Charlotte Bühler's idea of life-goal orientations that are pursued throughout the lifecourse often in an unconscious way (Bühler & Massarik,
1968). Bühler suggests that in the most general sense life-goal can be
understood as a person's desire to live a meaningful and self-fulfilling life.
Life-goals can be seen as vague and abstract values (e.g., "I want to live a
stimulating life" or "I need to be in control of my life"), but they can also
be relatively specific ideas about the direction of one's life (e.g., "I want to
have three children" or "I want to become a CEO before the age of 40").
Life-goals can be more or less immediate (e.g., "I want to start to study
art") or very long-term (e.g., "One day I want to return to my mother-
land"). As such, life-goals exist as socioculturally proposed, but personally negotiated, scenarios that people create about their unpredictable, yet
anticipated future. Life-goals enable people to make everyday decisions
about themselves within and in relation to the sociocultural context in
the present that connects their past with their imagined future.

In this book, building on Bühler's work, I talk about 'life-goal orientations' in order to emphasise the future-orientedness of human meaning-
making and the time perspective in the movement towards the goals that
people choose to have in their lives. I conceptualise life-goal orientations
as fields of highly generalised meanings, which allow people to define
who they are here and now that is consistent with who they were in the
past and who they are becoming in the future. As semiotic constructions
that enable people to manage their lifecourse, life-goal orientations are
understood as trans-situational, highly generalised meta-signs that are

integrated into the core of a person's self- system. In this sense, the processes of creating life-goal orientations are tightly interlinked with identity processes, and their construction can be conceptualised using Valsiner's laminal model (see above). Like other highly generalised signs, life-goal orientations are constructed by individuals based on their everyday experiences by way of combining social suggestions with individuals' personal histories in an idiosyncratic manner. Using Bühler's examples (Bühler & Massarik, 1968), having clear ideas about one's future professional career may be normal for a young man coming from an American middle-class family. However, a youngster, who has lived half of his life with his Indian-origin grandfather in the woods and the second half with his unemployed parents travelling from one place to another, may not have any long-term professional objectives but rather uses the job opportunities as these emerge. As hyper-generalised meta-signs, life-goal orientations function as semiotic regulators that enable one to make sense of one's life-trajectory. As such, they can be seen as relatively stable semiotic constructions that have the power to re-configure, integrate and give meaning to personal experiences across space and time (Valsiner, 2007b).

Ruptures and Transitions in the Lifecourse

In our ordinary flow of being, we constantly construct meanings about the world and ourselves within it, and we construct it ahead of time so that we are pre-adapted to our unpredictable but anticipated future. Importantly, human meaning-making does not canalise a person's actions and interpretations towards one desirable trajectory in the future, but multiple possible scenarios emerge from our negotiations between the AS-IS and AS-IF worlds, out of which we choose one as useful and meaningful for our current purposes (Valsiner, 2007a). Importantly though, the other possible and imagined trajectories that do not eventuate, do not disappear completely, but remain available as shadows of the actualised trajectories, creating a field of potential trajectories for the future (Bastos, 2017). As we function in a ceaseless and taken-for-granted flow, most of these shadows are dormant, while the dominant meanings enable us to respond spontaneously to the callings of others (Shotter, 2003, 2008).

Yet, the periods that are the focus of my attention in this book are not necessarily these moments of relative tranquillity but rather experiences that are challenging people's existing ways of making sense of their lives. That is, I am interested in exploring identity processes in relation to transitional experiences, at the heart of which is a sense of rupture.

Zittoun (2012) defines ruptures as "moments in which existing modes of progressive adjustment are interrupted" (p. 517). She writes: "The first criteria to consider an event as a significant rupture, is that it is subjectively, consciously or unconsciously perceived by a person as questioning her sense of self and sense of continuity" (Zittoun, 2007a, p. 190). In my reading then, a rupture is a felt break from the way life has been. It occurs when we sense that something that we are used to and have taken for granted does not flow anymore but is temporarily suspended. We encounter these moments all the time in our everyday experiences. In fact, as Marsico and Tateo's (2017) theorising about tensegrity suggests, tensions and ruptures, and dialogues about these tensions, are a normal and essential part of our self-system. These everyday breaks in our flow of being are not at the centre of my attention in this book. Instead, the ruptures that interest me here are the ones where the sense of temporary suspension or break is generalised into a significant rupture on the ontogenetic level as similar experiences of otherness or difference are gathered up. That is, my focus is on ruptures in the lifecourse that are typical in the context of developmental shifts and changes and amplified by significant life-events such as (repeated) migration.

As I explained above, in the ordinary flow of life, our sense of identity is backgrounded, as the hyper-generalised meta-signs guide our way of being in an implicit manner. Yet in the moments of rupture, this meaning field becomes foregrounded and the multiple meanings that are part of this fuzzy field become accessible. In Josephs's (2002) words: "The formerly taken-for-granted (and thus backgrounded) life-world suddenly becomes foregrounded and 'visible'" (p. 171). Thus, at the heart of a rupture is a sense of ambivalence and uncertainty, for the previously existing and order-providing semiotic architecture of the self-system—the hierarchically organised system of signs about one's self—becomes dismantled and the new structures that would provide guidance for moving towards the future have not been built yet. In other words, rupture makes the multiplicity of meanings visible. The shadow trajectories that so far existed only as part of the field of dormant possibilities become activated and destabilise our movement into the future (Bastos, 2017). Marsico and others (Español, Marsico, & Tateo, 2018; Marsico, 2016; Marsico & Tateo, 2017) suggest that in these moments of instability, where ambivalence becomes to dominate our ways of being, we need to re-create boundaries between self and others. In this sense, they suggest that identity can be conceptualised as a semiotic border-making process that helps to make sense of the self in relation to the difference and ambivalence that is activated by a rupture.

Greco and Stenner (2017) refer to these in-between situations, where the old structures do not hold anymore, but the new ones are not put in place yet, as liminal phases of transitions, suggesting that a liminal phase in the developmental trajectory emerges "where an existing form-of-process is suspended (becomes unviable) and a new one is not yet in place" (p. 152). In a liminal phase of transition, the existing borders are thus removed and the new ones have not yet been created. For liminality, as Szakolczai (2015) writes, is about "removing the limit" or being "at the limit": "Being "at the limit" is a genuine Alice-in-Wonderland experience, a situation where almost anything is possible" (p. 18). According to his reasoning, this liminal phase that is created by a rupture has two characteristics. On the one hand, being in a liminal phase creates a great deal of frustration, tension and anxiety for the individuals involved, for in the situation where old ways of being and doing are suspended while new ways are not yet place, robs people of their security and guidance regarding appropriate behaviour and acceptable ways forward. In other words, when the future is unknown and the signposts that used to regulate one's behaviour do not work anymore, then anxiety and worry prevail and a future-orientation that opens up a way forward and out of the liminality is hard to imagine. Szakolczai (2017) suggests that there are situations where liminality can become permanent and suggests that in these situations, all action can become paralysed, leading to the exhaustion of resources and eventually to devastation. Motzkau and Clinch (2017), for example, describe how police officers, who as part of their duties need to interview victims of child sexual abuse, find themselves in a situation of permanent liminality due to the uncertain and ambivalent, yet high-stakes nature of their work, that they seek to escape from by deskilling themselves and moving to another field of work within the police force.

On the other hand, liminality creates also a situation where new structures of meaning need to be created. Hence, liminal phases are also fertile grounds for innovation and creativity. The liminal phase of the transition is thus a period where alternative ways of being and doing and possibilities for becoming otherwise emerge out of ambivalence. It is in this sense that ruptures and liminal phases are closely linked to the process of becoming and development, for they trigger change and function as catalysts for things to become different and otherwise. In other words, ruptures should not be automatically seen as negative and problematic events that lead to unwanted tensions and changes, but they can also be seen as opportunities for change and development that lead to a new and more adaptive ways of functioning.

According to Zittoun (2007a), ruptures are followed by periods of transition, which "aim to restore one's sense of continuity and integrity of self beyond the rupture" (p. 191). Transitions, in this perspective, are seen as "moments of accelerated and catalyzed changes […] either from the perspective of a person's life-trajectory or from an observer's perspective" (Zittoun, 2012, p. 517). Transitions, as Stenner (2017) suggests, start with a liminal phase that typically starts to gradual fade, as the new structures of meaning become constructed. Zittoun suggests that during the transition following a rupture, people experience three types of changes: they develop new knowledge and acquire new skills, they redefine their identities and construct new, personal meanings of the experienced change. Ruptures and transitions are thus central to identity processes, which effectively entail experiencing a rupture and transitioning into a new, more optimal way of life after the rupture (Zittoun, 2007c). In fact, identity development can be seen as a process of creating a new sense of sameness and continuity beyond the rupture—a process that involves constructing new life-goal orientations that incorporate, in a meaningful way, the sense of identity before and after the rupture and can function as signposts for our movement into the future (Märtsin, 2010).

Ruptures and the related transitions can occur in every stage of one's life and can be brought along by different kinds of events such as illness, bereavement, change of employment, ending of a relationship, and so on (Crafter, Maunder, & Soulsby, 2019). In the focus of this book are these ruptures and related moments of accelerated change that are seen as significant shifts in one's lifecourse in the early years of adulthood and that have the power to impact the person's sense of self and identity. The book is organised around themes or dimensions of these transitions that require significant efforts if meaning-making—sense of belonging, relationships with peers, recognition and planning for the future. As the case studies discussed in this book suggest, these dimensions might be rather typical for the developmental transitions experienced by young adults. Yet, the experiences discussed in this book also suggest that the repeated movements between societies, cultures and institutions significantly amplify the experiencing of these ruptures and transitions. In short, this book is about the experiences of becoming. In conceptualising these experiences, I aim to take a close look at the dynamics of meaning-making and explore the processes of dismantling the existing and constructing the new meanings structures about the self and its relationship to the world.

Summary

In this chapter, I have given an overview of the conceptual ideas that form the basis of the research discussed in this book. At the heart of the conceptual framework used in this work is the idea that identity processes can be understood as part of our ongoing meaning-making processes that are always oriented towards the future. The central aim of the chapter was to explain what it means to conceptualise identity as a field of hyper-generalised meta-signs that organises and guides the person's movement into the future. Furthermore, the chapter aimed to introduce the related concepts of rupture and transition to provide a theoretical context for the kinds of experiences that will be unpacked through the eight case studies discussed in this book. I will return to some of these conceptual ideas and underlying theoretical assumptions again in the next chapter, where the methodological approach used in the study will be discussed.

References

Abbey, E. (2004). Circumventing ambivalence in identity: The importance of latent and overt aspects of symbolic meaning. *Culture & Psychology, 10*(3), 331–336.

Abbey, E. (2007a). At the boundary of me and you: Semiotic architecture of thinking and feeling the other. In L. M. Simão & J. Valsiner (Eds.), *Otherness in question. Labyrinths of the self* (pp. 73–92). Charlotte: Information Age Publishing.

Abbey, E. (2007b). Perpetual uncertainty of cultural life: Becoming reality. In J. Valsiner & A. Rosa (Eds.), *The Cambridge handbook of sociocultural psychology* (pp. 362–372). Cambridge: Cambridge University Press.

Abbey, E., & Valsiner, J. (2004). Emergence of meanings through ambivalence [58 paragraphs]. *Forum Qualitative Sozialforschung/Forum: Qualitative Social Research [Online Journal], 6*(1), Art 23.

Bakhtin, M. M. (1986). *Speech genres and other late essays.* Austin: University of Texas Press.

Bastos, A. C. (2017). Shadow trajectories: The poetic motion of motherhood meanings through the lens of lived temporality. *Culture & Psychology, 23*(3), 408–422. https://doi.org/10.1177/1354067X16655458

Bergson, H. (1907). *Loov evolutsioon [Creative evolution]* (M. Ott & H. Sahkai, Trans.). Tallinn: Imamaa.

Bertau, M.-C. (2007). Encountering objects and others as a means of passage. *Culture & Psychology, 13*(3), 335–352.

Bühler, C., & Massarik, F. (Eds.). (1968). *The course of human life. A study of goals in the humanistic perspective.* New York: Springer.

Cole, M. (1996). *Cultural psychology. A once and future discipline.* Cambridge, MA: Harvard University Press.

Costall, A. (2007). The windowless room: 'Mediationism' and how to get over it. In J. Valsiner & A. Rosa (Eds.), *The Cambridge handbook of sociocultural psychology* (pp. 109–123). Cambridge: Cambridge University Press.

Crafter, S., Maunder, R., & Soulsby, L. (2019). *Developmental transitions: Exploring stability and change through the lifespan.* London and New York: Routledge.

Daniels, H. (2001). *Vygotsky and pedagogy.* London and New York: Routledge Falmer.

Diriwächter, R., & Valsiner, J. (2005). Qualitative developmental research methods in their historical and epistemological contexts [53 paragraphs].

Forum Qualitative Sozialforschung/Forum: Qualitative Social Research [Online Journal], 7(1), Art 8.

Dodds, A. E., Lawrence, J. A., & Valsiner, J. (1997). The personal and the social: Mead's theory of the 'generalized other'. *Theory & Psychology, 7*(4), 483–503.

Edwards, A. (2005). Relational agency: Learning to be a resourceful practitioner. *International Journal of Educational Research, 43*(3), 168–182.

Español, A., Marsico, G., & Tateo, L. (2018). Maintaining borders: From border guards to diplomats. *Human Affairs: Postdisciplinary Humanities & Social Sciences Quarterly, 28*(4), 443–460. https://doi.org/10.1515/humaff-2018-0036

Falmagne, R. J. (2004). On the constitution of 'self' and 'mind'. *Theory & Psychology, 14*(6), 822–845.

Fuhrer, U. (2004). *Cultivating minds. Identity as meaning-making practice.* London and New York: Routledge.

Gibson, J. J. (1986). *The ecological approach to visual perception.* London: Lawrence Erlbaum Associates Publishers.

Gillespie, A. (2005). GH Mead: Theorist of the social act. *Journal for the Theory of Social Behaviour, 35*(1), 19–39.

Greco, M., & Stenner, P. (2017). From paradox to pattern shift: Conceptualising liminal hotspots and their affective dynamics. *Theory & Psychology, 27*(2), 147–166. https://doi.org/10.1177/0959354317693120

Holland, D., & Lave, J. (Eds.). (2001). *History in person. Enduring struggles, contentious practice, intimate identities.* Santa Fe: School of American Research Press.

Josephs, I. E. (2002). 'The hopi in me': The construction of a voice in the dialogical self from a cultural psychological perspective. *Theory & Psychology, 12*, 161–173.

Kloep, M., & Hendry, L. B. (2011). A systemic approach to the transitions to adulthood. In J. J. Arnett, M. Kloep, L. B. Hendry, & J. L. Tanner (Eds.), *Debating emerging adulthood: Stage or process?* (pp. 53–76). Oxford: Oxford University Press.

Kress, G. R. (2010). *Multimodality: A social semiotic approach to contemporary communication.* London: Routledge.

Lawrence, J. A., & Valsiner, J. (1993). Conceptual roots of internalization: From transmission to transformation. *Human Development, 36*(1), 150–167.

Lawrence, J. A., & Valsiner, J. (2003). Making personal sense. An account of basic internalization and externalization processes. *Theory & Psychology, 13*(6), 723–752.

Levine, D. N. (Ed.). (1971). *Georg Simmel on individuality and social forms. Selected writings.* Chicago: The University of Chicago Press.

Marková, I. (2003). Constitution of the self: Intersubjectivity and dialogicality. *Culture & Psychology, 9*(3), 249–259.

Marsico, G. (2016). The borderland. *Culture & Psychology, 22*(2), 206–215. https://doi.org/10.1177/1354067X15601199

Marsico, G., & Tateo, L. (2017). Borders, tensegrity and development in dialogue. *Integrative Psychological & Behavioral Science, 51*(4), 536–556. https://doi.org/10.1007/s12124-017-9398-2

Märtsin, M. (2010). Identity in dialogue: Identity as hyper-generalized personal sense. *Theory & Psychology, 20,* 436–450. https://doi.org/10.1177/0959354310363513

Märtsin, M. (2018). On the possibility of becoming otherwise. In B. Wagoner, I. Bresco, & S. Zadeh (Eds.), *Memory in the wild* (p. TBC). Charlotte, NC: Information Age.

Mead, G. H. (1934). *Mind, self and society from the standpoint of a social behaviorist.* Chicago: The University of Chicago Press.

Motzkau, J. F., & Clinch, M. (2017). Managing suspended transition in medicine and law: Liminal hotspots as resources for change. *Theory & Psychology, 27*(2), 270–289. https://doi.org/10.1177/0959354317700517

Peirce, C. S. (1932). On sign. In C. Hartshorne & P. Weiss (Eds.), *Collected papers of Charles Sanders Peirce (Volume II).* Cambridge, MA: Harvard University Press.

Rosa, A. (2007). Dramaturgical actuations and symbolic communication. Or how beliefs make up reality. In J. Valsiner & A. Rosa (Eds.), *The Cambridge handbook of sociocultural psychology* (pp. 293–317). Cambridge: Cambridge University Press.

Roth, W. M. (2007). The ethico-moral nature of identity: Prolegomena to the development of third-generation cultural-historical activity theory. *International Journal of Educational Research, 46*(1–2), 83–93.

Salvatore, S. (2015). *Psychology in black and white: The project of a theory-driven science.* Charlotte, NC: Information Age Publishing.

Salvatore, S. (2018). Culture as dynamics of sense-making. A semiotic and embodied framework for socio-cultural psychology. In J. Valsiner (Ed.), *Cambridge handbook of culture and psychology* (pp. 35–48). Cambridge: Cambridge University Press.

Sawyer, R. K. (2002). Unresolved tensions in sociocultural theory: Analogies with contemporary sociological debates. *Culture & Psychology, 8*(3), 283–305.

Shotter, J. (2003). 'Real presences': Meaning as living movement in a participatory world. *Theory & Psychology, 13*, 435–468.

Shotter, J. (2008). *Conversational realities revisited: Life, language, body and world.* Chagrin Falls, OH: Taos Institute.

Sonesson, G. (2010). Here comes the semiotic species: Reflections on the semiotic turn in the cognitive sciences. In B. Wagoner (Ed.), *Symbolic transformation. The mind in movement through culture and society* (pp. 38–58). London and New York: Routledge.

Stenner, P. (2017). *Liminality and experience. A transdisciplinary approach to the psychosocial.* London: Palgrave.

Stetsenko, A. (2005). Activity as object-related: Resolving the dichotomy of individual and collective planes of activity. *Mind, Culture and Activity, 12*(1), 70–88.

Stetsenko, A., & Arievitch, I. M. (2004). The self in cultural-historical activity theory. *Theory & Psychology, 14*(4), 475–503.

Szakolczai, A. (2015). Liminality and experience. Structuring transitory situations and transformative events. In A. Horvath, B. Thomassen, & H. Wydra (Eds.), *Breaking boundaries: Varieties of liminality* (pp. 11–38). New York: Berghahn Books.

Szakolczai, Á. (2017). Permanent (trickster) liminality: The reasons of the heart and of the mind. *Theory & Psychology, 27*(2), 231–248. https://doi.org/10.1177/0959354317694095

Tateo, L., & Marsico, G. (2013). The self as tension of wholeness and emptiness. *Interaccoes, 9*(24), 1–19.

Valsiner, J. (1998). *The guided mind. A sociogenetic approach to personality.* Cambridge: Harvard University Press.

Valsiner, J. (2001). Process structure of semiotic mediation in human development. *Human Development, 44*, 84–97.

Valsiner, J. (2002). Forms of dialogical relations and semiotic autoregulation within the self. *Theory & Psychology, 12*(2), 251–265.

Valsiner, J. (2005). Scaffolding within the structure of dialogical self: Hierarchical dynamics of semiotic mediation. *New Ideas in Psychology, 23*(3), 197–206.

Valsiner, J. (2007a). *Culture in minds and societies: Foundations of cultural psychology.* New Delhi: Sage Publications.

Valsiner, J. (2007b). Human development as migration: Striving toward the unknown. In *Otherness in question: Labyrinths of the self* (pp. 349–378). Charlotte: Information Age Publishing.

Valsiner, J. (2007c). Semiotic autoregulation: Dynamic sign hierarchies constraining the stream of consciousness. *Sign System Studies, 35*(1/2).

Valsiner, J. (2014). *An invitation to cultural psychology.* London: Sage.

Valsiner, J. (2017). *From methodology to methods in human psychology.* Cham: Springer.

Valsiner, J., & Diriwächter, R. (2008). Conclusion: Returning to the whole—A new theoretical synthesis in the social sciences. In *Striving for the whole: Creating theoretical synthesis* (pp. 211–237). New Brunswick: Transaction Publishers.

Valsiner, J., & Van der Veer, R. (2000). *The social mind: Construction of the idea.* Cambridge: Cambridge University Press.

Van der Veer, R. (1994). Pierre Janet's relevance for a socio-cultural approach. In A. Rosa & J. Valsiner (Eds.), *Explorations in socio-cultural studies. Vol. 1. Historical and theoretical discourse* (pp. 205–209). Madrid: Fundación Infancia y Aprendizaje.

Van der Veer, R., & Valsiner, J. (1991). *Understanding Vygotsky: A quest for synthesis.* Cambridge: Blackwell.

Vygotsky, L. S. (1978). *Mind in society. The development of higher psychological processes.* Cambridge: Harvard University Press.

Vygotsky, L. S. (1987). *The collected works of L. S. Vygotsky, volume I. Problems of general psychology.* New York: Plenum Press.

Vygotsky, L. S. (1989). Concrete human psychology. *Soviet Psychology, 27*(2), 53–77.

Wartofsky, M. (1979). *Models—Representations and the scientific understanding.* Dodrecht and Boston: Reidel.

Zittoun, T. (2004). Symbolic competencies for developmental transitions: The case of the choice of first names. *Culture & Psychology, 10*(2), 131.

Zittoun, T. (2007a). Dynamics of interiority. Ruptures and transitions in the self development. In L. M. Simão & J. Valsiner (Eds.), *Otherness in question. Labyrinths of the self* (pp. 187–214). Charlotte: Information Age Publishing.

Zittoun, T. (2007b). Symbolic resources in dialogue, dialogical symbolic resources. *Culture & Psychology, 13*(3), 365–377.

Zittoun, T. (2007c). The role of symbolic resources in human lives. In J. Valsiner & A. Rosa (Eds.), *The Cambridge handbook of sociocultural psychology* (pp. 343–361). Cambridge: Cambridge University Press.

Zittoun, T. (2012). Life-course: A socio-cultural perspective. In J. Valsiner (Ed.), *The Oxford handbook of culture and psychology* (pp. 513–535). New York: Oxford University Press.

Zittoun, T., Duveen, G., Gillespie, A., Ivinson, G., & Psaltis, C. (2003). The use of symbolic resources in developmental transitions. *Culture & Psychology, 9*(4), 415.

3

Studying Identity Development: Merging Theory and Phenomenon in the Methods

How does one study scientifically the processes that are highly unique and varied? How does one make meaningful generalisations about psychological processes based on examining the unique and idiosyncratic life experiences and trajectories of single individuals? And how does one study phenomena that are in the process of becoming, that are always changing and moving, not being quite there yet, but not being here anymore either?

These are the questions that guide the discussion in this chapter that considers the methodological challenges of studying the process of identity development from a semiotic cultural perspective. It builds on Valsiner's (2017) conceptualisation of the methodology cycle that is seen as a dynamic intertwinement between the theoretical assumptions of the researcher, the way the phenomenon is understood and the manner in which data collection methods are constructed. The cycle can be described as follows: the researcher defines her basic theoretical assumptions or axioms and, through that, outlines the phenomena under study; she then makes explicit her frame of reference and, through that, sets up the theoretical framework that she uses and develops in the research; she then uses all this to construct her methods that fuse together the theoretical

© The Author(s) 2019
M. Märtsin, *Identity Development in the Lifecourse*, Sociocultural Psychology of the Lifecourse, https://doi.org/10.1007/978-3-030-27753-6_3

underpinnings and views about the phenomenon. In this conceptualisation, methods are not seen as stand-alone tools of data collection but a
sub-part of methodology that works as a cycle, where the different elements or sub-parts are repeatedly considered and revisited. In other
words, methods are purposefully constructed based on the way the phenomena are seen and theory is used and developed in research. Elsewhere,
I have suggested that working within this cycle entails a continuous oscil-
lation between different sub-parts of the cycle that blurs their boundaries
and intertwines the sub-parts (Märtsin, 2012). I have used the metaphor
of jigsaw puzzle to refer to this cycle, considering underlying assumptions, frame of reference, theoretical underpinnings of the study, phenomenon and methods as pieces of a jigsaw puzzle that need to be
perfectly interlocked, and make sense only in relation to each other. These
relationships between theoretical ideas, phenomenon and methods and
how they were merged together in the methods construction will be discussed in this chapter.

Defining Underlying Assumptions and the Emergence of the Phenomenon

In the previous chapter, I discussed, at length, the theoretical ideas that
guided the study that forms the basis of this book and that were also
developed further based on the eight cases. To explain how these theoretical ideas led me to a specific view of the phenomenon of identity development and how they informed the construction of data collection methods,
I will briefly summarise the core theoretical ideas here again, explaining
how they informed my understanding of identity development.

1. **All human conduct takes place in the irreversible flow of time**. This
   is one of the cornerstones of research presented in this book. In
   essence, it means that we can view the present as a transient moment
   and should seek to understand human psychological functioning as
   occurring at the border between past and future (Bergson, 1907;
   Valsiner, 2017). According to this view, it is impossible to predict the
   future with certainty based on past experiences, for there can never be

two experiences that are exactly the same. However, we should never-theless conceptualise human psychological functioning as future-oriented, for we use our imagination to anticipate possible future scenarios and through that pre-adapt to the future. As Valsiner (2017) writes, psychology deals with "preadaptational semiosis of meaning making organisms who operate within irreversible time" (p. 89).

2. **Person and environment form a dynamic and interwoven whole**. As explained in Chap. 2 this research builds on the assumption that person and context are inseparable (Sawyer, 2002). That is, an individual and the surrounding sociocultural environment can be understood as intertwined, open dynamic systems which depend for their existence upon mutual exchanges (Kloep & Hendry, 2011; Valsiner & Diriwächter, 2008). These mutual exchanges take place through the reciprocal processes of internalisation and externalisation (Valsiner, 2007), where material from the outside is through transformations brought over to the intra-psychological system and thereafter reflected back to the collective meaning space. Analytically, the person/environment system can be separated into components that, in turn, can be conceived as open dynamic systems (Valsiner, 1998). Each of these systems is defined by the structural components within the system, by the relations between those internal components, and, importantly, also by the relations between the system and other dynamic systems. Hence, while being themselves wholes, person and environment are also interrelated parts of the same system at the next level of wholeness (Diriwächter, 2004).

3. **All human functioning is mediated by signs**. As described above, a border that simultaneously separates and connects the two components of the same whole separates person and environment from each other. This simultaneous connection and separation occurs through the process of semiotic mediation; that is, through ongoing sign construction (Hasan, 2002; Vygotsky, 1978; Wertsch, 2007). The simultaneous connection and separation function that semiotic mediation, as a border-making process, has is bound up with tension and conflict as the bringing-over and bringing-back-again is accompanied by resistance. Hence, the signs that become constructed in the process of creating and maintaining a functional relationship between person

and environment are always in the process of becoming and being constructed instead of being stable and fixed. Not only alteration but also maintenance, that is, the process of remaining, are considered to be developmental (Valsiner, 2007). Signs as they are created in the irreversible time make the pre-adaptation for the future possible and are, therefore, always "in a state of perpetual transition" (Valsiner, 2000, p. 105), as something that is moving, changing and fluctuating. The tension within the system is, therefore, not something that can be eliminated and resolved but, rather, it is the fundamental feature of the dynamic system that is always in a state of transition. As Marsico and Tateo (2017) suggest: "In this kind of system, endogenous and exogenous forces, tension and compression are at work to create a state of tensegrity (Tateo & Marsico, 2013) in which the organism's integrity is based on a state of constant dynamic pre-tension that ensures both flexibility and stability over time" (p. 538).

4. **Human conduct is organised by future-oriented goals**. As explained in the previous chapter, the unique feature of human meaning-making is the fact that humans are active sign-makers who create signs in order to imagine a certain kind of future state of affairs for themselves and then proceed to construct it. That is, humans constantly create AS-IF scenarios about how things should or could be based on their experiences in the AS-IS world. These scenarios are constantly changed and altered according to the ongoing dynamic relationship with the environment and the experiences of the person. Yet, they nevertheless function as important signposts for a person's movement towards the unknown but imagined and anticipated future. In the current work, these constantly modified guiding principles or semiotic regulators are referred to as life-goal orientations referring to the conceptualisation of Charlotte Bühler (Bühler & Massarik, 1968).

I have explained these underlying theoretical assumptions again in this chapter in order to explain how the phenomenon of identity development emerged out of these theoretical considerations. These assumptions pointed me towards investigating identity development not only as a process occurring within individuals but rather as a process that creates a relationship between individuals and their sociocultural environments.

This view led me to define also my phenomenon of identity development as a process of semiotic regulation. That is, when people construct identities, they try to make sense of their being here and now as it relates to their being in the past with their possible being in the future. I came to understand identity development as part of our ongoing meaning-making process that creates an episodic clarity on the levels of meanings in the flow of unique everyday experiences. That is, in our constant flow of experiences, we sometimes need to stop and stabilise our relation to the occurring events. What is going on here? What does this mean? Who am I? What am I doing here? Where am I going? These are the questions that identity development as a semiotic regulation process deals with. Hence, my attempt to study identity development was essentially an investigation of the dynamic process of meaning-making.

In addition to this, I saw identity development as something that becomes evident in situations where there is a mismatch between a person and the environment. In other words, people need to make sense of something when that something is new, different or unexpected. Hence, identities can be considered as tacit meaning spaces within a person's intra-psychological system, which regulate a person's functioning within a sociocultural environment without the individual being necessarily aware of them. The questions about one's identity are brought into the individual's awareness by a sudden change in the environment that brings along a rupture (Zittoun, 2007). Rupture creates an interruption, a break in the normal flow of events, where the present functions as a divide between known past and unknown, but imagined future. Rupture destabilises the self-system by making another perspective available in a person's meaning field. By this, the rupture generates tension, ambiguity and uncertainty within the self-system that needs to be dealt with. As a result of the rupture, a person becomes aware of his/her way of being, as well as realising that this way of being may not be functional under the changed circumstances. In this respect, rupture is a multi-furcation point that opens up different possible future trajectories for the person, out of which one becomes realised (Sato et al., 2007). The inner tension becomes controlled through the construction of new personal meaning and when this is achieved the questions of identity fade into the background. The answers to these questions that created a temporary state of clarity and stability enable the person to move on to the future. Until these newly constructed ways of making sense of the world and one's being in it are functional, they are actively not dealt with and semiotic regulation operates with these signs automatically (i.e., without the person's awareness).

As is evident from the way I have described the phenomenon of identity development here, I used the individual-socioecological frame of reference in this study (Valsiner, 2017). This frame of reference is different from intra- and inter-individual frames that are typically used in psychological research for it considers the person in relation to his or her sociocultural context. It also differs from the individual-ecological frame for it underlines the unique goal-oriented relationship with the environment that human beings have. This frame of reference thus fits with the psychological functioning of humans yet significantly complicates the construction of methods. Before discussing how I approached that complicated task, I will explain how these theoretical considerations guided my decisions about sampling, study design and theory building.

From Unique Trajectories to Generalised Understandings

According to the methodology cycle, there are several questions related to the study design and data collection that need to be resolved. The first of these has to do with the sample. Two immediate options come to mind—an aggregate or a single case. The preferred approach in contemporary psychological research has been the former. Most of the mainstream psychological research uses (representative) samples of individuals to make generalisations to populations. The most common practice is to carry out an inter-individual analysis with the aim of yielding an average and comparing the groups based on that average. As expected, the idiosyncrasies of individuals' answers are lost in this kind of research, as these become incorporated into the average or disregarded as unwanted outliers. Differently from this, these unique and idiosyncratic ways of making sense of one's experiences were the main focus in understanding the young adults' identity development in this study.

Idiographic Research

There has been a renaissance of interest in idiographic research in recent years, in many areas of social sciences, including psychology (Flyvberg, 2001; Gomm, Hammersley, & Foster, 2009; Valsiner, 2017; Yin, 2003). Molenaar and his colleagues, for example, have convincingly cast doubt on the practices of nomothetic psychological research that focuses on inter-individual variation and aims to make generalisations based on a sample to populations (Molenaar, 2004). They argue that according to mathematical laws, the structure of inter-individual variation is the same as the structure of intra-individual variation only in case of ergodic processes that are rarely found when psychological phenomena are considered (Molenaar et al., 2002). According to Valsiner (2017):

> Ergodicity is a mathematical characteristic of systems where the average of a synchronically derived sample average is considered to be equal to the average derived from the same phenomenon over time. […] If brought to psychology, ergodicity presumes that interindividual and intraindividual variations in a set are isomorphic. (p. 35)

In contrast to this, psychological phenomena are typically characterised by at least some level of growth and maturation, gain and loss or sudden 'jump' to a qualitatively different level and, therefore, are, by definition, varying in time. Vygotsky (1978) has described psychological processes as: "a complex dialectical process characterised by periodicity, unevenness […], metamorphosis or qualitative transformation of one form into another, intertwining of external and internal factors" (p. 73). Psychological processes so described and conceptualised are, therefore, nonergodic. They are developmental in nature and cannot be studied by the nomothetic approach, for the differences among individuals at a given moment in time (i.e., inter-individual variability) are not informative for understanding the changes in individuals' functioning during the course of their life (i.e., intra-individual variability). Based on this mathematical reasoning, Molenaar and his colleagues (Molenaar, 2004; Molenaar et al., 2002) suggest that idiographic approaches that use a time-series analysis of single cases should be utilised in order to understand time-dependent psychological processes.

In the semiotic cultural tradition, the idea that most psychological phenomena are always in the process of becoming, instead of being stable and fixed and thus developmental in their nature, is well-established and the need to study these processes through idiographic approach is generally accepted (Valsiner, 2017; Zittoun, 2017). In the current study, the focus too was on studying time-dependent psychological processes and this led to the usage of an idiographic approach. The aim was to carry out a multiple-case study in order to understand personal life trajectories and reveal intra-individual fluctuations and dynamics across time. Furthermore, the future-oriented nature of human conduct guided my research attention away from focusing only on past experiences and investigating how these were revisited and re-evaluated in my research encounters with my study participants. Instead, it led me to pay attention to the ways these revisits served my participants' possible movement forward into the future. In other words, it guided me to explore how past and future became intertwined in the present narratives and what kinds of futures were at stake for my participants in the retelling and reliving the past experiences. Yet, the aim of this study was not to remain at the level of describing the unique and idiosyncratic ontogenetic trajectories of individuals. Instead, the aim was to construct universal scientific knowledge based on an in-depth analysis of single cases.

Multiple-Case Study Approach

The case study research is based on the idea that behind individual uniqueness lay universal psychological processes that become realised in unique ways throughout a person's life (Molenaar & Valsiner, 2005). These universal processes can be revealed by the detailed investigation of a single case or of multiple single cases. The general aim of case study research is to develop a deep and multifaceted understanding of each case and its functioning using a variety of methods and data sources. The process of case study research is similar to that of case work in psychological practice or social work, where the understanding of a client's situation (e.g., child's behavioural issues) requires engagement with various perspectives (e.g., the child, his parents, teachers, peers) in various contexts (e.g., home, school, sports club) through a variety of methods (e.g., interviews, observations, analysis of test results). In case study research, the ultimate goal is not the creation of new knowledge about inter-group variability and making generalisations to populations, for the cases cannot usually be considered as representative in relation to the population. Instead, the goal is to get an in-depth understanding of the case and to use that insight to create novel theoretical or analytic generalisations. In other words, the goal is to build a new theory (Flick, 2014; Gomm et al., 2009; Yin, 2003).

While a single case analysis can often provide unique insights for theory building, sometimes several cases are analysed to arrive at an analytic generalisation. In the multiple-case study approach, the initial conceptual model becomes built using data from a repeated time-series analysis of a single case and this preliminary model is thereafter used to analyse other single cases, making necessary modifications and alterations to the model. As the model-building is embedded in the unique individual cases, the possibility of arriving at many similar, but slightly different, theoretical models is high. Therefore, the generalised model does not necessarily need to include a description of one single possible trajectory but, rather, should explain the emergence and interrelatedness of several possible unfolding trajectories of the same process (Sato et al., 2007). A good example of this kind of theory-building approach is Sato's trajectory equifinality approach/model (TEA/TEM), which aims to consider both actual and possible past trajectories (what happened and what else could have happened?) and connect these to the possible future trajectories (what can and should happen?) in irreversible time. Valsiner (2017) has described it as: "a method that is aimed at revealing the processes of a construction of a trajectory of movement of a system as it is happening" (p. 54). The focus on mapping all the possible trajectories in the past, including these that did not eventuate, and considering how these set up a field of possible trajectories for the future, makes Sato's model unique in idiographic research. However, the idea of seeking to explain all the possible cases and their particularities is common also to other ways of conducting idiographic research. Differently from nomothetic research that is based on the analysis of aggregates, the deviant cases that reveal a different kind of trajectory are not disregarded as outliers or unwanted exceptions when working within an idiographic approach but, instead, become highly informative in the theory-building process, where the model needs to accommodate all the differences and particularities of individual cases and their unique trajectories. This is achieved by focusing on the examination of universal psychological processes that explain their idiosyncratic occurrences by the constructed generalised conceptual model.

In this kind of analytic work, the role of the researcher is thus fundamental. For it is the researcher's intuition and their subjective relating to the world that is at the centre of the methodology cycle. Typically, in psychological research, we distinguish between the inductive and deductive approaches, positioning the multiple-case study research discussed here on the inductive side of things. Valsiner (2017) suggests that what is actually needed in this kind of research is neither the inductive nor the deductive reasoning but, rather, abduction that he defines as "educated intuition". Abduction, which was introduced by Charles S. Peirce as one of the three logical ways of arriving at new knowledge, is described by Zittoun (2017) as "the core mechanism that allows generalisations from case studies" (p. 171). She sees it as "creative synthesis—a new, unique creation based on the past and present semiotic resources" (p. 175). In my reading, abduction thus allows fusing together the existing theoretical assumptions, conceptualisations and views about the phenomenon in a new and creative way and allows new ideas and conceptual models to emerge, often suddenly as a flash of light.

In answering the question, how do we create generalised knowledge about phenomena that are highly personal and always in the process of becoming, I thus turned to these methodological considerations and chose to adopt a multiple-case study approach in the current study. It was important for me to use a study design that allowed me to observe change and development over time and I, therefore, used a semi-longitudinal design where the individuals who participated in the study were asked to do so during a one-year period. It is through considering the unique developmental trajectories of the eight young adults who participated in this study and viewing these through the lens of the initial theoretical ides that the new model of identity development emerged in this study. As the discussion so far indicates, it was obviously not a linear process of moving from theory to data to conclusions but, rather, a continuous iterative movement between theory, phenomenon and data, guided by my educated intuition. How these data were collected through the methods that were constructed for this study will be explained next.

Constructing Methods to Explore the Process of Becoming

The final question related to the study design and data collection that needs to be resolved within the methodology cycle has to do with the construction of specific data collection methods. As already mentioned, the individual-socioecological frame of reference that guided me to look at identity development as a movement and transformation complicated the construction of data collection methods. Much of the contemporary psychological research seems to ignore this complicated process of taking one's conceptualisation of the phenomenon seriously and trying to find ways how to translate theory into methods. Instead of taking up this challenge and trying to find novel ways of collecting data, a reverse translation, from available data collection methods back to the theory, is carried out. That is to say, the achieved operational definition of theoretical concepts is taken as a theoretical representation of the phenomenon (Valsiner, 2017).

Differently from this problematic reverse translation, the history of psychology offers many productive examples of the translation from theory to methods. The German-Austrian research tradition from the late-nineteenth, early-twentieth century is a good example to consider here (Toomela, 2007). The *Ganzheitspsychologie* approach, developed by the so-called Second School of Leipzig, was one of the first to investigate human psychological functioning by using the "dynamic whole with all its processes [...] as the unit of analysis" (Diriwächter, 2004, p. 7). *Ganzheitspsychologists* were interested in studying processes by way of which the perception moves from a diffused and undifferentiated condition to a state of clarity in real time. Their *Aktualgenese* method slowed down the occurring process by asking the study participants to report all their intermediate percepts as these occurred when looking at an initially blurry and gradually clearer image. By looking at these rich and constructive intermediate forms, through which the person strives towards a meaningful whole and which may be lost en-route, *Ganzheitspsychologists* could reconstruct the process of becoming and build a developmental model (Diriwächter & Valsiner, 2008). Using the same underlying ideas, Heinz Werner developed his microgenetic method that he applied to studying more complex social processes such as the development of word meaning (Wagoner, 2009).

The methods construction in the study discussed in this book was inspired by these strategies as they seemed to fit the underlying assumptions and the way the phenomenon was seen. Particularly relevant for the methods construction was the focus on the process of becoming, where the aim is to examine the personally relevant meanings, while paying attention to the intermediate forms of their emergence. However, the focus of the above-described methods was on the microgenesis of personal meanings; that is, how the experiences are made sense of in real time. The focus of this study, though, was on the creation and functioning of meanings between the mesogenetic and ontogenetic levels, with some links to the microgenetic level. That is, the study focused on understanding how people operate with different personal meanings in the course of their lives beyond the specific everyday experiences where these meanings emerge. I was interested in understanding how, at the mesogenetic level, certain personal signs become constructed as people combine similar reactions to everyday experiences that have emerged at the microgenetic level and how these signs sometimes feed into the construction of overwhelming generalised meta-signs at the ontogenetic level that have the power to guide person's functioning over the course of life. While offering useful suggestions about the methods construction, the microgenetic methods referred to above were, therefore, not directly transferable to this study, although they formed an important inspirational backdrop for the methods creation. Instead of a microgenetic design, a semi-longitudinal design, where the data collection took place over a one-year period, was used. In order to explore the ways the study participants made sense of their experiences during this period, the study combined repeated individual semi-structured interviews with repeated self-completed diary-type questionnaires. The questionnaires included a short sentence-completion exercise and the final interview included a drawing task. The methods were reflective and retrospective and focused on different timeframes, as explained below. Personal narratives in the form of spoken or written text that were sometimes complemented with drawn images were taken as externalisations of personal meanings and the repeated nature of these narratives helped to see the dynamics and fluctuation in one's meaning-making. The interviews and questionnaires include specific questions that focused on the moments of tension, conflict and interruption in the normal flow of being and this decision, as explained below, was informed by the idea that border-crossing processes are tied up with tension and resistance. All the methods used in the study will now be described in greater detail.

Individual Interviews

During the one-year study period, three individual interviews were conducted with each study participant. This gave me the opportunity to build good research relationship with the participants, as well as to compensate for the lack of details and depth in the descriptions of one's everyday experiences gathered through the questionnaires that was evident in some cases. All the interviews were non-directive and semi-structured, and I only decided upon general topics for each interview beforehand. This flexibility enabled me to focus on the themes that emerged during the interview and gave me the opportunity to take into account the uniqueness of each case. As usual, in case study research, the data collection and analysis phases of research overlapped and this continuous analysis of emerging data from previous interviews and questionnaires fed into the content of later interviews (Flick, 2014).

All the interviews were conducted in Estonian, which was the mother tongue of all the participants, with the exception of one participant whose mother tongue was Russian, but who considered herself to be bilingual and was fluent in Estonian. Each interview lasted approximately 1.5 hours, they were all tape-recorded and transcribed verbatim. The permission to do so was obtained from each participant at the beginning of the first interview and confirmed again at the start of each following interview.

My initial plan was to conduct the first interview before the participants' arrival to the UK, for it made sense to me to map their initial experiences and meanings before coming to the UK. However, due to their and my commitments and living and travel arrangements, this was not possible in all cases. This need to modify my initial plans and use opportunities to engage with my study participants as these were presented to me, often unexpectedly, became usual in the one-year data collection period. I will, therefore, describe the process of data collection here only in broad terms, leaving out some case-specific modifications that I had to introduce to my data collection strategy.

The data for this study was collected during the period of August 2006 to October 2007. The first interviews took place within the first two months of the study, and half of them took place in Tallinn, Estonia, while the other half were conducted in various cities in the UK. The aim of the first interview was to start building a research relationship with each participant. The first interview concentrated on understanding the personal background of the participant (e.g., information about one's family, educational trajectory and professional life, as well as intimate relations), as well as the motivation for undertaking a study abroad, ideas and expectations about the UK and one's forthcoming experience. The second interview was conducted with one of the participants in the end of January before she returned to Estonia at the end of her short-term study visit. With the remaining seven participants, the second interview was conducted in April. All the interviews were conducted in the UK, where the participants lived, with the exception of one interview, which took place in Tartu, Estonia. The aim of the second interview was to get a more detailed understanding of the participants' experiences abroad up to that point in the study. The interview concentrated on person-specific themes that had emerged from the questionnaires and aimed to collect deeper and more detailed accounts of the important life-events and their significance to the participant. The second interview also touched upon participants' future plans.

The time of the third interview depended largely on the commitments and travel and living arrangements of the participants, but they all took place approximately 12 months after the first interview. Some of the interviews took place in Estonia and some others in the UK, depending on the availability of the participants. The aim of the third interview was twofold: first, to look back at the experiences of the last period of the study and collect more detailed accounts of the significant events and their personal meanings from that period; second, to look back at the entire study period and analyse one's life-trajectory in terms of positive and negative periods throughout the year. In order to facilitate the discussion about this latter theme, a drawing task was used in the final interview. The aim of this task was to offer participants a tool that would enable them to talk about their experiences in a more structured and easily accessible, whilst playful manner.

In order to complete the task, the participants had to represent their experiences during the last 12 months by drawing a time-line on a sheet of A3 size white paper, using colour pencils. In this timeline, the 'hills' represented positive periods and the 'valleys' marked the negative periods in their lives. The participants were encouraged to use different colours when drawing the timeline. They were also asked to either write on the drawing or to explain orally what were the important events in each 'hill' or 'valley' that triggered the positive or negative emotions. The suggestion was also made to give names to the 'hills' or 'valleys' if these came to one's mind. The participants were also encouraged to use symbols, pictures or other means to illustrate the drawing. When the participant had finished working on the task, she or he was asked to explain what the timeline with its captions, colours and images meant for them. Figures 3.1 and 3.2 give two contrasting examples of the timelines that were produced in this study.

I have reflected upon the opportunities and challenges presented by the use of this drawing task elsewhere (Märtsin, 2017). Here, it is worth mentioning that the use of this task gave me an opportunity to offer the study participants a different way of accessing and expressing their meanings—an opportunity that was welcomed and eagerly taken up by some participants, like Lisa, whose image is shown in Fig. 3.1. In fact, some of

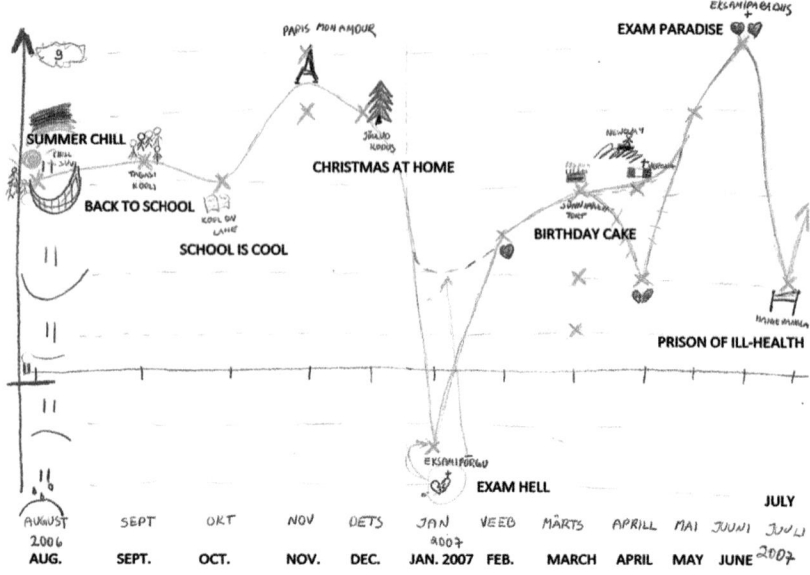

Fig. 3.1 Lisa's timeline drawing

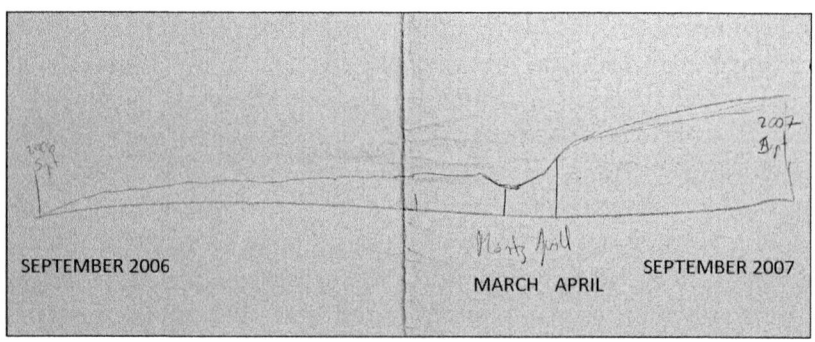

Fig. 3.2 Andres's timeline drawing

the reflections included in this book come from the explanations the participants gave about their drawings. At the same time, this mode of representing one's meanings did not work for everybody and some young adults, like Andres, whose image is shown in Fig. 3.2, used it only as a complementary mode to verbal narrative. In this book, I have decided to leave the timeline images created by the participants aside and concentrate only on the spoken text that accompanied their creation. I have decided not to discuss the opportunities and challenges of using the visual mode of meaning-making in this book, as it deserves a separate conceptual and analytical frame and space to reveal its uniqueness.

Questionnaires

In order to investigate the personal life experiences of the participants as these occurred and to discover critical moments in their life-trajectories during the one-year period, questionnaires were sent to the participants once a month via e-mail. The aim of the questionnaires was to collect personal narratives about personal life experiences and feelings and thoughts related to those. While the interviews enabled me to explore the life-events retrospectively within a longer timeframe, the usage of monthly questionnaires allowed gathering reflections on more recent events and sometimes immediate reactions to significant everyday situations. Estonian was used as the language of the questionnaires.

The questionnaires used in the study included up to five open-ended questions that enabled the participants to describe their life experiences during the previous month. Each questionnaire included some general questions that were asked to all the participants and some person-specific questions. Using the theoretical underpinnings of the study, the general questions used in the questionnaires concentrated, on many occasions, on situations where tension and struggle was evident (e.g., describe a situation from the last month where you felt that you were different from people around you). Many of the questions were used repeatedly in the questionnaires in order to see how persons construct meanings in relation to the same input in different moments in time.

As with the interviews, the data collection with questionnaires overlapped with the data analysis. The person-specific questions that were included in the monthly questionnaires aimed at following up the emerging topics and seeing how certain themes developed in relation to a person's flow of experiences.

In addition to the questions about daily experiences, every second questionnaire included a sentence-completion exercise. The beginnings of the sentences that needed to be completed by participants were the following:

- Estonians are …
- Estonia is …
- For an Estonian student in the UK, it is …
- Lately, I feel …
- My life is lately …

The aim of this exercise was to investigate the possible fluctuations and changes in a person's meanings in relation to her experiences. While the answers to open-ended questions were aimed at providing a general picture of the events happening in participants' lives and their reactions to these, the sentence-completion exercise was designed to bring out the changes in more general aspects of the personal meaning space. Furthermore, the sentence-completion exercise enabled the triangulation of the data (Eisenhardt, 1989) and seeing whether the periods of tension and conflict that were evident in the interview and questionnaire data were revealed also by the fluctuations in the sentence-completion task.

Principles of Data Analysis

So far in this chapter, I have explained the principles of the methodology cycle and described how the back and forth movement between theory and phenomenon led to the creation of specific methods used in the study that forms the core of this book. The same kind of back and forth movement between theory and phenomenon guided also the data analysis. In the following pages, I will explain the main steps of the data analysis, and although I will present these step in a linear manner, it is important to keep in mind that the analysis actually emerged through the iterative process of moving continuously between theoretical ideas, data and the phenomenon.

The data analysis carried out in the current study concentrated mostly on the intra-individual analysis and sought to reveal the dynamics of meaning-making within a single case across time.[1] At later stages of the analysis, I also compared the cases and through this inter-case analysis, selected the themes that are presented in this book. The principles of these analytical steps will be briefly described in this section.

Intra-Case Analysis

The within-case analysis consisted of the following stages:

1. **Identification of re-occurring themes within each case.** In this initial stage of analysis, I read and re-read the interview transcripts and questionnaires in order to identify the themes that were re-occurring throughout the study period. My aim in this first stage was to extract all the themes that re-emerged and thus appeared as significant for understanding the life experiences of the participants. At this stage, I did not pay attention to the fluctuations in the participants' self-understandings. Rather, I aimed to extract all the themes that were important for understanding each case.

2. **Identification of meaning-making episodes.** In this second stage, I read the transcripts and questionnaires once again in order to reveal the themes in case of which changes and fluctuations in meanings were evident and where it appeared that the participant was engaged in active meaning-making. In this stage, I abandoned the themes in case of which the data did not disclose any fluctuations, dynamics or movement between different perspectives. The analysis at this stage resulted in a list of quotations that were grouped together according to the general re-emerging themes. To help me in the analysis, I used tables and diagrams to map when exactly the different themes emerged and how they changed throughout the study period.

---

[1] The term *intra-individual analysis* is used in this book to refer to the analysis within a single case, as opposed to the *inter-individual analysis*, which investigates the differences and similarities between cases. I acknowledge that the former term may not fully represent the conceptualisation of meaning-making as a boundary-process that connects person and environment. However, as it enables to differentiate between the two types of analysis and maintains consistency with the relevant methodological literature, I use it here, despite its conceptual shortcomings.

3. **Triangulation**. Once the main themes for each case were identified and the trajectory of change for each of those themes was mapped out, these trajectories were compared with the timeline drawings that the participants had created. Equally, the responses to sentence-completion exercises from the questionnaires were used at this stage of analysis to understand whether the analysis across themes mapped to the fluctuations in participants' emotions and meaning-making, as revealed through this exercise. The discrepancies that this triangulation revealed fed into the further analysis and interpretation of the data. This stage of analysis resulted in a list of key themes for each case and an identification of a trajectory of change for each theme.

4. **Compiling the case summaries**. In this stage of analysis, I wrote analytical summaries for all the cases and for each theme within the case. In doing that, I built on the conceptual ideas discussed in the previous chapter. In particular, I aimed to identify the various rupture-transition episodes and then describe how the semiotic auto-regulation occurred during the transition phase. In describing the semiotic auto-regulation, I sought to identify which life-goal orientations, and self-understandings from past, present and future, and which meaning fields were created and re-created in order to regulate the inner tensions and reconstruct the shaken meaning structures. I also paid attention to the voices of others, trying to identify who were the most significant real and imaginary, present and absent dialogue partners for the participants in their efforts to make sense of their experiences.

Inter-Case Analysis

The cross-cases analysis consisted of the following two steps:

1. **Identification of the re-occurring themes across cases**. In this stage of the analysis, I revisited all the themes that were revealed by the intra-case analysis in order to identify similarities and differences in these themes across cases. This stage of analysis thus aimed to move beyond the idiosyncrasies in the dynamics of meaning-making that

were revealed by the intra-case analysis and, instead, look for general commonalities across cases in terms of the kinds of ruptures and meaning-making efforts experienced by the participants. This analysis across cases led to the identification of four broad themes that brought together similar meaning-making episodes from various cases. These four broad themes form the core of this book and were labelled as follows: (1) home, adventure and belonging; (2) reconstructing relationships; (3) competence, self-confidence and recognition, and (4) making plans.

2. **Selection of the cases across the themes**. In this final stage of the analysis, I chose the case studies to be discussed under each of these four themes in this book. I decided to choose two cases for each theme in order to allow space for explaining the cases in enough depth. The decision to unpack each theme through two cases does not mean that the same themes did not emerge also in other cases. On the contrary, the four themes emerged in various forms in all the eight cases. The two cases chosen for each theme are meant to offer new insights about the dynamics of meaning-making in relation to these themes, while also being somewhat different from each other and thus complementing each other within a theme.

The results of the analysis carried out is presented in the following four chapters, organised by the four main themes identified. But, before turning to these themes, I give a brief overview of the young adults who participated in this study.

Overview of Study Participants

The current study sought to explore the everyday experiences and life-trajectories of young people from Estonia living and studying in the UK. This specific group was chosen for the study for several reasons. First, I assumed that in order to investigate personal meaning-making processes, a situation where tension between personal and collective culture emerges would be suitable. I also reasoned that this kind of stress is more likely to occur in situations where a person comes into contact with a new sociocultural context and where she or he needs to move between cultural contexts repeatedly. I considered that a situation where a person moves to a foreign country for a short or medium-term period for studying purposes and then needs to return to their country of origin offered a suitable context for examining how these movements made one's identity development processes more 'visible'. I also assumed that sharing an ethno-cultural background with my study participants made it easier for me to understand some of their struggles and enabled a deeper understanding of their possible experiences in a new environment.

The recruitment of study participants started in May 2006. My initial plan was to include in the study only those young Estonians who had never lived in the UK before. In order to gain access to individuals coming to study in the UK, several institutions were contacted: Tallinn University, Tartu University, Tallinn Technical University, the British Council in Estonia, Archimedes Foundation in Estonia[2] and the Estonian Embassy in London. Each of these institutions provided me either with the names and e-mail addresses of young people who were planning to start studies in the UK or sent my invitation letter to the people whose contacts they had.

As a result of these contacts, it became increasingly clear that it would not be possible to limit the group of participants only to the people who had never lived in the UK. Hence, I made a decision to relax this inclusion criterion and include in the study also those persons who had previously lived in the UK. The negotiations with all the interested individuals resulted in a final group of eight people who committed to participating in the study over a one-year period. All these eight participants who stayed in the study received a gift voucher to thank them for their time and effort. The summary of the basic characteristics of the eight participants is provided in Table 3.1. More detailed background information about each participant is given throughout this book in the chapter where their experiences are discussed.

---

[2] Archimedes Foundation is responsible for providing scholarships for studies within the European Union.

Table 3.1   Summary of the basic characteristics of study participants

Pseudonym	Gender	Age at the start of the study	Time in the UK at the first interview	Planned period of stay in the UK
Andres	Male	31	2 years	4 years
Eva	Female	19	1 month	3 years
Mari	Female	23	0 months	6 months
Lisa	Female	20	9 months	3 years
Nora	Female	21	1 year	3 years
Säde	Female	25	0 months	1 year
Kersti	Female	25	0 months	1 year
Tania	Female	19	0 months	3 years

Researcher in the Methodology Cycle

Before drawing this chapter to the close, I will once again return to Valsiner's (2017) methodology cycle. So far, I have discussed how researcher's conceptual assumptions and theoretical ideas inform and shape the research design, construction of data collection methods and analysis of the data. But the researcher is at the centre of the methodology cycle also due to her unique position in relation to the research participants. A position that shapes the way participants are recruited, data collected, analysed and presented to the wider audiences in qualitative research as the one discussed in this book.

It is often argued that in order to enhance the accuracy of qualitative research and the credibility of the findings, qualitative researchers should be aware of their values, beliefs, knowledge and personal characteristics that they bring to the research context, and reflect on these continuously throughout the research process (Alvesson & Sköldberg, 2000; Berger, 2015; Flick, 2014). Berger (2015) defines reflexivity as "the process of a continual internal dialogue and critical self-evaluation of researcher's positionality as well as active acknowledgement and explicit recognition that this position may affect the research process and outcome" (p. 220). In other words, reflexivity entails turning the researcher's gaze that is ordinarily directed to the research participants towards oneself and interrogating one's own ideas, reasons, motivations and reactions to the formulation of certain research questions, collecting certain kind of data in a particular way and interpreting the data in a unique manner. The personal characteristics and positions that can affect these processes include among others, gender, race, age, experiences of mobility, political and ideological viewpoints, theoretical perspectives and various personal experiences. Berger (2015) suggests that these characteristics and positions can shape the research process in three major ways: (1) creating possibilities for access to the 'field'; (2) impacting the researcher-researched relationships; and (3) filtering the way data is interpreted. These characteristics can thus position the researcher as an insider or an outsider in relation to the participants and their experiences, creating certain kinds of opportunities for access, relationship building and data collection and interpretation.

In the research discussed in this book, I was positioned from the start as an 'insider' in relation to the study participants. I was relatively close to all of them in terms of my age, also being in the process of transitioning into adulthood. I came from the same geographical location and cultural system and shared with them experiences of relocating to the UK, having undertaken mobility for educational purposes. Therefore, their references to the peculiarities of living as a foreigner in the UK, especially as a female from a post-Soviet country in a place that was at the time flooded with immigrants from the former Eastern Bloc, made immediate sense to me and resonated with my own experiences (see Chap. 6 for examples of these experiences). Their distinctions between being Nordic vs being Scandinavian vs being Eastern-European (see for example in Chap. 6 and in Chap. 7) were also familiar to me and did not require an additional explanation. Furthermore, I was able to conduct the interviews in our native language that again made access to certain meaning fields easier if not possible. My insider position was thus very important in the first months of the study, as it gave me access to my participants and allowed building research relationships with them that were grounded in shared understandings and experiences.

Yet being so close to my participants in terms of the experiences also created certain challenges for the data collection. From the start, I made the decision of not sharing many of my own perspectives with my participants. I was interested in their views and experiences and thought that bringing my own 'material' explicitly into the research encounter will too strongly shape the meaning-making of my participants. Yet, this decision resulted in me having to deal with some awkward situations where my vague answers to their questions created mini-ruptures into the development of our research relationships. In these moments, the participants seemed to re-evaluate how to position themselves in relation to me as a researcher (and not a fellow migrant or a potential friend in the UK) and how much of their experiences to reveal to someone who is not responding with the same kind of revelations. While these ruptures could have shaped significantly a research process that relied on a single in-depth interview, I trusted my longitudinal design to give me further opportunities to repair these ruptures. By feeding the already collected data back to the participants for further reflection in every new questionnaire or interview (as explained above), they could start to see me as an empathic and attentive listener who was interested first and foremost in their experiences.

In fact, the longitudinal design became an important way for me to move between the 'insider' and 'outsider' position throughout the research process. This insider position was clearly foregrounded for me in the first months of the research where it allowed me to ask questions that 'made sense' and position me as someone who understood what it meant to be an Estonian student and young adult in the UK. However, as the months passed, I became more and more aware that, fundamentally, I was an 'outsider' to the personal lives and life-trajectories of my participants. In a way then, I had to reflect on this and backgound the insider position that made their experiences known and familiar on the surface, and instead try to foreground the outsider position to continue to ask the questions that 'made sense' and continue to learn about their unique and layered perspectives—their histories, their families, their motivations, desires and goals. In other words, I had to make the familiar seem unfamiliar in order to notice its uniqueness and understand its distinctiveness (Mannay, 2010). In a way then, although my research relationships developed over the one-year period that I was collecting my data and, in many ways, I moved closer to my participants, my continuous reflection allowed me to also move further away from them as I grew to know how diverse their experiences were from each other and from me.

Valsiner (2017), in conceptualising the methodology cycle, underscores the importance of continuously moving between theory, phenomenon and methods in the unfolding research process. I will add to this the constant movement between the various positions that one needs to occupy as a researcher in the research process and in relation to the research participants. For it is this movement that allows becoming aware of the unique perspectives of study participants and maintains the rigour of the researcher's work.

Summary

In this chapter, I have discussed the methodological approach used in the study that provided the empirical material for the development of the conceptual model of identity development presented in this book. The central aim of this chapter was to describe how the methodology cycle, as described by Valsiner (2017), could be put to practice and how the creation of specific data collection methods emerges from the complex interplay between theory, phenomenon and methods. The chapter has underlined the idea that methods are not tools that can be picked up from the researcher's toolbox and used without considering the theoretical and phenomenological context in which they are used. Equally, it has underlined the idea that methodology is an evolving process, a cycle, a movement, where new decisions need to be constantly made and new relationships need to be constantly negotiated as novel features of theory, phenomenon or data emerge. I also explained how these negotiations and movement between theory, phenomenon and data led to the identification of four broad themes that will be discussed in the following chapters that build on the unique experiences of the eight emerging adults who participated in this study.

References

Alvesson, M., & Sköldberg, K. (2000). *Reflexive methodology. New vistas for qualitative research*. London: Sage.

Berger, R. (2015). Now I see it, now I don't: Researcher's position and reflexivity in qualitative research. *Qualitative Research, 15*(2), 219–234. https://doi.org/10.1177/1468794112468475

Bergson, H. (1907). *Loov evolutsioon [Creative evolution]* (M. Ott & H. Sahkai, Trans.). Tallinn: Imamaa.

Bühler, C., & Massarik, F. (Eds.). (1968). *The course of human life. A study of goals in the humanistic perspective.* New York: Springer.

Diriwächter, R. (2004). Ganzheitspsychologie: The doctrine. *From Past to Future. Clark Papers on the History of Psychology, 5*(1), 3–16.

Diriwächter, R., & Valsiner, J. (Eds.). (2008). *Striving for the whole. Creating theoretical syntheses.* New Brunswick, NJ: Transaction Publishers.

Eisenhardt, K. M. (1989). Building theories from case study research. *Academy of Management Review, 14*(4), 532–550.

Flick, U. (2014). *An introduction to qualitative research* (5th ed.). London: Sage.

Flyvberg, B. (2001). *Making social science matter. Why social inquiry fails and how it can succeed again.* Cambridge: Cambridge University Press.

Gomm, R., Hammersley, M., & Foster, P. (Eds.). (2009). *Case study method.* London: Sage.

Hasan, R. (2002). Semiotic mediation and mental development in pluralistic societies: Some implications for tomorrow's schooling. In G. Wells & G. Claxton (Eds.), *Learning for life in the 21st century: Sociocultural perspectives on the future of education* (pp. 112–126). Oxford, UK: Blackwell.

Kloep, M., & Hendry, L. B. (2011). A systemic approach to the transitions to adulthood. In J. J. Arnett, M. Kloep, L. B. Hendry, & J. L. Tanner (Eds.), *Debating emerging adulthood: Stage or process?* (pp. 53–76). Oxford: Oxford University Press.

Mannay, D. (2010). Making the familiar strange: Can visual research methods render the familiar setting more perceptible? *Qualitative Research, 10*(1), 91–111. https://doi.org/10.1177/1468794109348684

Marsico, G., & Tateo, L. (2017). Borders, tensegrity and development in dialogue. *Integrative Psychological & Behavioral Science, 51*(4), 536–556. https://doi.org/10.1007/s12124-017-9398-2

Märtsin, M. (2012). A dismantled jigsaw: Making sense of the complex intertwinement of theory, phenomena and methods. In E. Abbey & S. Surgan (Eds.), *Emerging methods in psychology* (pp. 101–119). New Brunswick, NJ: Transaction Publishers.

Märtsin, M. (2017). Beyond verbal narratives: Using timeline images in the semiotic cultural study of meaning making. *Integrative Psychological and Behavioral Science.* https://doi.org/10.1007/s12124-017-9409-3

Molenaar, P. C. M. (2004). A manifesto on psychology as idiographic science: Brining the person back into scientific psychology, this time forever. *Measurement, 2*(4), 201–218.

Molenaar, P. C. M., Huizenga, H. M., & Nesselroade, J. R. (2002). The relationship between the structure of inter-individual and intra-individual variability. In U. Staudinger & U. Lindenberger (Eds.), *Understanding human development* (pp. 339–360). Dordrecht: Klüwer.

Molenaar, P. C. M., & Valsiner, J. (2005). How generalization works through the single case: A simple idiographic process analysis of an individual psychotherapy [40 paragraphs]. *International Journal of Idiographic Science* [Online Journal], Art. 1. Retrieved April 4, 2008, from http://www.valsiner.com/articles/molenvals.htm

Sato, T., Yasuda, Y., Kido, A., Arakawa, A., Mizoguchi, H., & Valsiner, J. (2007). Sampling reconsidered: Idiographic science and the analysis of personal life trajectories. In J. Valsiner & A. Rosa (Eds.), *The Cambridge handbook of sociocultural psychology* (pp. 82–106). Cambridge: Cambridge University Press.

Sawyer, R. K. (2002). Unresolved tensions in sociocultural theory: Analogies with contemporary sociological debates. *Culture & Psychology, 8*(3), 283–305.

Tateo, L., & Marsico, G. (2013). The self as tension of wholeness and emptiness. *Interaccoes, 9*(24), 1–19.

Toomela, A. (2007). Culture of science: Strange history of the methodological thinking in psychology. *Integrative Psychological and Behavioral Science, 41*, 6–20.

Valsiner, J. (1998). *The guided mind. A sociogenetic approach to personality*. Cambridge: Harvard University Press.

Valsiner, J. (2000). Data as representations: Contextualizing qualitative and quantitative research strategies. *Social Science Information, 39*(1), 99–113.

Valsiner, J. (2005). Scaffolding within the structure of dialogical self: Hierarchical dynamics of semiotic mediation. *New Ideas in Psychology, 23*(3), 197–206.

Valsiner, J. (2007). *Culture in minds and societies: Foundations of cultural psychology*. New Delhi: Sage Publications.

Valsiner, J. (2017). *From methodology to methods in human psychology*. Cham: Springer.

Valsiner, J., & Diriwächter, R. (2008). Conclusion: Returning to the whole—A new theoretical synthesis in the social sciences. In *Striving for the whole: Creating theoretical synthesis* (pp. 211–237). New Brunswick: Transaction Publishers.

Vygotsky, L. S. (1978). *Mind in society. The development of higher psychological processes*. Cambridge: Harvard University Press.

Wagoner, B. (2009). The experimental methodology of constructive microgenesis. In J. Valsiner, P. Molenaar, N. Chaudhary, & M. Lyra (Eds.), *Handbook of dynamic process methodology in the social and developmental sciences* (pp. 99–121). New York: Springer.

Wertsch, J. V. (2007). Mediation. In H. Daniels, M. Cole, & J. V. Wertsch (Eds.), *The Cambridge companion to Vygotsky* (pp. 178–192). New York: Cambridge University Press.

Yin, R. K. (2003). *Case study research: Design and methods* (3rd ed.). Newbury Park: Sage Publications.

Zittoun, T. (2007). Dynamics of interiority. Ruptures and transitions in the self development. In L. M. Simão & J. Valsiner (Eds.), *Otherness in question. Labyrinths of the self* (pp. 187–214). Charlotte: Information Age Publishing.

Zittoun, T. (2017). Modalities of generalization through single case studies. *Integrative Psychological and Behavioral Science, 51*(2), 171–194. https://doi.org/10.1007/s12124-016-9367-1

4

Home, Adventure and Belonging

Introduction

The meanings of home are multiple and varied. As Mallett (2004) suggests, "The term home functions as a repository for complex, inter-related and at times contradictory socio-cultural ideas about people's relationship with one another, especially family, and with places, spaces, and things" (p. 84) (see also Roy, Dubé, Després, Freitas, & Légaré, 2018). Home can be understood as a physical space, a house, a dwelling where one was born and lives or that one seeks to create, acquire and own. This physical space is actual and real, but it is also imagined and ideal; it is lived, it is remembered and it is imagined. The meaning of home is strongly interlinked with the idea of family, as home becomes the centre of family life from one's past or for one's future (Henderson, Holland, McGrellis, Sharpe, & Thomson, 2007). Home is seen as the nexus of relationships with others from this and previous generations, creating a relational bridge between past, present and future (Dahinden, 2012; Manzo, 2005). The interconnection between family and home also conjures up feelings and experiences related to comfort, safety and security, as home is experienced as a private space, a retreat, a haven, a safe place

© The Author(s) 2019
M. Märtsin, *Identity Development in the Lifecourse*, Sociocultural Psychology of the Lifecourse, https://doi.org/10.1007/978-3-030-27753-6_4

where one can escape the gaze of the others, relax and be free (Després, 1991). But home also includes others beyond one's family, for it can also be understood as homeland, the land of one's ancestors (Mallett, 2004). Ethnicity or nationality can thus become important in the processes of identification and creating a sense of belonging as a way of drawing boundaries between self and others, between home and non-home (Dahinden, 2012, 2013).

Furthermore, notions of home are also related to ideas of staying and leaving, journeying and returning (Moore, 2000). Home is thus not merely a place of origin, but also a destination, an imagined objective of journeying where a better life and being can begin to unfold. Home thus contains both memories and dreams, and it is an important site through which a sense of self and identity is experienced and constructed (Crafter, Maunder, & Soulsby, 2019; Kylén, Löfqvist, Haak, & Iwarsson, 2019). In fact, home and identity can be seen as mutually defining: we gain our identity, our sense of sameness, continuity and rootedness from the experiences of being at home, while home becomes a significant place precisely due to these meaningful experiences (Märtsin & Mahmoud, 2012). In other words, we are who we are partly because we come from a certain locale in space and time, and we call this locale our home because we derive our sense of identity from the experiences within and in relation to it.

Yet, as many feminist writers have pointed out, the meanings of home are not always positive, for this private space can also become a site of oppression, a site that hides violence and abuse from others (Jones, 1995; Wardhaugh, 1999; Woodhall-Melnik et al., 2017). For many children, young people and women, it can conceal traumatic experiences and be associated with fear, danger and insecurity, emerging as a prison instead of a haven (Jones, 2000). Also, as home gains its meaning through unique lived experiences, it may not refer to one physical location (dwelling, neighbourhood, city or country) but to a bricolage of multiple and varied experiences in and of home—places involving several significant others. The extensive research about home suggests that it has bodily, spatial, kinesthetic, sensual, emotional, rational and irrational, personal and interpersonal qualities and combines speakable with unspeakable, explicit with tacit, and reflective, prereflective and hyperreflective meanings, not all of them necessarily positive (Mallett, 2004; Manzo, 2014).

Together with Hala Mahmoud, I have suggested that the complex assemblage of meanings related to home may become accessible only when home is not available anymore, when we have voluntarily or unwillingly moved away from it (Märtsin & Mahmoud, 2012). According to this line of reasoning, the meaning and value of home is awakened in its absence, where the ordinarily taken-for-granted meaning field of 'home' emerges in relation to a meaning field of 'non-home'. It is thus activated by the tension between home and journeying, security in an insecure world, inside in relation to outside, the feeling of being at home as opposed to yearning-for-home, self in relation to the other, and private in relation to the public (Dovey, 1985; Manzo, 2005, 2014). According to Dovey (1985), to experience home is to experience such dialectics: "There is no sense of home unless there is also journeying. [...] Without a public realm there is no privacy. And in a sense, without homelessness, we would not be concerned with what home means" (p. 48).

Home and adventure thus emerge as complementary meaning fields that are mutually constitutive and, through that, home with its many meanings and associations becomes simultaneously enabling and constraining. It helps us to build self-continuity within and beyond novelty, but it also holds us back and distances us from newness. Following this dialectic logic, I will examine mobility and the process of identity development it triggers as a painful, yet possibly exhilarating, experience that makes us lose our centre of security and familiarity, yet also opens up opportunities for transformation and re-invention. While moving between places and cultural systems is demanding and exhausting, because of the encountered novelty and foreignness, it is also filled with possibilities for re-establishing familiar patterns of everyday life in a new way. Therefore, the process of moving between home and away is not necessarily characterised by initial disruption, loss and pain that is followed by efforts to cope and reconstruct new stability by merging old and new ways of being as some cross-cultural models would suggest (Berry, 2009). Instead, for mobile individuals as the young adults in this study, the current country of residence may be the first but not the final destination in their mobile trajectory (Dahinden, 2012; Plöger & Kubiak, 2019). In light of this, I explore the mobility between home and away as a fundamentally ambiguous experience of loss in relation to finding, change against the backdrop of everydayness and disruption within continuity that has implications for the way we see ourselves and imagine our futures.

The ideas of staying and leaving home, journeying and returning in relation to home are also linked to notions of dependency, interdependence, autonomy and independence (Crafter et al., 2019; Mallett, 2004). Being at home, we are protected and sheltered by the familiarity and relational interconnectedness in which we are situated. Yet, being at home and situated within our familiar networks, we are also kept away from possibilities to venture out into the world and do things in our own way, for our own purposes. It is in this sense that moving away from home can be exciting and exhilarating, for it allows us to reconstruct our ways of being independently, to become otherwise without the constraints of the family and home. In this way, moving away from home tells us something about the kind of person we want to be and become in the future. As such, moving away from one's home becomes an important marker in the transition to adulthood (Arnett, Kloep, Hendry, & Tanner, 2011; Henderson et al., 2007). Becoming independent, moving physically and psychologically away from the family home and settling down in order to create one's own family thus emerge as important milestones in the transition to adulthood. And although this conflation of home, house and family across different timescales and in relation to one's lifecourse has been criticised as a manner in which neoliberal and individualist ideological agendas aimed at increasing economic efficiency and growth are imposed on individuals (Mallett, 2004), the meanings related to home and moving away remain vital in the transition to adulthood.

These themes are unpacked in this chapter by drawing upon examples from two case studies—Säde and Tania. The case of Säde allows an examination of the ways in which meanings about belonging to a specific ethnic group are constructed, challenged, suspended and reconstructed in relation to the experience of moving away from home and being away from the home community. The case of Tania, instead, allows an exploration of how the adventure away from home and the journey into adulthood can become intertwined and create simultaneously identities of a child and an adult. Both cases thus enable a focus on the idea that identities emerge as a result of our semiotic border-making processes. There is a growing body of anthropological and sociological literature that problematises the use of ethnicity and nationality as pre-existing categories in mobility research and, instead, examines how these and other categories, such as gender or professional status, emerge as significant categories through individuals' boundary-work that enables the creation of a sense of identification and belonging (see, for example, Dahinden, 2012, 2013; Eade, 2013). While this body of work is foremost focused on analysing the role of various social actors in using such categories and revealing the consequences of this usage for individuals and groups in society, my analysis here is more concerned with individual development as it seeks to explore the dynamics of the emergence of identities in such semiotic border-making processes and how this enables individuals to make sense of their experiences and imagine a trajectory into the future. In my analysis, I thus build on the work of Marsico and others (Español, Marsico, & Tateo, 2018; Marsico, 2016; Marsico & Tateo, 2017) who consider these dynamics from a semiotic perspective and suggest conceptualising identity as a semiotic border-making process. With the help of the two case studies discussed in this chapter, I want to explore this suggestion and see how semiotic border-making between different others, between self and others, and within the self emerges through and supports the movement between home and away. I also want to discuss how this process of border-making leads to the reconstruction of the meaning of home and the sense of being 'at home'.

Homeland, Journeying and Ambiguous Belongings

It is not a coincidence that I introduce Säde first in relation to the topic of ethnicity in this book, for she is unique amongst the eight study participants in terms of her relationship to her homeland. At the beginning of the study, Säde is 25 years old. She comes from a big Estonian family and is the oldest among six children, having one sister and four brothers. She was born in a small town but moved to a city in Estonia when she was 15. Since then, she has lived alone, away from her parents and family home. Säde reports not having very close relationships with her family; in fact, her interactions with me suggest that she calls and writes to her friends in Estonia more frequently than using these means to stay in touch with her parents and siblings. Despite this, it is clear from our interactions that she has deeply internalised some of the values of her parents, especially those that are related to the way she relates to nature and the environment and the way she makes sense of her ethnic heritage and her connection to the homeland.

While a majority of the study participants move to the UK to undertake their undergraduate studies, Säde moves to England to undertake her Master's studies. This decision to go back to university comes after working several years in Estonia in the public sector, in an area that she is very passionate about and has been very successful in. Prior to her arrival, Säde has never been to the UK. Now she moves to one of the oldest cities and embarks on studies that are meant to last for one year in one of the most prestigious universities in the country.

"Being Estonian Is a Full-Time Job"

Although Säde has not been to the UK before, her movement away from home and into this new cultural environment does not seem to create a significant rupture into her way of being immediately. While her first couple of months abroad are characterised by active semiotic border-crossing and making processes, which position and reposition her in relation to her peers and homeland, these movements do not seem to result in a strong sense of rupture that suspends her belonging to these groups. Instead, it seems that these positionings and re-positionings initially emerge through calm observations and reflections. For example, she reflects on the differences between the way Estonian and American students behave in lectures, revealing how adventure impacts our ordinary everyday activities and practices and allows us to notice things that are usually insignificant and taken for granted:

> A thing I'm still not used to and probably will never get used to, is Americans eating in lectures! […] In Estonia you had to keep quiet unless you had something very important to say. Here Americans (more than

half of my course-mates are Americans so they use their majority) are constantly making comments and asking, so that the lecturer often runs out of time. And the questions are not terribly intelligent. (Questionnaire, November 2006)

Säde's initial experiences thus guide her border-making processes where she draws a demarcation line between others, who eat and talk in lectures, and herself who would do no such things. Yet, these experiences also make her rethink her own perspectives and ideas:

I've understood that I've somehow completely ignored America and know nothing about it […] So it's funny—I've thought I'm not familiar with exotic cultures, but it appears I know nothing of America. (Questionnaire, December 2006)

Säde thus finds herself in a border zone, where the border between 'me' and 'them' is not as rigid and impermeable as it may seem but, instead, appears as porous, enabling the slippage of semiotic resources that start to influence Säde's self-positioning. Through this process, Säde constructs two new oppositional meaning fields—'them—speakers' and 'us—non-speakers':

I invented 'speakers' to contrast these course-mates who speak English as their mother tongue (hence native speakers) to those who don't (non-native speakers) […] A small rift between 'speakers' and 'non- speakers' has appeared […]. This categorization is definitely not neutral, although it is also not meant to denigrate one and praise the other side. I have friends on both fronts, perhaps even more among 'speakers', while many 'non-speakers' don't or have friends only among themselves. At the same time I feel that 'non-speakers' are deeper and you can discuss other matters with them. (Questionnaire, March 2007)

Säde's position in relation to these meaning fields is interesting. On the one hand, she obviously belongs to the category of 'non-speakers', as English is not her mother tongue. On the other hand, she also seems to differentiate herself from other 'non-speakers' as someone who has 'friends on both fronts'. She thus appears as someone who is a kind of broker between the two camps, enjoying the benefits of being able to cross the border, 'the rift' between them. Yet, when it comes to evaluating these two groups, then Säde's belonging to the 'non-speaker' group is crucial, for they are the ones that discuss 'deeper matters' not like the 'speakers', who ask not 'terribly intelligent' questions. The experiences in her new university and in her new cultural context thus start to feed into Säde's meaning-making, making her fluctuate between different ways of thinking about her belonging to her new peer groups.

Belonging to the category of 'non-speakers' has several functions for Säde. In Chap. 6, I will discuss how her performance in the new educational environment creates turmoil in her self-confidence. Belonging to the category of 'non-speakers' enables her to make sense of some of those negative experiences for she can refer to external factors (i.e., her language skills and her perception that lecturers prefer to work with native speakers) in an attempt to explain away her perceived failures. Further, as she is the only Estonian in her course, then being a 'non-speaker' gives her a possibility to be part of something bigger, to belong to a real group in her new environment, instead of relying only on her existing relationships with Estonian friends that are merely virtual in that new environment. As a 'non-speaker', she is not alone; there are others like her. Yet, in an interesting semiotic move, this belonging does not eliminate her uniqueness but rather allows her to emphasise it. In other words, being a 'non-speaker' enables her to be Estonian, to reveal her belonging to a unique group within the bigger group that people are interested in. Being a 'non-speaker' thus creates sameness and difference at the same time, allowing Säde to belong to two different groups—peer group in England and ethnic group in Estonia—simultaneously:

> With my lecturers I feel that … Estonians, or in general people from small nations, they meet and then they ask: "Oh, you come from Estonia, how are things there? What do you have there?" And then the Estonian is already prepared to give a long presentation about Estonia […] They don't really care about the information though. They just speak about these X countries but they don't learn from their audience. (Second interview, April 2007)

Although Säde is aware of the disinterest from 'speakers' who ask, but do not care about the answer, their questions nevertheless allow her to have "a full-time job as Estonian", even if it comes with certain frustrations. In order to explain this expression, she retells me a story about an American who is married to an Estonian:

> When he wants to make his wife upset, he says: "Being Estonian is a full-time job". Because his wife [...] is also accustomed that everybody comes and asks and then she explains how things are in Estonia. And the wife is quite disappointed that nobody really cares. (Second interview, April 2007)

Säde's own reflections seem to indicate that while she enjoys having this 'full-time job', she is also somewhat removed from this ethnic group belonging, for she is able to look at it from a somewhat self-critical and ironic position of an outsider. The physical distance from Estonia and other Estonians seems to thus create a border between her and other Estonians. In fact, the anecdote above is not the only occasion on which she uses humour to talk about her ethnicity from this distanced position:

> An American, a Russian and an Estonian are in the zoo and are staring at a huge elephant. The American thinks: "Really cool giant creature. Should take it back to the States, show it to people for money and become rich". The Russian thinks: "Really cool creature. Should take it back to Russia, would be nice to drink vodka together. It's big, so wouldn't get drunk too fast". The Estonian thinks: "I wonder what this elephant thinks of me?" (Questionnaire, March 2007)

The experience of adventuring into a new cultural environment thus leads to the creation of a complex web of borders that simultaneously connect and separate Säde from others around her. In terms of her meaning-making, she takes full use of being in the border zone of this complex web, where her self-positioning can be reconstructed and lead to her being different and otherwise. It is in the fertile space of the border zone where different semiotic moves that simultaneously separate and connect her are possible, being supported by various semiotic resources such as humour and self-criticism.

Becoming 'Less Estonian'

Journeying into a new cultural environment thus leads to the creation of borders between Säde and others. These processes of border-making and crossing allow Säde to strengthen her Estonian identity, position herself away from other 'non-speakers' and closer to other Estonians. Yet, equally, it leads to the creation of borders within the self, allowing distinguishing ways how she has been, currently is and is becoming. For being away from Estonia awakens the fuzzy meaning field of her ethnic identity and allows dialoguing about it with herself and with other Estonians. In some of these dialogues, she positions herself as a patriotic Estonian:

> By now I've already had three occasions when I realise, after meeting my friends and talking to them in Estonian, how important they and that language is for me. And how few Estonians there are. And Estonian men. I really get all patriotic. (Questionnaire, November 2006)

Being away from her ordinary cultural and linguistic environment and then having access to it again thus activates a sense of longing for home and foregrounds her ethnic heritage that has been passed on to her by her parents and grandparents. However, while feeling close to that sociocultural context, the encounters with Estonia from the distance make her also question her patriotism. She follows eagerly the coalition negotiations that take place after the local elections in Estonia in 2007. Her questionnaires reveal that she "cannot understand the mess that is going on around that" (Questionnaire, March 2007). She is clearly disappointed about the political situation in her homeland, for she returns to this topic also in our last interview:

> I can't stand this, first, this tremendous ambition, and second, this narrow-mindedness and this bigotry that is there in Estonian politics and in all the discussions [...] I would like to get back my faith in the Republic and in this kind of thing, but now I rather feel a total counter-reaction towards all this. [...] I definitely feel less Estonian, vastly less Estonian than before. [...] I'd like to stay away for a bit longer and get back the faith and positivism. I've lost it along the way. (Third and last interview, September 2007)

Säde finds herself in an interesting position in her new cultural environment. On the one hand, her distance from home and the attention she receives from her others about her homeland awaken and strengthen her ethnic identification. In relation to the non-Estonians, she is thus 'more Estonian' than she was before. On the other hand, her connections with her homeland make her disappointed about the situation in the country and thus distance her from her identification with it. In relation to Estonia and the country she thinks it is increasingly becoming, she is thus 'less Estonian' than before. Moving away from home thus opens up an ambiguous space of being in-between different ways of belonging. In another interesting semiotic move, the mobility that has created this ambiguity seems to also be the resource that enables Säde to manage it. For as she explains above, she thinks that she will get back her "faith and positivism" if she stays away for a bit longer in order to "contribute to general human values and environmental issues on international level" (Third and last interview, September 2007). As the home she imagines seems to be no longer there, she prefers to stay away, instead of returning.

Home, Away and Becoming Independent

The second case study I introduce in this chapter in relation to the theme of home, adventure and belonging is that of Tania. At the outset of the study, Tania is 19 years old. She moves to the UK to undertake undergraduate studies in a male-dominated field. Our first encounter takes place in her university city about a month after her arrival to the UK. Prior to this, she had never lived away from home and never visited the UK. However, the summer before starting her studies, she lived and worked as an *au pair* in Ireland for two months to earn and save some money for her upcoming study period. For, as some other participants in this research project, she starts her studies without a scholarship or other kind of stable financial support that would give her financial security for the entire study period. Her family is not in the position to support her financially and, therefore, she needs to find a part-time job to cover her living expenses. Finding a balance between study, work and entertainment thus becomes an important element in her experiences. Furthermore, the topic of gaining and maintaining financial independence from her family makes Tania's case unique in providing a view of the ways movement between home and away becomes intertwined with the movement out of adolescence and into adulthood.

Becoming Independent and Responsible

As for many participants in this study, the move away from home and into a new sociocultural context is marked by a sense of excitement and joy for Tania. Yet, this initial exhilarating experience of meeting new places, people and ways of being, becomes soon interrupted by worries about her financial situation. In our last interview, Tania reflects back on those initial experiences in this way:

> The beginning was very positive, I came here and all those new people and especially the first week. That was really interesting and I liked it. […] And then the next month was like … I didn't have a job; the money that I'd earned in the summer was starting to end. […] It was really, well, a lot of worrying and insecurity. (Third and final interview, September 2007)

In a way then, Tania's move away from home does not only place her into a new sociocultural environment where she has to make sense of foreign and novel ways of being and doing things. It also catapults her into a new and independent way of life. It throws her into a life, where she does not only need to make independent decisions about her everyday activities in relation to her studies and social life but where she also has to find a job, earn her own living and support herself financially. By moving away from home, she thus leaves behind a life where she was taken care of by others, and rapidly moves into a life where she is completely in charge. This sudden break from the way things have been brings with it tensions and worries that become simultaneously deepened and softened through her contacts with home and her family. On the one hand, the tensions are heightened by the conversations with her father, who being worried about her daughter and not being able to support her financially, suggests her to return home. On the other hand, her worries are softened by discussions with her mother who encourages her and supports her emotionally. In trying to deal with the tensions and pressures that come from this sudden change, Tania clings to her identity as a hard-working person who is not afraid of difficulties:

> When my father told me at some point that you have to return if you cannot find the job, I said: "Why are you saying those things, you know perfectly that I'm not coming back, I will find a way or I don't know". [...] At some point I thought, well, what will I do if it gets very difficult, perhaps I can't do it. But nobody said that it has to be always easy. I am used to this. I like it. When things go too easily then I become lazy and don't work anymore or something. (Second interview, April 2007)

Her identity as a person who is not afraid of difficulties thus guides her movement through the uncertainty and helps her to relate the difficult present in a meaningful manner with the past and, through that, provide a positive input for the movement into the unknown future (e.g., "I've managed difficulties before, I'll be fine this time too"). Soon enough, she finds two jobs, and this gives her the possibility to make ends meet. In this way, her life in the UK becomes a life of a responsible and independent adult:

> The word 'hard-working' has more meaning to me now, now I actually do work. And I could also add that I am more responsible now. I have so many ... and more independent. [...] I have always been quite independent [...] but now I have to also earn my living. Perhaps I don't even realise yet how independent I actually am. (Third and final interview, September 2007)

Tania's movement away from home and into a new sociocultural environment is thus coupled with her rapid and sudden transition out of adolescence and into adulthood. This new independent life that is filled with studying and working brings along new tensions and stresses that come from her very busy schedule and many competing responsibilities. In the midst of this stress, Tania dreams of home as a place where she can rest and relax:

> It is so nice to rest at home ... when mother is always close ... and cooks ... and is very, very NICE with me!!! ☺ (Questionnaire, January 2007)

I bought my tickets to home… to go home in the end of March and I cannot wait to go … […] Since I returned, I have been to the classes every day and then at work during the weekends and sometimes also in the evenings … and I am a bit tired … […] and then HOME … TO REST!!! […] For me it is simply the time when I don't have to think about the university, work, cooking, finances … I just want my parents to take care of me once again for a while ☺. (Questionnaire, March 2007, original emphasis in capital letters)

In Tania's meaning-making then, 'home' and 'non-home' emerge as oppositional meaning fields. The latter is related to university, work, cooking, finances, stress and worries. The former, in contrast, is seen as the place where the family is close, where Tania can rest and relax, where she does not have to be stressed and worried and where she does not have to be an independent adult and can just enjoy being a child again. Home thus emerges as an anchor from the past that allows managing the tensions and troubles in the present; it is a place where she can go back in time to the period of her life that was happy and stress-free. Home thus emerges as a place where she is cared. And this anchor from the past does not only help to regulate the tensions in the present but also guides Tania's movement forward into the future. Being at home—in reality or in imagination—makes the stress more manageable; it is no longer an overwhelming feeling, but a period that has an end. It ends when Tania finally goes home. For as Tania, looking back at her first year in the UK suggests in our last interview:

A lot of positive time is related to my being at home. It was like every time I had, something negative happened, I went home and things turned positive again. […] Sometimes I just get tired of studying and everything, working. Then I need to go somewhere for a change. Home. (Third and final interview, September 2007)

Becoming and Remaining

The move away from home thus creates a rupture in Tania's usual way of being and pushes her to develop new behaviours and acquire new skills, while also setting in motion the process of identity development. On the one hand, the need to earn her own living catapults her into independence and responsibilities, creating a sudden break from the way she lived her life at home. On the other hand, her values and ways of seeing herself as a person lag behind this rapid change, being slowly influenced by the encounter with the otherness. She thus simultaneously breaks free from home and her family by being economically independent and continues to be closely tied to them through the values and worldviews that they share.

Tania recalls her life at home as a life of a well-educated girl who went to church every Sunday with her mother. The life in her university city is very different. It is characterised by active social life, meeting new people, smoking and drinking—all the things that Tania's previous life did not include. She thus needs to figure out how to relate to these new experiences:

> I've been before quite conservative in everything, in behaviour and everything. When I came here, I started to … All these people that surround you, they take things very easily … If there is a party, then it is a party, if we drink, then we drink, that kind of thing … And I feel I've started to take things more easily as well. I'm not sure yet, if it is right or wrong. Sometimes I feel guilty. How come? Before I would've never had parties like this or something. But now it's like… Sometimes I don't know what's happening to me. […] Initially I thought, I'd come here and I'd study and work and behave very properly and this kind of thing. Now it's like, I even see myself that sometimes I feel guilty. But then you start to think that we have a nice company, friends, why not go out, to some party or something. (Second interview, April 2007)

Just like Säde whose experiences were described above, Tania finds herself in a border zone between her old and new ways of being. She realises that the boundaries she has drawn between herself and others are not solid enough to keep her old ways of being a 'conservative' person intact, instead the novelty with its excitement and promise for difference slips through the pores of these boundaries and starts to infiltrate her ways of feeling, thinking and acting. In the process, the borders between self and others are being reconstructed and removed, while the borders within the self are starting to emerge—between the person she used to be and the person she is becoming.

Being in this border zone, Tania is thus in between different ways of being, in a liminal phase of a transition, where some of the old structures of meaning have been dismantled, while solid new ones have not yet been built. Her reflections also indicate that in order to do this construction work, she needs to draw up some new borders. For in order to protect the space where she can try out new ways of being and build up new meaning structures, including her life-goal orientations, she needs a space away from her mother. Her mother is an important dialogue partner in Tania's inner discussions. She seems to be the moral anchor for Tania, representing the right and good way of living. Disappointing her mother by tearing down some of the meaning structures that she worked so hard to build over the years for Tania is thus hard and makes Tania feel guilty:

> When I went to church in Estonia together with my mum. My mother doesn't drink or smoke or anything like that [...] When I came here I'm more free and I can't tell my mother all the things that I do here because I know she would, it has a bad influence, and I know she would be very worried. That if I feel myself that it is not that big of a threat. But sometimes I do think what if my mother knew or something like that. [...] That church where I used to go ... When I came here I really wanted to go there. But now I notice that I take the church more easily too. It starts to fade to the background, all the things my mother taught me. I do go to the church still, but it's a bit different. I have friends there now and so on. But sometimes I feel strange that I go to the church in a different way. (Second interview, April 2007)

Home thus emerges as an important anchor for Tania's meaning-making also through her relationship with her mother. Yet, in the process of identity development, it emerges not as a safe haven to return to in the moment of trouble but rather as a place of stagnation that holds her back. Through the association with her mother and her conservative values, home emerges not as enabling but rather as a constraining site for Tania in her encounter with the otherness. She needs to move psychologically away from home and her mother in order to let herself experience some of the new ways of being and make sense of these. In this movement away, the meanings about independence, being conservative, being at home, being away, being with mother and being with others, being a child and being an adult become reworked and placed in meaningful relationships with each other, allowing Tania to start making sense of her new experiences and new ways of being:

> I always know what I'm doing and I somehow have this self-confidence that I can, I don't know, control myself. […] It's not like I've forgotten all my previous principles. Came here and now I do what I feel. Freedom! Freedom! I don't feel like now I'm so … I notice that many of those people with whom I live, when they come here, they say it is so good, the parents are far away, I can do what I want. This kind of childish attitude. I don't see this kind of attitude in myself. (Second interview, April 2007)

Tania's reflections here indicate that her movement into adulthood in terms of her identity development has started to catch up with her accelerated transition into financial independence. She is starting to draw up new borders between herself as a 'self-confident' adult who is in control of herself and some of her friends who have a 'childish attitude'. In doing that, she secures a special place in her own trajectory into adulthood for her home that emerges as a place that represents the values and principles that she continues to hold dear. She has moved away from home and her mother in order to move towards them again, connecting her to her old ways of being in Estonia with her new ways of being at home and away from home. In this way, she maintains the connection with the moral teachings of her mother and the church, while also relating to her new environment and the opportunities it provides for her development, creating a sense of sameness and continuity beyond the dual rupture of moving away from home and into adulthood:

> I don't feel that I've changed so much. Yes, my environment has changed, people around me, I have new friends, I am in the university now, it is not a high school anymore, I don't live with my parents, I cook for myself, I work. Yes, this is what has changed. But inside, I don't feel that I'm a completely different person now. I'm still the same, just the things around me have changed, the work and everything, I have more responsibilities now. (Third and final interview, September 2007)

Summary

In this chapter, I examined the dialectics of home and adventure and considered how mobility impacts the sense of belonging by taking a closer look at two case studies. Säde's case allowed examining the ambiguous sense of belonging to one's ethnic and national group that emerges in relation to the movements between home and away in reality and in imagination. In contrast, Tania's case study provided an opportunity to see the dynamics of identity development in the context where the movement away from home is coupled with the movement into adulthood.

In unpacking the two case studies in this chapter, I conceptually built on the idea that human meaning-making in the context of mobility is characterised by the tension between home that is known and faraway that is unknown (Boesch, 1991). Based on this line of reasoning, being within the familiarity and comfort of home makes people long for the excitement and joy that comes from journeying into the unknown. Yet, as Tania's case study shows, moving away from home makes us homesick; it makes us long for our intimate, hidden, secure and safe haven in the world. Home, then, is simultaneously intimate and safe, but also known and unexciting, while faraway can be attractive with its promise of the discovery of unknown yet also threatening due to its strangeness. I have argued in this chapter that recognising this tension between home and away is essential in understanding the experience of mobility.

The case studies I have discussed have shown that the experience of moving away activates the dialectics of home and non-home as these become simultaneously present and absent in our everyday experiences. On the one hand, by moving away from home, we become acutely aware of the things we usually take for granted but now no longer have. Yet, through its absence, we also come to understand the meaning of home and thus home becomes very much present in our everyday life in the new environment. On the other hand, in our new environment, we are bombarded with encounters with difference and otherness. That otherness, if very actively present in our environment, demanding responses from us, which are absent from our structures of thinking, feeling and acting. Thus, the sense of being in-between the two ways of being emerges, a sense of being in transition, not any more here but also not yet there

(Bhatia & Ram, 2001). And this sense of transition is characterised by feelings of liminality, ambiguity, and ambivalence (Abbey, 2012; Greco & Stenner, 2017; Stenner, 2017). While this space of in-betweenness is conceptualised as a space where everything is possible and where one can experiment with different ways of being, the promise of liminality can also be overshadowed by a sense of loss, sadness, tension and doubt as in the case of Tania who questions her decisions and choices in the light of the inner dialogues with her mother. How the movement out of this liminal phase of transition depends largely on the support we receive from others and how it is guided by our general life-goal orientations will be discussed in the following chapters.

Both case studies discussed in this chapter suggest that movement between home and away, coupled with developmental shifts lead to the inevitable change in the way we see ourselves and our sociocultural environments. They also suggest that although this process of change and development can start before the actual move, the process of self-discovery and knowledge accumulation, including the renegotiated sense of being at home and the reconstruction of the taken-for-granted everydayness may not be fully realised until an actual new encounter or physical return home (Märtsin & Mahmoud, 2012). Yet, as Tania's and Säde's experiences suggest homecoming, as an attempt to re-establish meaningful connections with the known environment, people, and with one's own way of being in relation to home, may never really occur. For home does not stand still waiting for their return but also moves, changes and undergoes transformations. Säde, for example, finds that she cannot relate to her homeland the way she used to, not only because she has changed but also because her homeland has changed and some of its new directions are not in accordance with her ideals and values. Instead of imagining a return home, she thus has to reconstruct her connection with home and away and find a way to continue existing in-between places. It is in this sense that people like Säde, Tania and others in this study can find that they will never be 'at home' again but instead live in-between places, being simultaneously here and there, not in one place, but always on the move. They conduct a mobile life that is characterised by multiple and various forms of repeated movement between various sociocultural environments (Elliott & Urry, 2010). As existing research suggests, being on the move, trying to settle down, while preparing for the next move can be a challenging experience (Levitan, 2019). Some of these challenges in building relationships, engaging with educational opportunities and planning for the future will be discussed in the following chapters.

References

Abbey, E. (2012). Ambivalences and its transformations. In J. Valsiner (Ed.), *Oxford handbook of cultural psychology* (pp. 989–997). New York: Oxford University Press.

Arnett, J. J., Kloep, M., Hendry, L. B., & Tanner, J. L. (2011). *Debating emerging adulthood: Stage or process*. New York: Oxford University Press.

Berry, J. W. (2009). A critique of critical acculturation. *International Journal of Intercultural Relations, 33*(5), 361–371.

Bhatia, S., & Ram, A. (2001). Rethinking 'acculturation' in relation to diasporic cultures and postcolonial identities. *Human Development, 44*(1), 1–18.

Boesch, E. E. (1991). *Symbolic action theory and cultural psychology*. Berlin: Springer-Verlag.

Crafter, S., Maunder, R., & Soulsby, L. (2019). *Developmental transitions: Exploring stability and change through the lifespan*. London and New York: Routledge.

Dahinden, J. (2012). Transnational belonging, non-ethnic forms of identification and diverse mobilities: Rethinking migrant integration? In M. Messer, R. Schroeder, & R. Wodak (Eds.), *Migrations: Interdisciplinary perspectives* (pp. 117–128). Wien: Springer-Verlag.

Dahinden, J. (2013). Cities, migrant incorporation, and ethnicity: A network perspective on boundary work. *International Migration & Integration, 14*, 39–60. https://doi.org/10.1007/s12134-011-0224-2

Després, C. (1991). The meaning of home: Literature review and directions for future research and theoretical development. *Journal of Architectural and Planning Research, 8*(2), 96–115.

Dovey, K. (1985). Home and homelessness. In I. Altman & C. M. Werner (Eds.), *Home environments* (pp. 33–64). New York: Plenum Press.

Eade, J. (2013). Crossing boundaries and identification processes. *Integrative Psychological & Behavioral Science, 47*, 509–515. https://doi.org/10.1007/s12124-013-9244-0

Elliott, A., & Urry, J. (2010). *Mobile lives*. New York: Routledge.

Español, A., Marsico, G., & Tateo, L. (2018). Maintaining borders: From border guards to diplomats. *Human Affairs: Postdisciplinary Humanities & Social Sciences Quarterly, 28*(4), 443–460. https://doi.org/10.1515/humaff-2018-0036

Greco, M., & Stenner, P. (2017). From paradox to pattern shift: Conceptualising liminal hotspots and their affective dynamics. *Theory & Psychology, 27*(2), 147–166. https://doi.org/10.1177/0959354317693120

Henderson, S., Holland, J., McGrellis, S., Sharpe, S., & Thomson, R. (2007). *Inventing adulthoods: A biographical approach to youth transitions.* London: Sage.

Jones, G. (1995). *Leaving home.* Buckingham: Open University Press.

Jones, G. (2000). Experimenting with households and inventing 'home'. *International Social Science Journal, 52*(2), 183–194.

Kylén, M., Löfqvist, C., Haak, M., & Iwarsson, S. (2019). Meaning of home and health dynamics among younger older people in Sweden. *European Journal of Ageing*, 1–11. https://doi.org/10.1007/s10433-019-00501-5

Levitan, D. (2019). The art of living in transitoriness: Strategies of families in repeated geographical mobility. *Integrative Psychological & Behavioral Science, 53*, 258–282. https://doi.org/10.1007/s12124-018-9448-4

Mallett, S. (2004). Understanding home: A critical review of the literature. *The Sociological Review, 52*(1), 62–89. https://doi.org/10.1111/j.1467-954X.2004.00442.x

Manzo, L. C. (2005). For better or worse: Exploring multiple dimensions of place meaning. *Journal of Environmental Psychology, 25*(1), 67–86.

Manzo, L. C. (2014). On uncertain ground: Being at home in the context of public housing redevelopment. *Journal of Housing Policy, 14*(4), 389–410. https://doi.org/10.1080/14616718.2014.947125

Marsico, G. (2016). The borderland. *Culture & Psychology, 22*(2), 206–215. https://doi.org/10.1177/1354067X15601199

Marsico, G., & Tateo, L. (2017). Borders, tensegrity and development in dialogue. *Integrative Psychological & Behavioral Science, 51*(4), 536–556. https://doi.org/10.1007/s12124-017-9398-2

Märtsin, M., & Mahmoud, H. (2012). Never at home? Migrants between societies. In J. Valsiner (Ed.), *The Oxford handbook of culture and psychology* (pp. 730–745). Oxford: Oxford University Press.

Moore, J. (2000). Placing home in context. *Journal of Environmental Psychology, 20*, 207–217.

Plöger, J., & Kubiak, S. (2019). Becoming 'the internationals'—How place shapes the sense of belonging and group formation of high-skilled migrants. *Journal of International Migration and Integration, 20*, 307–321. https://doi.org/10.1007/s12134-018-0608-7

Roy, N., Dubé, R., Després, C., Freitas, A., & Légaré, F. (2018). Choosing between staying at home or moving: A systematic review of factors influencing housing decisions among frail older adults. *PLoS ONE, 13*(1), e0189266. https://doi.org/10.1371/journal.pone.0189266

Stenner, P. (2017). *Liminality and experience. A transdisciplinary approach to the psychosocial.* London: Palgrave.

Wardhaugh, J. (1999). The unaccommodated woman: Home, homelessness and identity. *The Sociological Review, 47*(1), 91–109.

Woodhall-Melnik, J., Hamilton-Wright, S., Daoud, N., Matheson, F. I., Dunn, J. R., & O'Campo, P. (2017). Establishing stability: Exploring the meaning of 'home' for women who have experienced intimate partner violence. *Journal of Housing and the Built Environment, 32*(2), 253–268. https://doi.org/10.1007/s10901-016-9511-8

5

Reconstructing Relationships

Introduction

Transitions do not occur in a vacuum but always in a social context. Existing research suggests that peer relationships can be important resources for people who go through significant lifecourse transitions, including those that are related to mobility, education and work (Henderson, Holland, McGrellis, Sharpe, & Thomson, 2007; Thomson, 2011). Friendships are shown to provide companionship, intimacy and affection, they offer opportunities for increasing self-knowledge and affirming one's self-worth, and they are important in integrating individuals into wider supportive networks that provide the basis for resource exchanges. Although some of these functions, especially those related to intimacy, are also fulfilled by romantic relationships that become increasingly important in young adulthood (McNamara Barry, Madsen, Nelson, Carroll, & Badger, 2009), research shows that friendships continue to provide companionship and support transitions throughout the lifespan (Crafter, Maunder, & Soulsby, 2019). Existing research suggests that the nature and functions of close relationships in early adulthood do not differ greatly from those in adolescence, and the apparent differ-

© The Author(s) 2019
M. Märtsin, *Identity Development in the Lifecourse*, Sociocultural Psychology of the Lifecourse, https://doi.org/10.1007/978-3-030-27753-6_5

ences may refer mostly to refinement, rather than redirection or disjunction of social and psychological functioning (Collins & van Dulmen, 2006). Some scholars suggest that friendships reach their peak of functional significance in the early years of adulthood (Arnett, Kloep, Hendry, & Tanner, 2011), where they are vital in assisting persons in their identity explorations and in navigating new educational and professional scenes in the context of transitions to higher education and work (Henderson et al., 2007; Koontz Anthony & McCabe, 2015). Recent studies suggest that university students, for example, rely heavily on their existing and emerging relationships with peers in order to find comfort and support for navigating educational transitions but also use these to find information and ideas in order to carve out their place within the chosen profession (Baldry, Märtsin, & Eivers, 2018; Märtsin, Chang, & Obst, 2016; Swenson, Nordstrom, & Hiester, 2008). At the same time, friendships can also be a source of tensions and trigger self-searching. Furthermore, friendships are not static and fixed relationships but dynamic and changing. In this sense, relationships also undergo transitions that can create tension and self-exploration for individuals. In fact, the ending of an important friendship can create a significant rupture in one's normal flow of being and require efforts to make sense of this experience and its impact on one's sense of self and identity (Stein et al., 2018).

In this chapter, I examine how the back and forth movement between home and away impacts young adults' relationships with peers and how this, in turn, influences the way they make sense of their experiences and of themselves. I will thus focus on the role of relationships in transitions that are related to mobility and developmental shifts and not on transitions within relationships, although as the examples below will show, the two are often interlinked.

The topic of relationships in the context of being on the move will be approached through the lens of border-crossing processes as these relate to identity development (Español, Marsico, & Tateo, 2018; Marsico, 2016; Marsico & Tateo, 2017). Borders and border-making processes, including the processes of creating, crossing, maintaining and dismantling borders, will be discussed in several different ways. First, the context and consequences of being on the move from one cultural world to another and back again—crossing the cultural-political borders between countries—will be highlighted. Second, building borders between 'self' and 'others'—creating demarcation lines between in-group and out-group, as a result of these movements and border-crossings will be discussed. Third, border-construction between groups of others—'real friends' and 'non-real friends', for example, will be examined, as it supports the process of reconstructing a sense of self and identity following the rupture of moving away from and back to home again. Finally, the borders within the self, the developmental dimension from a rupture to the reconstruction of one's semiotic structures with the support of peer relationships will be discussed. Conceptually, this focus on border-making allows examining the idea of identity as a semiotic border-making process that guides and is guided by the way we experience and make sense of our relationships.

These ideas will be unpacked by building on examples from two case studies—Mari and Eva. While the importance of peer relationships emerged in all the eight case studies, it was particularly pronounced in the two cases chosen for this chapter. Mari's case is unique amongst the eight in terms of the nature of her physical border-crossings and allows exploring the semiotic work required to draw new semiotic borders within the self and between the others. Eva's case enables examining these semiotic moves further, offering an opportunity to explore the role of social others in the construction of one's life-goal orientations.

Travelling Between 'Fake' and 'Real'

Mari's case is unique among the eight cases discussed in this book. While all the participants of the study experienced repeated mobility, the period that they spent abroad was typically between 1 and 3 years. In contrast, Mari's study visit was truly short term, for she lived in the UK only six months. The challenges of repeated mobility that stem from the situation where a person has to adjust to a new cultural environment while maintaining their readiness to move again in the near future (Zittoun, Levitan, & Cangiá, 2018) were thus particularly pronounced in her case.

At the outset of the current study, Mari was 23 years old. She was born in a small town in Estonia but had lived most of her life in the capital city of Tallinn. This is where she went to high school and started her university studies. Her single mother raised Mari, and she had always lived at home with her mother. At the beginning of the study, Mari started her final year of the Master's programme in the field of social sciences. She moved to the UK in order to undertake a half-a-year exchange programme before returning to Tallinn and to her home university to finish her degree. Being in the UK was Mari's first experience of living away from home and living abroad and her first time to visit the UK.

From 'Fake Life' to 'Real Life' and Back Again

In order to understand how Mari's views about her relationships change, it is important to consider the ways in which she makes sense of her experiences of moving between Estonia and the UK. Moving to the UK as an exchange student presents itself as an important rupture in Mari's life that creates a divide between her life as it used to be and her life as it would and could be. The repeated mobility that she experiences—moving back and forth between Estonia and England within the short timeframe of six months, creates unique challenges for her meaning-making. She needs to adjust to the new environment and make sense of her experiences in that environment, while also keeping in mind the temporary nature of her move and thus the need to soon leave the 'new' ways of doing and being behind, in order to return to the 'old' context and the 'old' ways. For Mari, this dynamic becomes externalised in her talk about 'real' and 'fake' life, where 'fake life' emerges as a complementary and opposite meaning field to 'real life' (i.e., 'fake' as 'non-real'). In one of the first questionnaires, she describes her initial experiences of being in the UK through these paired meaning fields in the following manner:

> In some moments I felt that everything here was fake because at some point I had to return to my real life. But now I rather think that this is the life I have designed and I can continue it also later. It is the life I want to live and I enjoy fully. And it is true that I couldn't live this life in Estonia, but I have all the possibilities to do it here […] The life here in England has become the 'real life' during the last month. It is not anymore simply a temporary phase. (Questionnaire, November 2006)

Mari thus draws a demarcation line between 'real life' and fake life', and her narrative suggests that she shrinks her experiences and the related meanings into one or the other. Yet, as the two meaning fields become separated from each other, they also remain fundamentally connected as oppositional meaning fields. Mari thus finds herself in the border zone between 'real' and 'fake' life, where the two meaning fields are simultaneously separated and connected by a porous border that allows the semiotic resources to move through in both directions. This space where Mari finds herself as a result of her repeated physical crossing of borders between Estonia and England—the initial move to England, a short visit to Estonia during Christmas, the return to England and then the final move back to Estonia can be conceptualised as liminal (Greco & Stenner, 2017). It is liminal as the old meaning structures are starting to be dismantled and don't hold anymore (i.e., what was 'fake' is becoming 'real' and what was 'real' is becoming 'restricted'), while new structures are not yet in place (i.e., how can this 'new' life that she has 'designed' for herself continue in the 'old' and 'restricted' cultural context):

> I feel that in Estonia I'm very different kind of person and live very different kind of life. And it's very difficult to combine the two of them—in Estonia nobody knows what I've experienced, what I've done, how I've lived. […] There I'm still the person who I was before leaving. Here, instead, I am who I want to be. Probably it's difficult to understand, but I mean that coming here, I had a choice what to do, where to go, with whom to be, how to live. The choices are much more restricted in Estonia. (Questionnaire, December 2006)

Finding herself in this liminal in-between border zone thus unsettles the ways Mari has seen her life and herself in it and calls for new and alternative ways of making sense of her experiences. It brings to the fore some of the meanings about her life and herself that she had backgrounded and started to take for granted in her flow of being. She thus needs to find new ways to make sense of her experiences (i.e., How should my life be? What is fake and what is real?) and her self-understandings in relation to this new life (i.e., What kind of person should I be now that I have experienced this?). The two sociocultural contexts—

Estonia and England—function as important markers for Mari's meaning-making:

> When you go to live in a new place, then you are kind of a blank page, there you can develop and be exactly the way you want to be. You can create a picture of yourself and you like that new picture. And then you go back and you have to be who you were before. And it's so difficult to stay who you have become, because all the people are different and they see you the way you used to be. Perhaps, I don't know, it's difficult to explain, but this is the way I felt. I moved on and then I had to move back to be able to be here [...] It's not that I moved back. Perhaps initially I felt that way. But now I think it's like a stable line, but I haven't moved forward. (Third and final interview, August 2007)

Mari's reflections clearly evidence the ambivalence and tensions related to transitional experiences. On the one hand, she describes her experiences as transformative and focuses on the fact that she has become otherwise. She feels that her experiences in the UK allowed her to grow as a person, gave her opportunities to move on, become a different and better person. On the other hand, as Szakolczai (2017) reminds us, liminal situations are not only about opportunities to create something novel and find a trajectory to become otherwise. Instead, they are also situations where old ways of being and doing do not stand anymore and, therefore, uncertainty and tension about the unknown future emerge, being hard to resolve through reason and rationality. The tensions and uncertainty are evident in Mari's reports about her experiences, for she is unclear how her new ways of being, which she wants to maintain and continue, fit into the sociocultural context where she lives. Her reflections indicate that she has experienced a positive break from the previous trajectory, a shift to a qualitatively different level. Yet, this new trajectory has become blocked by the experience of moving back to Estonia and this block forces her to stay within the liminal phase of the transition, unable to integrate her new structures of meaning with the cultural contexts and its semiotic guidance. Mari thus experiences the need to adapt to a 'new' collective culture once more. Only this time, the 'new' context is the one she knows too well and that has not moved on while she has. When she moved to

England, she changed her meaning space in order to fit in, and now, moving back to Estonia, she faces the same challenge all over again. This new challenge is particularly pronounced, as the adjustment needs to be permanent this time. As a result of this difference in the future-orientation—temporary vs permanent—Mari experiences the adaptation as more tense and uncertain. The newly created ways of seeing her life and her own position in it have very positive connotations for her and it is thus difficult to let go of them or even modify them. They function as a highly abstract vision of oneself and one's life that guides the movement from the present to the future.

The process of transitioning back to the life in Estonia thus requires the breaking down and reconstructing of the meta-sign field that Mari had created through her experiences in England. In this field, the signs "This is the person who I want to be" and "England is the place I want to be" are strongly linked, and it is this link that needs to be broken in the light of new life experiences until a new sign "I can be a better person also elsewhere" becomes created. This semiotic move requires the expansion and merger of the meaning fields 'real life' and 'fake life' so that Mari can be both this and that. This merger occurs in the border zone between the two oppositional meaning fields that are simultaneously separated and connected. After the initial turmoil of returning to Estonia has settled, Mari writes:

> I feel that I respect myself more. It is difficult to explain, but I don't feel anymore this feeling of obligation in relation to others and I think it's been important for me. Before going to England I was afraid of all the things that could happen or go wrong if I don't do something. […] Now I'm more courageous not to play the role others impose on me, but to be myself. Before leaving I was always searching for love, to have someone to be with. Now it's not the most important thing for me. I want to do so many other things in my life and feel good about it. Especially feel good also when I'm on my own. […] I feel like a better person and I hope these values will not disappear. (Questionnaire, March 2007)

The transformation of the meta-sign complex enables Mari to function effectively in different contexts; the definition of oneself through the opposition between places (e.g., 'I am this in England, but I cannot be that in Estonia') loses its relevance and becomes replaced with a self-definition through activities and values that she prioritises, as the reconstructed meaning fields become disconnected from particular geographical locations.

In Search of 'Real Friends'

Mari's struggles to make sense of her experiences as 'fake' or 'real' go hand in hand with her struggles to figure out who are the important people in her life that relate to these experiences. In other words, by constructing the oppositional meaning fields of 'real life' and 'fake life', Mari constructs related meaning fields about 'real friends' and 'non-real friends' that also initially appear as firmly separated either/or constructions which are linked to specific geographical contexts.

Initially, Mari's 'real friends' are in Estonia. In her questionnaires, Mari tells me how her contacts with her friends back home help to regulate the tension that accompanies her transition to the new cultural context. It appears that talking to her friends creates a link to the known past and that builds a sense of stability and security also in the present that is moving towards the unpredictable future. Yet, Mari also reports that these contacts create tension, for they make Mari homesick. However, as time goes by, the friends Mari finds in England become more important and the meaning field of 'real friends' starts to encompass both groups:

> I feel that they [friends from Estonia] are the closest friends I have. Initially it was more difficult, because contacts with them made me homesick. Now it is simply very good to know that many people are waiting for me to come to Estonia, and have not forgotten me. […] I couldn't say anymore, as I did in the first month, that my friends here will never be as close to me as my friends back at home. […] Now I think that they are both very good friends, no difference between my friends here or at home. (Questionnaire, November 2006)

Yet, this expanded meaning field of 'real friends' undergoes important shifts upon Mari's final return to Estonia. As Estonia becomes a place where her life is 'restricted' and gains a negative connotation, so do the relationships that are linked to that place. For Mari, the meaning field of 'real friends' shrinks to include only those friends who she met in England, while the 'old' Estonian friends appear as those who are not able to understand her and are thus placed outside of that group, into the category of 'non-real friends' with whom her relationships are 'broken':

> I feel that many of my relationships here are broken and I have been trying for many years to repair them. I feel that most of the people in Estonia are spiritually broken, their principles and values are very different [from mine]. […] The most important change for me is that when before leaving I wanted to change everything, then now I don't want anything anymore. Many people don't understand me and when I try to describe my feelings to my Estonian friends they misunderstand me and think that I don't value them enough. And I guess majority of them don't understand me right now. I like being alone, working on my Master's thesis and keeping myself busy with my voluntary work. But I don't feel that I need anybody here. […] My friends from England are still very important to me […] It's so much easier to talk to them, because they are experiencing the same feelings. […] It's so easy to talk to them, but so difficult to open up to people here. (Questionnaire, February 2007)

In the transition back to Estonia where Mari's newly created structures of meaning and ways of making sense of herself are being threatened, Mari distances herself from her old social networks and moves closer to the newly created friendships. She thus focuses on her most recent experiences that she shares with her friends from England and that are related to her 'new' self and identity, while pushing aside the shared experiences with her friends from Estonia that go back to her childhood, in some cases, and are linked to her 'old' self.

Mari's transition back to Estonia is thus simultaneously supported and blocked by her friendships. On the one hand, the new friendships that she developed in England offer companionship and affirm her new ways of seeing herself in the midst of changes and shifts in her environment. They allow her to deal with the rupture of moving back home and enable building a bridge from the past to present and into the future. On the other hand, the friendships at home create tensions and dilemmas, for her new experiences and self-understandings remain unnoticed by her old Estonian friends. At the same time, the shared history makes it hard for Mari to let go of these relationships completely. Transitioning back to Estonia and to her existing social networks thus requires a redefinition of her friendships in relation to the experiences she has had and the self-understandings she has created through those experiences:

> My relations with friends from home are so and so. There are some people with whom it is easy to talk and share my thoughts and ask for advice. At the same time there are others with whom I often have different opinions. I still feel that I expect more from my Estonian friends than they are willing or able to give. (Questionnaire, June 2007)

In her efforts to make sense of her social network, Mari constructs two groups of friends: friends from England and those Estonian friends with 'whom it is easy to talk', and 'others' with whom she often disagrees. The voices of those two groups remain somewhat antagonistic in Mari's meaning-making. The voices of the 'others' represent the opposition through which Mari defines herself, whereas the friends from England (and some friends from Estonia) represent a voice that strengthens and supports Mari's new self-understandings. This is the group that is similar to Mari and thus affirms her new identity:

> I felt that we think in the same way, that we have similar goals in life, exactly these girls also felt that they want to travel and see the world and experience different things and so on. [...] Here my friends are, everybody is already living in co-habitation and are having children and in this respect have a very different life. I tell them that I'm going to Sweden [to do some voluntary work] and they ask: Why? What is wrong here? You should start to think about children and should find yourself somebody and should move in with somebody. Perhaps this is the reason you feel bad here, that you're living alone, like, without a boyfriend. So it's like, different worldviews perhaps. So sometimes it's difficult. I love my friends very much and everything, but to meet them and then everybody is with their boyfriends and talk about baby stuff. So it's different. (Third and final interview, August 2007)

Transitioning out of the experience of being in-between different friendships requires semiotic moves to reconstruct the meaning fields about 'real' and 'non-real' friends. In these new meaning fields, geographical locations lose their definitional power and, instead, the values and worldviews become relevant in characterising different groups. An emerging meaning field that brings together meanings around Mari's identity and life-goal orientations thus guides her reconstruction of friendships, while this meaning field also becomes increasingly more generalised and 'powerful' through this process.

Staying on the Chosen Path?

The second example of the ways in which peer relationships can simultaneously trigger transitions and support them comes from Eva. Eva is one of the youngest participants in the current study, being 19 years old at the beginning of the research project. Despite her young age, she has lived a relatively independent life. Her parents divorced when she was small and in her first interview, she told me that she did not have a close relationship with her parents. Despite her young age, she used to live alone after her parents' divorce, studying and working part-time throughout her high school years and thus being economically relatively independent. In her first interview, she tells me that she sees this experience as good preparation for her upcoming life in England.

Eva used to attend a local public school in Tallinn but transitioned to one of the most prestigious high schools for the last three years of her studies. She remembers this transition as somewhat difficult, yet stimulating, because the level of teaching was higher and her new friends were very motivated and success-oriented. She graduated from high school with the silver medal, the second-highest graduation grade in Estonia. Despite the strong emphasis on science and technology that she had in high school, Eva decides to study fine arts at university. She moves to London to undertake her studies without any financial support. Working part-time thus becomes essential for her to be able to live and study in London.

In Search of a Stimulating Life

In order to understand how Eva's relationships support and challenge her transitions, it is important to consider the ways in which she makes sense of her decision to move to London. Differently from Mari, Eva moves to London for three years and although she makes repeated and rather frequent trips back to Estonia, her case study does not allow seeing the impact of a rapid return to the old context. Instead, the focus in her case study is on long-term adaptation that is guided by her life-goal orientations.

As the description above suggests, Eva showed some strength and determination in her life-decisions despite her young age. She seemed to have already experienced several ruptures in her lifecourse (e.g., parents' divorce, transition to a new and demanding high school) and seemed to have managed these successfully, becoming an independent young woman, who is not afraid to take on challenges and make bold decisions. Her interactions with me suggest that she has rather strong, albeit abstract, ideas about the kind of life she wants to live, even if it potentially creates serious challenges for her. For moving to London to undertake her studies without financial support is difficult, and Eva struggles to combine work, studies and social life. It takes her a while to find an arrangement that works for her in terms of living, work and study arrangements. In our last interview, looking back at her experiences, she tells me:

> Well, if you have everything under control, if everything is organised, then it's nice and interesting to live in London. But me, I'm always running around and then it's a bit too much. […] At some point I was again worried that I'll not manage to work that much, because the second year will be tougher than the first one. How will I manage money-wise? That I wouldn't spend too much again. Because sometimes I really feel that I can't do it anymore […] I have my life here that I am happy with. Things have fallen into place … I live in a nice neighbourhood; have normal job, superb co-workers, stable income, and friends here and there. (Third and final interview, September 2007)

The fluctuations between struggles and happiness in Eva's narrative evidence the tensions and dilemmas that she experiences in the first year of living in London. The struggles to make ends meet, to balance the time and money spent on entertainment, study and work appear constantly in the reflections that Eva sends to me via questionnaires and discussions in her interviews. Yet, the references to these struggles are always accompanied by her references to her life-goal orientations that centre around her desire to live an interesting and stimulating life and suggestions that living in London gives her opportunities to achieve that. These generalised meta-signs that seem to guide her decision to move to London and regulate the way she makes sense of her experiences during the time in London become clear in our first interview:

> I'm telling you, I have always felt out of place in Estonia. [...] There is nothing pushing me towards Estonia. Tiny. Everybody knows everybody. What I don't like about Estonia, Tallinn, is that there is nowhere to go. Nothing new to see. (First interview, September 2006)

In the case study of Mari above, I described her semiotic moves of constructing two oppositional meaning fields of 'fake' and 'real' life, connecting these to specific geographical locations. In a similar manner, Eva draws demarcation lines between Estonia and London, connecting the former with such meanings as 'tiny' and 'boring' and, through that, creating an opposite meaning field for London. London thus emerges as the place that supports her desire to live stimulating and interesting life, while Estonia remains the one that holds her back and does not offer her the opportunities she craves for. Eva's way of seeing her new cultural environment is, therefore, similar to that of Mari. Yet, with time and through the flow of diverse experiences, the meaning field related to London loses the completely positive value that it had in the beginning and becomes more varied:

> Initially the scenery was unusual for me, I liked it. Now it starts to get on my nerves. [...] I am getting tired. [...] Sometimes London makes me angry already. Please move! I'm in a hurry! Or something like that. I'm getting tired of this city. Being always in a hurry and there is always something wrong somewhere, the trains don't run or something. (Second interview, April 2007)

Yet, despite these shifts, it is still seen as the location that supports Eva's life-goal orientations. And this semiotic assemblage will start to guide her movements between different relationships that she maintains and creates at home and elsewhere.

Supporting and Challenging Relationships

From the point of view of living a stimulating life, the move to London is thus seen as a positive and progressive experience for Eva. It is a move that supports her becoming the kind of person she wants to become. Even if the life in London is stressful, it is in accordance with her life-goal orientation and, therefore, worth continuing. However, being in London means that Eva has to be away from her social network at home, and that is difficult for her. So the topic of friendships emerges strongly already in our first interview that occurs about a month after Eva's relocation:

> Sometimes I feel incomplete. And I want to feel complete here, find someone; be tied to someone somehow. Feel that somebody cares for me and looks after me. (First interview, September 2006)

Hence, in her meaning-making London emerges as a place that is interesting and inspiring, but equally a place where she is alone. And while Eva's reflections suggest that she manages to repress these tensions in her everyday functioning in London, her first trip back to Estonia after a couple of months in London creates a rupture and brings all those contrasting emotions to the surface of her awareness:

> Already on the first day I wanted to return to London that I've got so much used to. I felt awkward all the time. But at the same time it was so nice to see friends and relatives. Now I have a dilemma: I like this metropolitan life and freedom hugely, not to mention my studies, but my loved ones are in Estonia. I've thought a lot how to change this situation. Haven't reached a decision yet. (Questionnaire, December 2006)

The ambivalence and tension of this first trip back to Estonia is brought to life again in my last interview with Eva:

I was crying there in Estonia, I want to go home. But then everybody asked, to what home do you want to go. And I didn't know. It was painful to see the loved-ones, and I wanted to return. [...] Everybody cared for me and it hurt so much that I wanted to get away. That moment I thought again, that I should come back [...] back to Estonia. [...] doesn't matter, I don't like the life in Estonia, but these people are so important for me and I want to be with them. (Third and final interview, September 2007)

The pain of being away from her social networks is evident in Eva's narrative. The existing social relationships at home pull her back into that environment and away from the new environment in London where she is cut off from those networks and needs to figure out her trajectory into the unpredictable future alone. The relationships at home thus simultaneously support and challenge her as she moves between home and away and towards her goals. This experience triggers the creation of several possible scenarios that would allow moving out from this painful situation. In the first scenario, Eva imagines leaving Estonia and thus leaving also the pain behind. In the second, she imagines abandoning her life-goal orientation in order to be with the people she cares about and who care for her. The two trajectories appear as separated and exclusive, with Eva having to choose one or the other but not being able to combine them into one acceptable trajectory that can be followed. The potential pursuit of either of these scenarios has implications for Eva's identity development, for abandoning her life-goal orientations would challenge the kind of person she was, is and wants to become, while being without the support and companionship of her friends and the affirmation they provide to her as a person is also difficult to imagine.

The creation and pursuit of these AS-IF scenarios is obviously interlinked with Eva's experiences in the AS-IS world and so the experience of returning to London to continue her studies feeds into the process of regulating these imaginative moves. Although Eva's narratives throughout the year strongly foreground her relationships with her Estonian friends, she also talks about the role that her new friendships in England play in supporting her transitions:

When I returned I was calm. I left the emotions behind, to Estonia. I thought, okay I'm here, shall I stay or shall I go back. And then I had a lunch with friends and I came back and thought, what do I want to do. Am I ... Do I want to finish the university or do I want to return there, to Estonia ... I knew that at some point I would feel again the need to leave Estonia. Then I thought, okay let's try for couple of more weeks. If it doesn't get better, then I'll go back. But then somehow everything, the job, I met David [a friend] and everything went up-hill again. (Third and final interview, September 2007)

The possible scenario of returning to Estonia and leaving the life in London behind is still present in Eva's narrative despite her being physically in London. However, the physical distance and new friendships make her feel that the life in London may not be that lonely after all. Her narrative suggests that she uses meanings related to different temporal scales—the future need to move away from 'boring' and 'tiny' Estonia, and a short-term deadline of 'couple of more weeks', in order to regulate the inner tensions and continue on the trajectory that she has chosen for herself. The relationships she has created in her new environment thus support her transition into that environment and affirm her orientation towards her life-goals. Furthermore, while the friends at home remain highly important for her, she starts to reconsider these relationships in the light of her new experiences:

Friends there are still so important. I would have liked to pack them and take them with me. I think, if they were here, everything would be perfect. Perfect ... but then I'd know that I'd stay only with them and wouldn't meet anybody else. (Second interview, April 2007)

Eva's reflection here shows how she is starting to reconstruct her relationships with her friends in Estonia. Differently from Mari, Eva does not feel the need to distance herself from her old friends because they don't understand the person she is becoming. These relationships are still highly important for her but the meaning field related to those relationships starts to become more differentiated and diverse as a result of her new experiences in the new environment. The fact that she would be supported by these relationships is constructed as a positive aspect, yet the possibility that the availability of these relationships would keep her from forming new relationships starts to emerge as a potentially negative aspect in her meaning field. These semiotic moves are here once again guided by the life-goal orientations that Eva has constructed and that guide her towards the kind of person she wants to become.

Summary

In this chapter, I used examples from two case studies to interrogate the idea that transitions always occur in the social context. Both cases show how movement between cultural environments creates challenges for identity development, as well as creates the need to redefine the relationships with peers. Mari's case suggests that, sometimes, this leads to an initial distancing from or even an abandoning of the existing relationships in favour of the newly acquired social networks, while Eva's experiences suggest that it can lead to the strengthening of existing relationships as well as the creation of new ones in light of new experiences and related self-understandings.

While most research in the area of young people's migration focuses on relationships with family and friends as important resources in supporting people's mobility (see, for example, de Abreu & Hale, 2011; Gillespie, Kadianaki, & O'Sullivan-Lago, 2012; Levitan, 2019; Plöger & Kubiak, 2019), the findings discussed here suggest that relationships can also make the transition harder. In fact, the micro-level analysis of the dynamics of meaning-making related to the two case studies enabled exploring how young adults' relationships with their friends simultaneously trigger self-exploration and provide semiotic resources for managing these in the context of repeated mobility. The case studies showed how the physical border-crossings are coupled with semiotic border-making on different levels. First, the physical moves lead to the drawing of boundaries between cultural environments and to the creation of meaning fields related to these geographic locations. These border-making moves are particularly evident in the case of Mari whose transitions are largely guided by the construction of meaning fields about 'fake' and 'real' life. Second, the case studies also show how borders between self and others become created in the process of transition. Again, Mari's redefinition of her relationships with Estonian friends is a good example of those border-making processes, where some friendships are reconstructed as not affirming her new self-understandings and, therefore, distanced from the self. Third, the case studies allow examining the semiotic border-construction between groups of others—'real friends' and 'non-real friends' in the case of Mari or 'friends here' and 'friends there' instead of a more generic 'my friends' in the case of Eva. Finally, the case studies enable examining semiotic moves in relation to one's own developmental trajectory, where borders between one's life and identity before and after the move abroad emerge as important markers in the process of becoming. Mari's case offers an opportunity to observe new life-goal orientations and identity in the making, while Eva's case provides an opportunity to explore the maintenance of existing orientations despite the pain of being away from one's ordinary social scene. Both case studies show how these processes are supported by but also triggered by relationships that either support or not the construction and maintenance of life-goal orientations and related self-understandings.

I will return to the importance of peer relationships in challenging and supporting transitions in the next chapter that will focus on the topic of recognition and examine how it needs to be established or re-created as young adults move between different cultural worlds and cross boundaries between different institutional contexts.

References

Arnett, J. J., Kloep, M., Hendry, L. B., & Tanner, J. L. (2011). *Debating emerging adulthood: Stage or process*. New York: Oxford University Press.

Baldry, S., Märtsin, M., & Eivers, A. (2018). Travelling without a destination? A dialogical analysis of professional identity construction among Australian psychology double degree students. *Identity: An International Journal of Theory and Research, 18*, 94–108. https://doi.org/10.1080/15283488. 2018.1447483

Collins, W. A., & van Dulmen, M. (2006). Friendships and romance in emerging adulthood: Assessing distinctiveness in close relationships. In

J. J. Arnett & J. L. Tanner (Eds.), *Emerging adults in America: Coming of age in the 21st century* (pp. 219–234). Washington, DC: American Psychological Association.

Crafter, S., Maunder, R., & Soulsby, L. (2019). *Developmental transitions: Exploring stability and change through the lifespan*. London and New York: Routledge.

de Abreu, G., & Hale, H. (2011). Trajectories of cultural identity development of young immigrant people: The impact of family practices. *Psychological Studies, 56*(1), 53–61. https://doi.org/10.1007/s12646-011-0061-6

Español, A., Marsico, G., & Tateo, L. (2018). Maintaining borders: From border guards to diplomats. *Human Affairs: Postdisciplinary Humanities & Social Sciences Quarterly, 28*(4), 443–460. https://doi.org/10.1515/humaff-2018-0036

Gillespie, A., Kadianaki, I., & O'Sullivan-Lago, R. (2012). Encountering alterity: Geographic and semantic movements. In J. Valsiner (Ed.), *The Oxford handbook of culture and psychology* (pp. 695–709). Oxford: Oxford University Press.

Greco, M., & Stenner, P. (2017). From paradox to pattern shift: Conceptualising liminal hotspots and their affective dynamics. *Theory & Psychology, 27*(2), 147–166. https://doi.org/10.1177/0959354317693120

Henderson, S., Holland, J., McGrellis, S., Sharpe, S., & Thomson, R. (2007). *Inventing adulthoods: A biographical approach to youth transitions*. London: Sage.

Koontz Anthony, A., & McCabe, J. (2015). Friendship talk as identity work: Defining the self through friend relationships. *Symbolic Interaction, 38*(1), 64–82. https://doi.org/10.1002/SYMB.138

Levitan, D. (2019). The art of living in transitoriness: Strategies of families in repeated geographical mobility. *Integrative Psychological & Behavioral Science, 53*, 258–282. https://doi.org/10.1007/s12124-018-9448-4

Marsico, G. (2016). The borderland. *Culture & Psychology, 22*(2), 206–215. https://doi.org/10.1177/1354067X15601199

Marsico, G., & Tateo, L. (2017). Borders, tensegrity and development in dialogue. *Integrative Psychological & Behavioral Science, 51*(4), 536–556. https://doi.org/10.1007/s12124-017-9398-2

Märtsin, M., Chang, I., & Obst, P. (2016). Using culture to manage the transition into university: Conceptualising the dynamics of withdrawal and engagement. *Culture & Psychology, 22*, 276–295. https://doi.org/10.1177/1354067X15621476

McNamara Barry, C., Madsen, S. D., Nelson, L. J., Carroll, J. S., & Badger, S. (2009). Friendship and romantic relationship qualities in emerging adulthood: Differential associations with identity development and achieved adulthood criteria. *Journal of Adult Development, 16*, 209–222.

Plöger, J., & Kubiak, S. (2019). Becoming 'the internationals'—How place shapes the sense of belonging and group formation of high-skilled migrants. *Journal of International Migration and Integration, 20*, 307–321. https://doi.org/10.1007/s12134-018-0608-7

Stein, C. H., Petrowski, C. E., Gonzales, S. M., Mattei, G. M., Hratl Majcher, J., Froemming, M. W., et al. (2018). A matter of life and death: Understanding continuing bonds and post-traumatic growth when young adults experience the loss of a close friend. *Journal of Child and Family Studies, 27*(3), 725–738. https://doi.org/10.1007/s10826-017-0943-x

Swenson, L. M., Nordstrom, A., & Hiester, M. (2008). The role of peer relationships in adjustment to college. *Journal of College Student Development, 49*(6), 551–567.

Szakolczai, Á. (2017). Permanent (trickster) liminality: The reasons of the heart and of the mind. *Theory & Psychology, 27*(2), 231–248. https://doi.org/10.1177/0959354317694095

Thomson, R. (2011). *Unfolding lives: Youth, gender and change.* Bristol: The Policy Press.

Zittoun, T., Levitan, D., & Cangiá, F. (2018). A sociocultural approach to mobile families: A case study. *Peace and Conflict: Journal of Peace Psychology, 24*(4), 424–432. https://doi.org/10.1037/pac0000313

6

Competence, Self-confidence and Recognition

Introduction

The study discussed in this book is about identity development in the context of mobility and transition to adulthood. But in many ways it is also about educational transitions, for all the participants in this study were experiencing not only movements between home and away and journeying into adulthood but also movements into new educational environments with their own unique rules, norms, assumed social characters and shared practices. How the encounter with this novelty impacted the participants' sense of self and identity, in particular, their sense of self-confidence and self-worth and how these experiences were made sense of, will be discussed in this chapter.

Education holds a special place in the contemporary debates about the transition to adulthood. On the one hand, it has been suggested that the main reason for the prolongation of the transition to adulthood lies with education, as it takes significantly longer for young people today to pass through further and higher education than for previous generations (Benson, 2014). On the other hand, in our late modern risk society with its heterogeneous, non-linear and destan-

© The Author(s) 2019
M. Märtsin, *Identity Development in the Lifecourse*, Sociocultural Psychology of the Lifecourse, https://doi.org/10.1007/978-3-030-27753-6_6

dardised life-trajectories, the motivation to learn and accumulate knowledge has also been hailed as the most "potent steering wheel for navigating the ship of life through good and bad weather" (du Bois-Reymond, 2009, p. 34).

Within the plethora of studies that have examined the experiences of young people as they move through education, the topic of university transitions has gained particular significance in recent decades due to the emphasis on the widening participation in western societies. The journeys into and through university can be highly idiosyncratic and depend on the unique educational, cultural, gender and social class backgrounds of the students (Leese, 2010). But despite these differences, transition to university has typically been seen as a period when young adults make multiple adjustments across a range of social, emotional and academic domains, which can be experienced not only as exciting opportunities for personal growth and development but also as challenges that create tensions and stress (Crafter, Maunder, & Soulsby, 2019; Leese, 2010; Märtsin, Chang, & Obst, 2016). While the first year of university is undoubtedly crucial, changes and adjustments continue to occur beyond the first year of studies, for students are expected to become increasingly independent and responsible for their own learning, adopt new academic and study skills, get used to heavier workloads and higher expectations regarding their work, as well as start preparing for graduation and planning their life beyond university and in a professional area (Baldry, Märtsin, & Eivers, 2018; Maunder, Cunliffe, Galvin, Mjali, & Rogers, 2013). As discussed in the Introduction and evidenced by the case studies unpacked in Chap. 7, this future planning can be particularly challenging due to the unpredictability of the labour market in late modernity and due to the mobility that some young adults experience. In addition to the tensions stemming from the studies and future career prospects, students need to also navigate their developing personal relationships, living arrangements, lifestyles and other changes that extend beyond the university context (Arnett, 2000). Existing studies have found that becoming socially integrated into university life and community and engaging in social support in and beyond university are essential in increasing the likelihood that students remain enrolled in university, particularly within their first year of study (Buote et al., 2007; Crafter et al., 2019;

Wilcox, Winn, & Fyvie-Gauld, 2005). Building friendships with other students, engaging with academic staff and participating in study groups and extracurricular activities, as well as having supportive relationships with family and friends outside of university, have been found to reduce attrition rates and maintain enrolments (Bowles, Fisher, McPhail, Rosenstreich, & Dobson, 2014; Briggs, Clark, & Hall, 2012; Maunder et al., 2013).

It is suggested that successful transition into and through university does not only require developing new skills and abilities but also involves constructing a new sense of self and identity that can be shaken by the experience of entering a new educational environment (Azmitia, Syed, & Radmacher, 2013; Maunder et al., 2013; Symonds, 2015). Moving into a new academic environment with new tasks and demands often questions one's self-confidence and requires re-evaluation of one's abilities and competence. It also involves developing a sense of oneself as a university student who belongs to the university, its community and practices. Significant social others in and outside university play an important role in this process. They can be important sources of information for coping with new ways of being and doing at university. But they are also vital in the process of figuring out what are the expectations and where one fits. For developing a sense of identity in a new context requires being recognised as a certain kind of person by others (Gee, 2000; Holland, Lachicotte, Skinner, & Cain, 2001). Positioning oneself in relation to others in an unknown context and comparing one's performance with them, but also receiving affirmation and recognition about one's participation in the new context from others, allows young people to see if and how they have changed and remained the same beyond the rupture of entering into and moving through a new educational environment. Furthermore, others within the university are not the only ones that need to be related to during university studies. It is equally important to develop connections with one's (imagined) future professional community. Imagining oneself as moving towards a particular professional pathway and gaining recognition from others for the chosen direction and for the progress in the movement towards it—being seen as someone who is becoming a professional in their chosen field—is also an important part of the identity development process that occurs during university studies (Baldry et al., 2018).

In this chapter, I will consider how the movement away from one's ordinary sociocultural environment and into a new educational institution can rupture and dismantle the meaning structures related to self-worth and self-confidence and leave young adults to question their decisions, their competence and life-goal orientations. Recognition—gaining and lacking recognition from others—becomes a central feature in my discussion. Kompridis (2007) suggests that recognition is usually seen as "an explicit act of affirmation that can be expressed in various ways in various social contexts" (p. 285) and claims that "We do not just *desire* recognition, we *need* multiple forms of recognition—respect in the political sphere, esteem in the social sphere, and care in the intimate sphere of the family. Lacking these interlocking experiences of recognition, we cannot achieve full 'self-realization': we cannot become who we want to be, cannot realize the kind of life we want for ourselves" (p. 278, original emphasis). It is the esteem that we gain from social others that is particularly relevant for my discussion in this chapter, for I will consider how the young adults struggle to be recognised as competent and intelligent persons by those around them in their new educational context and how this supports their movement towards the trajectory into future that they have imagined for themselves. In my discussion, I will build on two case studies. First, I will return to the case of Säde and then introduce the case of Kersti. I will travel with these two young women as they question their decisions to suspend their emerging careers in Estonia and embark on postgraduate studies in a new educational and sociocultural environment. I will discuss the ways in which they reconstruct their sense of self-confidence and competence that shapes and is shaped by their life-goals orientations beyond the rupture of moving into a new educational environment. In the case of Säde, I will also discuss how lack of recognition regarding one's trajectory thus far by the new academic context creates doubts about her life-goal orientations. In the case of Kersti, I will consider the complex interlacing of different contexts within which we conduct our lives and explore how the question of recognition from various imagined others shapes our sense of competence and self-confidence and sense of self and identity.

Rebuilding a Shaken Self-confidence

As already said, in this chapter, I will once again return to the case of Säde. In Chap. 4, I examined her transitions in relation to her sense of belonging to her homeland. Here, my focus will be on the ways in which her movement away from home and into a new sociocultural and, in particular, into a new educational environment shakes her sense of academic competence and self-confidence and thus creates a rupture into her sense of identity.

As I explained in Chap. 4, Säde was a successful public sector professional in her homeland before moving to the UK. I also explained that she moved to the UK to undertake a Master's degree in one of the most prestigious universities in the country. This combination creates a unique context to explore the topic of recognition through her case.

"I Have Never Felt So Stupid and Insecure in My Entire Life"

As explained in Chap. 4, the move to a new sociocultural context does not create a serious and immediate rupture into Säde's ways of being. By the time she moves to the UK, she has lived away from her family home for several years, has established herself as an independent and self-sufficient young adult and proven herself as a very good university student and a successful professional in a field that she is passionate about. She thus comes to the UK as a person who is secure in herself, who knows what she is doing and why she is doing it. She has made a decision to put her professional career temporarily on hold in order to gain a postgraduate degree in a very good university and, through that, widen her knowledge base and career prospects for the future. While all her experiences so far have confirmed her identity as an intelligent and capable young woman, including her acceptance into a prestigious study programme, academic experiences in her new university give her a new perspective for evaluating her performance. For her first presentations and assignments in her new university do not get the praise that she has got used to receiving:

I didn't go through that much not even in October when I moved here. Emotions have jumped up and down, from one extreme to another and at the moment I feel rather confused. In short, I have never felt so stupid and insecure in my entire life. I think they gave us too much time to settle in in autumn and the whole 'prestigious university thing' didn't seem that scary at the beginning. But the real demands, expectations and performance levels are starting to become clearer now. [...] I heard that my essay was 'not bad'. And then I heard that it was 'not good'. And this comment was very hard for me because I had spent weeks writing this essay and thought the result was quite good [...] After this meeting on Tuesday night I walked in the rain for two hours and tried to cool down. Thereafter I spent 2–3 days in a complete emotional hole. All the pride I had about my essay was smashed into pieces [...] Unfortunately this was not all. I met Professor A. another three times and Professor D. one more time during the writing of my project proposal. And as I said the real expectations are starting to emerge. The two of them in our first meeting basically tore my little proposal apart. Especially Professor D. who is otherwise very kind and caring. It is just awful when your sincere writing is judged so harshly. (Questionnaire, February 2007)

While these academic experiences may be objectively rather mixed and reflect the ordinary gap that exists between the view that students hold about the university life and the actual university life, Säde interprets these experiences in purely negative terms as her lack of competence. These experiences touch the core of her being and shake the basis on which she has built her sense of identity. The experiences with the first essay and project proposal and the meanings created through them thus become generalised beyond the specific contexts in which they emerged and start to guide the way Säde thinks about herself and her performance more broadly: Who am I if I am not the intelligent and capable person I thought I was? What am I doing here if I am not able to perform as well as I thought I could? And if I fail in this programme, what will I do? How will I move forward into the future towards my life-goals?

In order to find answers to these questions and manage the tensions that arise from the shaking of the meaning field she had constructed about herself, Säde turns her gaze towards the experiences of others. She finds that the ones who performed better during the first exams were 'the speakers' who "independently read a pile of books during the Christmas and tried to use this knowledge to orientate themselves" (Questionnaire, February 2007). But overall, she finds that others, especially other 'non-speakers', had experiences similar to hers:

> It has helped me a lot to hear that others—both course-mates and Ph.D. students—have had similar experiences in relation to the feedback and atmosphere in general. And there is nothing unique about my experience. [...] Professor A, who gave the feedback about my essay and who is now going to be my thesis supervisor is the most chaotic, emotional and non-structured person around here. But I'm a big fan. Due to our similar disciplinary backgrounds it is easier for me to understand him, while several of my course mates have changed their project topics because their initial projects would have gone to him for supervision. [...] But I'll try to take on the challenge. (Questionnaire, February 2007)

In an attempt to regulate the tensions that emerge from the encounter with a different view about her performance and move out of the resulting chaos, Säde compares her performance to that of others and finds that her experiences are not so unique. On the one hand, she is able to attribute her failures to external factors that are out of her control (i.e., her language ability as a 'non-speaker' and the supervisors' perceived preference to work with 'speakers'; see also Chap. 4). On the other hand, she refers to some hyper-generalised meta-signs about herself and her life-goal orientations to manage these tensions: the supervisor and the final project are made sense of as challenges that an intelligent and capable woman like Säde can handle. Furthermore, as she shares the disciplinary background with her supervisor, she cannot only take on the challenge, she is well-equipped for it. Making sense of the situation in this way serves two purposes at the same time: on the one hand, it allows Säde to keep some of the core meanings about herself and her life-goal orientations intact, on the other, it differentiates her from the others in her group. In this way, the boundaries within self and between self and others confirm her existing self-understandings: she is still the Säde she has always been. And this reconstructed sense of sameness and continuity is soon supported by other experiences in her ordinary flow of everyday experiences:

So this repeated 'swallowing' lasted for two and half weeks. And partly still continues. But I have had couple of moments based on which I've tried to rebuild my destroyed self-confidence. (Questionnaire, February 2007)

It was one of the best reading groups during these language-and-abilities related somersaults. I was in a good form, was able to think along, make intelligent comments, be clever and even flirt. It gave me back a lot of my self-confidence. (Questionnaire, March 2007)

Moving Beyond Silenced Competence

While these new experiences and the recognition from others allow Säde to rebuild her 'destroyed self-confidence', the questions about her identity re-emerge again when she starts to think about the life beyond her studies in the UK. The world of work in this new sociocultural environment is yet another new context for her, and she is not sure whether her self-understandings and the trajectory that she has imagined for herself in the future will be appropriate and recognised in her new environment. For she feels that the experiences and knowledge she had gained previously in Estonia through her professional career are seen differently in her new sociocultural environment:

You know who you are in Estonia and it is relatively easy to be somebody. There are not so many job opportunities and the community is so small. You know everybody in your field. I really was having meetings and exchanging emails with deputy ministers […] In this context it is absolutely unthinkable. […] But at the same time you do have job experience and in terms of practical experience I do feel like I am somewhat above the others in my group. […] At the same time I feel that the lecturers have the same attitude, they won't say it explicitly or think about it, but it seems that for them it is inappropriate or they pay no attention to it. It almost feels like you are bluffing or it is unthinkable [that you can have these experiences]. (Second interview, April 2007)

In describing her experiences in her new academic environment, Säde tells me about two occasions of meeting prominent European Union officials who she knew from her previous work in Estonia at conferences in her university and the perception that it was inappropriate for her, as a student, to know these people and talk to them in an academic context:

> I feel that some of my lecturers think that its arrogant or they are strangely silent or don't develop this topic further. Which gives me the impression that perhaps they don't believe it or that my behavior seems to them arrogant or inappropriate, which it is not. (Second interview, April 2007)

Säde's previous work experience is highly important for her, for it helps her to define who she is and where she is going in terms of her career. Yet, this experience goes unnoticed and unrecognised in her new academic context, where she is seen merely as another student. The silence that she receives undermines Säde's previous professional experience and, in this way her new academic environment instead of reinforcing her identity as a successful professional renders her ways of being arrogant and inappropriate. This silencing and lack of recognition creates a break into her professional trajectory and makes her confused about her future professional pathway:

> It is confusing for me in relation to the future, that I don't really understand who am I here. [...] At the moment I just don't understand how to position myself. Am I too ambitious if I want to have a normal job here, some sort of specialist position? Or do I devalue myself? (Second interview, April 2007)

While the university is often the place where an image of oneself as a particular kind of professional and possible pathways towards this image become created, it is not what happens for Säde. She does not need to create this image, for it is already rather clear in her mind and she has started to move towards it. And although her academic experience gives her plenty of knowledge to keep moving forward on that trajectory, it also interrupts that movement for she does not receive recognition for the part of the journey that she has already undertaken. And this makes the decision to pursue the chosen goals and continue on the chosen path uncertain.

In many ways then, Säde's time in the university as a Master's student functions as a multi-furcation point in her lifecourse, opening up many different pathways into the future. There is the option of going back to Estonia and continuing her professional career there. There is also the option of staying in the UK and finding a job as a specialist in her field there. But there are also some new pathways that were previously not available for Säde. In the end, she chooses one of these, as she decides to stay in her university, take a year off and then continue as a PhD student:

> My supervisor is rather excited about the topic I chose for my thesis and wants to continue with that. He thought that I should now take it easy for a year, write my project proposal and then start to apply for external funding. The way it goes, couple of years in advance. I am not quite sure yet, whether this is what I want to plan for my next 4 years. I'm afraid that if I find a job, then I will not leave it anymore. (Third and final interview, September 2007)

Säde's hesitations about this possible pathway are evident in her reflections. However, as her movement on this trajectory is clearly supported and recognised by the people, whose opinion matters to her, and as it allows her to create a sense of sameness and continuity with her previous sense of identity as an intelligent and capable young woman, she is willing to give it a go.

Becoming Intelligent Again

The second case study introduced in this chapter discusses the experiences of Kersti. Together with Säde, Kersti is one of the older participants in this study, being 25 years old at the start of the study. Like Säde, she comes from Tartu, where she spent her childhood, went to school and graduated from the university. Kersti has never lived away from home and the relationships with her family, especially with her younger sister to whom she is very attached to, are very important for her. So it is no surprise that Kersti wants to use the time abroad as a platform to "become more independent, to see the world. Not only for the studies, but also to develop personally", as she explains in our first interview.

Kersti's school journey is marked with achievement and success. She studied in one of the most prestigious high schools in Tartu that specialises in science. Although she achieved very high results in high school, she decided to study humanities at Tartu University. She was very successful in her studies and was considered to be a promising young researcher in her department. She was almost at the end of her Master's studies at Tartu, when she decided to move to the UK to start a one-year Master's programme in the same field. She reveals that she was probably accepted to the programme thanks to the recommendation from one of her supervisors at Tartu, pointing to the success she had in that academic environment. Prior to her arrival to her university city, she had never visited the UK.

Balancing on the Crest of the Wave

My interactions with Kersti evidence that through her previous academic experiences, she has come to think of herself as an intelligent and academically successful young woman. She comes across as a calm, even a shy, person, but underneath that façade, is an ambitious young woman who knows what she wants and where she is heading. For Kersti is not in the UK to simply experience something different; she is there to do well in her study course and prove herself also in her new sociocultural and academic environment, keeping an eye on the possibility of continuing her academic career in the UK beyond the Master's studies. Similarly to Säde, her transition into the new educational context with its new language environment, different ways of studying and different expectations and demands, is not smooth but brings along experiences that make her question the ways in which she is used to seeing herself. Similarly to Säde, the rupture in her identity is not immediate but builds up over time as she acquires different experiences in her new university. For example, she is rather optimistic after her first presentation:

> It was okay as an introductory attempt—in the future I'll try to take on more serious challenges like at Tartu. In reality I have never liked to be

treated differently due to my gender or nationality. (Questionnaire, October 2006)

However, as time passes and new experiences accumulate, this initial optimism starts to be replaced by worries about her academic performance:

> I feel like I'm on the crest of a wave—sometimes at the bottom, sometimes a bit higher up. Still very far from the top. Self-confidence academically is still zero. Some presentations go well; in other cases I somehow manage to read my part, and I'm ashamed of it for several days afterwards. One of my problems is that I'm scared to speak in the seminars. I am simply scared. I haven't been much of a talker in Estonia either, but here I'm completely blocked. (Questionnaire, November 2006)

Similarly to Säde, then, Kersti too experiences that her language skills do not allow her to perform as well as she would like to in her new academic environment. She finds that this feeds into her shyness, turning it into a bigger challenge than it has previously been. In light of these new experiences, Kersti's existing field of hyper-generalised meta-signs about herself that, among others, include signs that relate to her competence (i.e., "I am a smart and successful person") starts to tremble and does not work anymore as a guide for her movement into the future. In her attempt to deal with this trembling, she, on the one hand, seeks out opportunities to demonstrate her abilities and prove to herself that her way of seeing herself holds true also in the new environment; on the other hand she, is anxious about these challenges:

> I need to write essays in some of the courses. I am already quite anxious about it—I want to succeed so badly that it can harm my performance. (Questionnaire, November 2006)

In the process of transitioning into her new academic environment, Kersti thus has to reconstruct some of the meaning structures about her abilities and confidence in light of the new experiences she gains. Positive feedback to her first assignments and the fact that her department accepts her application of doctorate studies are important in helping her to rebuild some of those meaning structures, allowing her to see that the self-understandings she utilised to make sense of herself in her home environment are functional also in the new context:

> If before I thought that I was one of the most clueless and most narrow-minded people in our department, then I don't think like that anymore. I'm just over-critical about myself, compare myself even with the English native speakers and presume that I should be on the same level with them on everything. It feels like, not considering the grammar mistakes and less fluent speech, I can compete with them. In that sense I'm a bit more self-confident. But I cannot slack away; I still need to write three big essays and the dissertation, so I have to keep on stretching. (Questionnaire, April 2007)

Comparisons with others are, therefore, an important way for Kersti to figure out where she fits, although she needs some time to figure out who would be the best people to compare herself with. Her initial choice of comparing herself with 'English native speakers' does not seem to give her accurate estimates, pushing her to be 'over-critical' about herself. Yet, despite these efforts to find appropriate comparison groups and be balanced in her self-evaluations, her self-confidence fluctuates depending on her performance. As she struggles to achieve consistently high results throughout the year, the tensions in her self-system are not resolved once and for all, but she keeps coming back to the questions about her academic competence again and again:

> It did inhibit my academic self-confidence, but at the same time, I have written many good things in my life and I'm already old enough not to take these failures as proof that I'm a failure as a person. I blame different factors for these failures—three essays is too much, stress etc. (Questionnaire, July 2007)

> Academically I couldn't pull myself together and so everything has gone wrong this year. In Estonia I got an A for my BA dissertation, also for most of my Master's subject. In the end of my BA, I had only A-s, 4.7 was the average grade in Master's, I think [maximum is 5 in the Estonian system]. Now all of it has disappeared. […] I have this paranoia that I will fail with my dissertation. I just feel so bad, because it was below any of my standards

[…] But actually all this year I have felt that it has been a bad year in some sense […] Somehow it feels that with this number everything goes wrong […] Should even start to believe in astrology. (Third and final interview, October 2007)

Kersti's efforts to make sense of these fluctuations in her performance, her efforts to interpret these away in order to maintain her belief in her competence and abilities and avoid the decline in her self-confidence are evident in her discussions with me. Similarly to Säde, Kersti too attributes some of her failures to the external factors: in her case, it has been a 'bad year'. Making sense of her experiences in this way allows Kersti to hold on to the existing meaning structures about herself. She does not need to build a completely new meaning field but can restructure the existing one, building a bridge from the past through the present and into the future, as she continues her journey towards her life-goals orientations: "I feel a bit bad, so starting my doctorate studies, if I pass the Master's thesis, I need to become better" (Third and final interview, October 2007).

"I Cannot Disgrace Estonia and Womankind Here"

The tensions that Kersti experiences in relation to her performance have multiple layers. On the one hand, her ways of seeing herself are challenged by the experiences in her academic environment, the feedback she receives to her performance in the seminars and through the assignments. On the other hand, they are also challenged by the experiences in her new sociocultural environment more broadly. She comes to the UK as a proud Estonian woman, who thinks highly of her cultural heritage, including her background as an Eastern-European woman:

I don't consider myself to be Nordic, not to mention Scandinavian. I do think I am Eastern-European […] These days it is more fashionable to consider ourselves, Estonia to be part of Nordic countries. But I am not ashamed of our Eastern-European heritage or anything. For me, Estonia is Eastern-Europe and there is nothing to do about it. (First interview, August 2006)

Yet, these views about Eastern-Europe and herself as an Eastern-European become challenged in her new sociocultural context as Kersti realises that the label 'Eastern-European' might have a rather negative connotation for British people, who have experienced a recent influx of foreign workers to the country:

> It seems they don't have a good opinion about Polish […] I didn't think anything bad of Poland […] for me, I thought Poland was more developed than Estonia, what is there to be ashamed of. But yeah, it seems Polish are simple workers here. Typical Eastern-Europeans … (Second interview, April 2007)

Kersti's self-understandings related to her belonging to the group 'Eastern-Europeans' thus become challenged in her new sociocultural environment, for being part of that group creates questions about her motivations for being in the UK and about her competence as a young successful academic. Kersti thus needs to draw boundaries between herself and other 'typical Eastern-Europeans', for as she says: "I don't want to classify myself as part of the gang who is earning easy money with simply jobs here in England" (Second interview, April 2007). Kersti is not in the UK to 'earn easy money' but to continue on her trajectory towards a life-goal orientation of becoming a brilliant female academic, and it is important for her that others recognise this difference between her and other Eastern-Europeans. So this challenge of gaining recognition as an Eastern-European woman becomes interlaced with her challenges of remaining an intelligent and capable student:

> I feel the obligation to perform well. Even more, I cannot disgrace Estonia and womankind here. […] I was proud to tell my friends here that I'm going to visit a friend who is studying at Oxford—as if it is a proof that Estonians, and women are not that clueless after all. (Questionnaire, November 2006)

> In general I think I'm not considered too ignorant here. But I need to still work hard, because among other things I still want to improve the image the English have of Eastern-European women. (Questionnaire, March 2007)

The challenge of gaining recognition from others about her competence and capabilities thus goes beyond her academic environment. The way she sees it, she has more to prove than simply her own worth. There is much more at stake—the reputation of Eastern-European women in general. In other words, as she positions herself within the group of Eastern-European women, it becomes her obligation not only to show that she, as a person, is still intelligent and capable beyond the rupture of moving to the new academic environment, but also that the entire group can be differently seen. She thus enters into a dialogue with an imagined generalised other, who she is trying to convince and from who she is trying to get recognition to her difference. The transition into and through university and the challenges it creates for her self-understandings thus become layered and more complex than dealing with the ruptured academic identity.

Summary

In this chapter, I built on two case studies to examine the ways in which the transition to university that is paired with international mobility can be experienced by young adults. I focused on the case studies of two older female participants in the study—Säde and Kersti, whose decision to move abroad to undertake Master's studies suspended their emerging professional careers at home and created challenges for them in terms of their perceived sense of competence, self-confidence, identity and life-goal orientations. In line with the previous research, the case studies suggested that transition into and through university is not only related to learning new skills and acquiring new knowledge, but it is also a period for identity explorations and configurations of new self-understandings as students need to figure out where they fit in relation to others and in relation to their own previous self (Baldry et al., 2018). The case studies discussed in this chapter also support previous research that underlines the importance of others—real and imaginary, specific and generalised—in triggering some of these challenges but also in supporting the process of moving through and out of the transition. In particular, they point to the importance of real and imagined others in providing recognition for one's experiences from the past, present and for the future and, through that, supporting or inhibiting the reconstruction of the sense of identity in the new educational environment.

Säde's case brings to the fore the idea that students do not enter universities as blank pages ready to be written on but, instead, bring with them a plethora of unique knowledge and experience that they use and refer to when making sense of their experiences in the new academic context and rebuilding their sense of sameness and continuity beyond the rupture of starting a new study course. As Säde's case evidences, the knowledge and experience can remain unnoticed by the universities, and this lack of recognition can seriously undermine students' sense of identity and their chosen trajectories into the future, creating a rupture into their professional and personal pathways. These findings echo the results of existing educational research that has explored the experiences of indigenous and minority group children in mainstream schools. Singh, Brown and Märtsin (2012), for example, report how the knowledge and experiences of Australian indigenous children are rendered invisible in their schools, where their competence is merely built around their (low) performance in the classroom (see also case studies in Hviid & Märtsin, 2019). What these studies and the findings discussed in this book foreground is the problematic silencing of the students' past in their present educational context that can make them question their past, but importantly also their chosen pathways into the future towards their life-goals that are linked to the past. Transition through university, just like transition through school, can thus become a journey of figuring out how one's past should be seen in light of the present and the future, which parts of it are worthy of recognition and which should remain hidden, making it harder for students to build a bridge between where one has been and where one is heading.

Kersti's case too provided opportunities to see students as entering university not in isolation from their social and cultural backgrounds and personal histories but, instead, embedded in a complex web of connections with real and imaginary others, from who they expect to receive affirmation and recognition to their chosen ways of seeing themselves and ways of creating pathways into the future. Her case shows that transition to university is not only about the new educational context but, instead, can become interlaced with the transition away from home that introduces new ideas about one's belonging and background. These new meanings that may not emerge from the university context and may not be at all related to one's experiences in and of university nevertheless feed into one's educational transition, either supporting or challenging it.

Contemporary universities are increasingly welcoming students from a variety of backgrounds. The case studies discussed in this chapter provide further evidence of the need for universities to recognise the complex webs of knowledge and experiences related to their social and cultural backgrounds and the personal histories students are embedded in, use them to make sense of their experiences in and outside of university and create meaningful developmental trajectories through university studies into their chosen futures.

References

Arnett, J. J. (2000). Emerging adulthood: A theory of development from late teens through the twenties. *American Psychologist, 55*(5), 469–480.

Azmitia, M., Syed, M., & Radmacher, K. (2013). Finding your niche: Identity and emotional support in emerging adults' adjustment to the transition to college. *Journal of Research on Adolescence, 23*(4), 744–761. https://doi.org/10.1111/jora.12037

Baldry, S., Märtsin, M., & Eivers, A. (2018). Travelling without a destination? A dialogical analysis of professional identity construction among Australian psychology double degree students. *Identity: An International Journal of Theory and Research, 18*, 94–108. https://doi.org/10.1080/15283488.2018.1447483

Benson, J. (2014). Transition to adulthood. In A. Ben-Arieh, F. Casas, I. Frønes, & J. Korbin (Eds.), *Handbook of child well-being* (pp. 1763–1783). Dordrecht: Springer.

Bowles, A., Fisher, R., McPhail, R., Rosenstreich, D., & Dobson, A. (2014). Staying the distance: Students' perceptions of enablers of transition to higher education. *Higher Education Research & Development, 33*(2), 212–225. https://doi.org/10.1080/07294360.2013.832157

Briggs, A. R. J., Clark, J., & Hall, I. (2012). Building bridges: Understanding student transition to university. *Quality in Higher Education, 18*(1), 3–21. https://doi.org/10.1080/13538322.2011.614468

Buote, V. M., Pancer, S. M., Pratt, M. W., Adams, G., Birnie-Lefcovitch, S., Polivy, J., et al. (2007). The importance of friends: Friendship and adjustment among 1st-year university students. *Journal of Adolescent Research, 22*(6), 665–689. https://doi.org/10.1177/0743558407306344

Crafter, S., Maunder, R., & Soulsby, L. (2019). *Developmental transitions: Exploring stability and change through the lifespan.* London and New York: Routledge.

du Bois-Reymond, M. (2009). Models of navigation and life management. In A. Furlong (Ed.), *Handbook of youth and young adulthood. New perspectives and agendas* (pp. 31–38). New York: Routledge.

Gee, J. P. (2000). Identity as an analytic lens for research in education. *Review of Research in Education, 25*, 99–125. https://doi.org/10.2307/1167322

Holland, D., Lachicotte, W., Skinner, D., & Cain, C. (2001). *Identity and agency in cultural worlds.* Cambridge: Harvard University Press.

Hviid, P., & Märtsin, M. (Eds.). (2019). *Culture in education and education in cultures: Tensioned dialogues and creative constructions.* Cham: Springer.

Kompridis, N. (2007). Struggling over the meaning of recognition: A matter of identity, justice, or freedom? *European Journal of Political Theory, 6*(3), 277–289. https://doi.org/10.1177/1474885107077311

Leese, M. (2010). Bridging the gap: Supporting student transitions into higher education. *Journal of Further and Higher Education, 34*(2), 239–251. https://doi.org/10.1080/03098771003695494

Märtsin, M. (2012). A dismantled jigsaw: Making sense of the complex intertwinement of theory, phenomena and methods. In E. Abbey & S. Surgan (Eds.), *Emerging methods in psychology* (pp. 101–119). New Brunswick, NJ: Transaction Publishers.

Märtsin, M., Chang, I., & Obst, P. (2016). Using culture to manage the transition into university: Conceptualising the dynamics of withdrawal and engagement. *Culture & Psychology, 22*, 276–295. https://doi.org/10.1177/1354067X15621476

Maunder, R. E., Cunliffe, M., Galvin, J., Mjali, S., & Rogers, J. (2013). Listening to student voices: Student researchers exploring undergraduate experiences of university transition. *Higher Education, 66*(2), 139–152. https://doi.org/10.1007/s10734-012-9595-3

Symonds, J. (2015). *Understanding school transition: What happens to children and how to help them.* London: Routledge.

Wilcox, P., Winn, S., & Fyvie-Gauld, M. (2005). 'It was nothing to do with the university, it was just the people': The role of social support in the first-year experience of higher education. *Studies in Higher Education, 30*(6), 707–722. https://doi.org/10.1080/03075070500340036

7

Making Plans

Introduction

As discussed in the introduction of this book, the transition to adulthood
has become prolonged, destandardised, heterogeneous and non-linear in
recent decades (Benson, 2014; Blatterer, 2007; Furlong, 2009). It is
claimed that, nowadays, there are many different pathways and trajectories that can lead young people into adulthood. Making plans and decisions about one's future in relation to education, work and family that
help to navigate between these various trajectories and detours have
become one of the crucial elements in transition to adulthood (Heinz,
2009). On the one hand, young people' lifecourses are believed to be
more 'open'; there are more options and opportunities that they can
choose from instead of following a pre-set pathway. On the other hand,
this openness also creates more contingencies: opportunities go hand in
hand with uncertainty and one is constantly left to wonder whether the
right decision at the right time has been made (du Bois-Reymond, 2009).
It has been suggested that young people react to this constant need to
choose and decide in two different ways. One is to draw up long-term
plans and follow these, while the other one is to avoid long-term plan-

© The Author(s) 2019
M. Märtsin, *Identity Development in the Lifecourse*, Sociocultural Psychology of the
Lifecourse, https://doi.org/10.1007/978-3-030-27753-6_7

ning, stick to short-term plans or to make no plans at all (du Bois-Reymond, 2009). Both strategies seem sensible in the context of late modernity with its constantly emerging and disappearing risks and opportunities. Empirical evidence suggest that these general trends are indeed shaping young people's lifecourses, although the openness of their future is often dependent on cultural, ethnic, gender and economic factors, with some young people experiencing rather restricted opportunities, while others can experience 'choice dilemmas' because of the abundance of alternatives in their lives (Henderson, Holland, McGrellis, Sharpe, & Thomson, 2007; Thomson, 2011).

Charlotte Bühler (Bühler & Massarik, 1968) has suggested that human life is not a random and disconnected sequence of events and efforts to make sense of these but tied together by certain life-goals that individuals pursue throughout their lifecourse in their unique ways. As explained in Chap. 2, Bühler conceptualises life-goals, in a general sense, as a person's desire to live a meaningful and self-fulfilling life. She suggests that life-goals can guide one's life in the form of rather vague and abstract values or as relatively specific ideas about the direction of one's lifecourse. They can be immediate or long-term, and they can be explicitly articulated, although mostly they guide the decisions about the direction of one's lifecourse in an implicit and unconscious manner. For Bühler (Bühler & Massarik, 1968), an individual's lifecourse can be divided into several developmental stages and active life-goal construction is characteristic to only some of these periods. She suggests that active exploration of one's life-goals starts in late adolescence (ages 15–25), when many tentative attempts to define one's future trajectory are made. But the main period of life-goal setting is adulthood (ages 25–45) when life-goals in relation to one's education, work, family, passions and general life-values become constructed, reconstructed and finally defined. Late adulthood (ages 45–65) is the time for evaluation when people tend to look back at their lives through the prism of their life-goals and assess whether they have been successful in fulfilling these or not. In this period, people still have time to set themselves new life-goals to pursue in their late age. After the age of 65, however, life-goal construction is highly unlikely, for people rather start to settle in their feelings of fulfilment, resignation or failure. Bühler's ideas about life-goals and their development across the lifespan have been picked up by other developmental psychologists interested in adult development, especially by Daniel Levinson (1986) whose model of the seasons of life clearly echoes Bühler's conceptualisation. However, recent work in sociocultural tradition has indicated that Bühler's focus on adulthood in relation to life-goal construction may be misleading, for human conduct and meaning-making is, by essence, future-orientated, irrespective of the life-stage (Hviid & Villadsen, 2018; Villadsen, 2019). While the content of life-goals, as well as their specificity or abstractness, may vary through lifecourse, it nevertheless forms an important part of the intra-psychological system that enables people to make sense of themselves within and in relation to their sociocultural environment. Furthermore, as the social and cultural conditions in which people conduct their lives have changed considerably since Bühler and Levinson conducted their studies and developed their theories, there is a need to re-examine the age normativity of the models they proposed.

Bühler's suggestion that human life is always guided towards future and human agents are always pursuing plans and goals that they have constructed for themselves has been influential also for the theoretical perspective developed in this book. However, in my interpretation life-goals are not set targets or objectives to be achieved, but rather orientations towards a certain kind of future where we want to be certain kinds of people. In this sense processes of constructing life-goal orientations are interlaced with processes of identity development. For life-goal orientations are semiotic constructions that form part of the field of highly generalised meta-signs that allow people to define who they are here and now, have been in the past and are becoming in the future.

These ideas about life-goal orientations and identity processes are unpacked in this chapter by referring to two case studies—Nora and Andres. For both of them, the uncertainty and unpredictability that comes from the pairing of repeated mobility with the transition to adulthood lead to the creation of dilemmas and tensions that temporarily suspend their planning and movement into the future. Stability related to home—its absence in the present and availability in the imagined future thus emerges as an important topic for both of these case studies, leading to the reintroduction of some of the topics already discussed in Chap. 4. While mirroring similar dilemmas, the two case studies also allow examining how the tensions and worries emerging from this suspension are shaped by young people's age and gender. Taken together, the two case studies allow developing further the idea that goal-orientation and future-orientation are essential dimensions in the conceptualisation of identity as a field of hyper-generalised meta-signs that orchestrates our ways of understanding, imagining and acting in the world with and in relation to others in the present, past and imagined future.

Making Plans While on the Move

Nora is 21 years old at the beginning of the study and is probably the most 'mobile' participant in the study discussed in this book. She was born in Tartu but moved to Tallinn with her family when she was a child. At the age of 14, Nora moved to the United States for half a year due to her father's studies. Five years prior to the beginning of this study, she again left Estonia and moved to one of the European capitals as her father made an important career move. She graduated from high school in that city and then spent half a year in Belgium, working as an *au pair*. Despite her initial plan to go to study in France, she moved to London to start her undergraduate studies. While being partly financially supported by her family, she also aimed to achieve some economic independence in London and thus found a part-time job in a local pub. At the onset of the study, Nora had lived in London for one year.

Nora is the only participant in this study who tended to switch between Estonian and English in her interviews evidencing the impact of her mobile lifestyle on her life. However, despite this mobile lifestyle, the question of home seems to be relatively clear for Nora: her home is in Estonia. That is the place where she "need[s] to return to one day" (Questionnaire, June 2007). It seems that this stable idea of home compensates the lack of real-life stability in relation to home that she has experienced in recent years. Having a place where she 'needs' to return offers a sense of continuity in her insecure and uncertain mobile life. Even if she has not lived in Estonia for the last five years, the thought of that place functions as an anchor that also connects other strands of her life; the questions about a possible career and stable intimate relationships are considered through the possibility of returning and staying in Estonia, as becomes clear in the following analysis.

Moving Towards an Open Future

As for many young people, graduation from high school is an important multi-furcation point for Nora, opening up many different directions and possibilities for the future. Coming from a rather affluent family, Nora is in a privileged position to choose which direction she would like to move. But instead of welcoming this opportunity to choose and embark on a journey of explorations and experimentations, as the advocates of the emerging adulthood theory suggest (Arnett, 2000), Nora feels the pressure to decide. Instead of liberating her to learn who she is and where she is going, this abundance of choices paralyses her and makes her 'stressed' about her future:

> I was a mess [said in English in an interview conducted in Estonian]! Like… in my head [last three words said again in English] [...] I was very stressed all the time and all the time I thought: what will become of me, what will I be! [...] There was also pressure from my parents, like what will you do and do this and do that and you know, really … a pressure. (First interview, September 2006)

While being seemingly free to choose whatever she wants, Nora nevertheless feels the pressure to make a 'good' decision. And this is very hard for her, for she does not have a clear and strong image of herself in the future that pulls her towards it. Furthermore, she needs to respond to the callings and demands of the others, namely, her parents, to make the 'right' choice. In our first interview, she reveals to me that her father becomes an important dialogue partner for her in this period, where she is 'a mess in her head'. Through the conversations with her father, the idea to pursue a law degree emerges, allowing Nora to calm her inner storm and move out of the state of a mess that paralysed her and stopped her from moving forward into the future:

> Now I have a clear thing to do and I don't have to worry about things all the time and … Well, okay, I do need to worry about certain things, but I don't have a fear, like: Help! I will not make it! Or something like that. (First interview, September 2006)

Nora's experiences are thus opposite to the carefree emerging adulthood characterised by extensive explorations and experimentations (Arnett, 2000). Instead, she feels a strong pressure to decide how to move forward and not being able to make a decision is equated with a sense of failure: a sense that she 'will not make it'. So Nora's decision to study law, made with the help of her father, gives her a direction away from this imagined failure and orientation towards a future. However, this orientation, perhaps because it is born out of parental pressure and advice, remains rather nonconcrete, not providing her with a direction long-term and enabling her to make a clear plan in terms of her professional trajectory. Although Nora is undertaking studies in the area with a rather well-defined professional pathway that could guide her movement towards a future professional identity as a lawyer (Baldry, Märtsin, & Eivers, 2018), the signposts and suggestions that her future professional area gives her seem to be insufficient and unconvincing for her. Instead, her professional trajectory emerges as vague and not well integrated into her self-system where other self-understandings would support her choices and push her towards an image of herself in the future. For the uncertainty related to the possible future trajectories becomes acute again in the second year of studies, where the choices regarding her study programme bring the questions about the future to the surface of her consciousness again. And this time, her mobile lifestyle becomes the factor that destabilises the meaning structures about the future that she had tentatively built through the choice of her study degree:

> There is nothing certain, I don't have this strong and clear goal, I don't have this that I know what to do, so … […] I guess I don't know yet who I want to be and like this. There is no goal. I have a small goal, but the future is open. In that sense. […] Where do I want to settle down eventually when I grow up [laughs]? […] I don't know if I want to go back to Estonia or stay here or I don't know. […] I have found myself thinking, just like I said before, that I don't know where I will be. I like it here a lot, to be honest, but I don't know if I want to live here my entire life or should I live here another five years. Or where shall I do the Master's—here or somewhere else or will I go to Estonia. Lately I have all these questions in my mind. (Second interview, April 2007)

Nora's reflections suggest that not only is she unable to commit to a professional pathway that would orient her towards a certain kind of future, she is also unable to make a decision about the place where she will live in the future. Until recently, Nora has followed her parents as they were moving between different places, and now being on her own, she finds it hard to imagine whether she should continue to be on the move or should settle down. In her deliberations, Estonia emerges as a rather solid anchor in her AS-IF world of imagined future. It emerges as her home where she used to live as a child and could return to when she 'grows up'. It emerges as a place that builds a bridge between known past and unknown future and, as such, gives an orientation for her movement. However, as the return to Estonia is imagined as a possible future long-term scenario, it does not provide certainty in the here-and-now and keeps Nora in a state where her planning is suspended by a possible, next short-term move to a next unknown place.

Interestingly, Estonia as a home is not the only signpost that guides Nora's movement towards an imagined future. Another abstract sign about womanhood emerges as an orientation that guides her meaning-making and imagination:

Some of the students are like this that they have already … One girl from my course is already working for a human rights organization and is active in that field […] But I don't have… okay human rights, but I don't know if I'd like that. I don't know if I'm that interested in that. […] I think I don't want to imagine life like this that I'm doing some sort of work … I am a woman, I don't want to sit somewhere… Because these positions there in the City are, like you are working 16 hours a day in the office and you have no life other than work. I am a woman, my goal is to have a family and children and things like that one day. Because, I'm afraid that simply becoming rich will not make me happy. (Second interview, April 2007)

Nora thus creates two oppositional meaning fields that guide her movement towards an imagined future. On the one hand, she imagines the life of a lawyer, who sits in an office 16 hours a day, does not have a family and kids, but earns enough to become rich. On the other, she imagines the life of a woman who does not work 16 hours a day in an office, does not become rich, but has a family and children. The latter meaning field is perceived as more attractive by Nora and, therefore, provides an orientation towards the future for her. The creation of these oppositional meaning fields reveals how strong is the appeal of a traditional conception of adulthood and its gendered character for Nora, despite the abundance of choices she has and possible future trajectories she can construct. In other words, struggling to imagine a future where her life-goal orientations of having a family and having a professional career are merged, she seems to revert back to meanings of adulthood that are traditional and deeply gendered. Furthermore, this imagined future is also related to the idea of settling down, something that, for her, could happen once she moves back home to Estonia.

"I Do Not Want to Be Alone When I Am 30"

After the end of her second year at university, Nora goes back to Estonia to spend her summer there. In a different sociocultural context, where she is not engaged in studies, her dilemmas about her future career seem to fade into the background. However, being in her old sociocultural environment for a longer period after a year away adds another dimension to the tensions Nora experiences in relation to the uncertainty of her future, for Nora finds herself dealing with questions about romantic relationships:

> You see, that is another surprise. I came here and everybody has a child, or not everybody. But people who I would never have thought could have a child already or something. And everybody is living together or is already married […] Or, you know, old stories with some people here and some old love stories that have remained. See, these remain, they come back again. (Third and final interview, July 2007)

The image of a future as a woman with a family thus resurfaces for Nora as she encounters her old friends and romantic partners and pushes her to make sense of her own experiences and decision in relation to theirs. She cannot help but notice the difference between her mobile lifestyle and the stability of their lives that, among other things, allows creating long-terms romantic relationships:

> And I know that I can't allow myself [pause] a relationship, I cannot afford such a thing, because I am always moving from one place to another and people will not just sit and wait for me for two years. [...] Well in this sense it is a bit sad, that I cannot have a more serious relationship with anybody. That I'm always moving. [...] My lifestyle is very mobile, it is like, well sometimes I feel like bad, lonely ... I feel lonely ... But what can I do [...] The others have it and it's good and before you have had yourself a longer relationship and so you know what it means and that it is good and you have someone to be with. But at this point in my life it doesn't make any sense. (Third and final interview, July 2007)

Nora's reflections evidence that she is missing the closeness and intimacy that comes from being in a long-term romantic relationship. Furthermore, she also realises that her mobile lifestyle that does not allow her to have a stable relationship gets in the way of moving towards her life-goal orientation of having a family and kids one day. In order to regulate that tension and make sense of her choices, she draws boundaries between self and others that allow perceiving her own experiences and decisions in a positive light, while distancing herself from those of the others:

> Thoughts about settling down and creating a home and my friends also say that they want to love somebody and give themselves to somebody. They are 22–23, want to have children and build a family and want to have this calm life and just take it easy. Then I think that I wouldn't imagine something like that now. Let my life be as it is now. I still have time for this. [...] At the same time I have this, I look at other girls of my age and I think that they are not at all independent, they are so attached to their men. [...] I cannot understand how it is possible. I really need my distance; that I am independent and can do my things. That I don't depend on anybody, you see, I don't want to be, I can't imagine being like that [...] I can't imagine that I buy a house and have to pay the mortgage for 30 years. That I can't go, I can't go even to France in the summer for three months. I don't know, to study French, because I have a mortgage I can't do that. I can't imagine something like that. (Third and final interview, July 2007)

Being at home thus allows Nora to encounter a version of her imagined future—a future where she settles down in Estonia, has a family and kids, takes on a mortgage and is thus tied down and unable to experience the things that she has become used to experiencing. Instead of affirming her future life-goal orientation and making her act in relation to it in the present, this view of her possible future pushes Nora away from it. She positions this scenario as something that is not in accordance with her life as a mobile and independent young woman who can do her own things and this negative connotation helps to make her own current position more desirable. Another pair of oppositional meaning fields becomes created, where one refers to her friends who 'have this calm life and just take it easy' and 'are so attached to their men', and the other that refers to her choices and allows her to be 'independent' and do her 'own things'. The sadness that comes from being alone and not having 'somebody to be with' is thus regulated by a field of higher-order meta-signs, where being independent and mobile emerges as more important than being tied down by someone. In other words, the meanings about the kind of life in the present and in the future that she would like to have, and meanings about the kind of person she would like to be, become intertwined as the AS-IS and AS-IF worlds become connected and help her to make sense of her experiences.

However, as with the dilemmas that Nora is experiencing in relation to her career trajectory, the life-goal orientation of having a family and kids regulates also her dilemmas in terms of positioning herself in relation to her Estonian friends. While their position is undesirable from the perspective of her current life, it makes sense from the distant perspective. While, in the present, it is in contradiction with her identity that is closely linked to her mobile lifestyle, in the imagined future where she has settled down (in Estonia), there is no such contradiction. From this future perspective, having a stable relationship becomes a prerequisite for having a family and kids. Thus, as a life-goal orientation, it provides a direction, albeit a distant one, for Nora's meaning-making:

> I don't know exactly who I am, what I'm doing here, what I will be. Like what would I be and what the future will bring. And this is one of the wor-

ries. Okay, I am 22 now and also if I want to have a more serious relationship. It is actually a thing that makes me to think a bit, that at some point it would be nice to have something more serious. But when I return, then I will be 24. Okay, I'm not in a hurry yet. Well, 25 almost and then and … 23, 24. Well, yes, 24 more or less. Should have something more serious already. I don't want to be alone when I am 30. (Third and final interview, July 2007)

Suspended Transitions to Adulthood?

Andres is the only male participant in the study that is discussed in this book. He is also the oldest participant, being 31 years old at the outset of the study. He grew up in the capital city of Estonia but spent his university years in Tartu. He claims to identify mostly with that place and to have a less strong connection with Tallinn, where his parents and sister live. Andres has lived away from his family for many years already, as he moved abroad after completing his undergraduate studies in order to undertake a Master's degree. During the research project discussed in this book, he is continuing his PhD studies in one of the best-known universities in London and at the beginning of the study, he is starting his third and final year.

It appears from our interactions that Andres is very much dedicated to his academic career. He says that he is ambitious and wants to prove to himself that he can be a successful researcher not only in Estonia but also internationally. Yet, our interactions also reveal that this life-goal orientation is in tension with another goal of his—to have a stable intimate relationship. For he suggests that the pursuit of academic success that has brought him away from home and made him move repeatedly between countries has made it hard for him to create and maintain relationships (see Plöger & Kubiak, 2019, for similar findings). In many ways then, Andres's dilemmas are similar to the ones experienced by Nora. However, when Nora only imagines her life when she is 30, Andres is already living it, and this gives a somewhat different flavour to his experiences of transitioning to adulthood while on the move.

Living Between Estonia and Europe

Similarly to Nora, the study period does not reveal any strong and significant ruptures in Andres's flow of being that are related to his repeated mobility. As he has lived away from home for several years already and is starting his third year in London, the experience of being in a different cultural environment does not lead anymore to any serious breaks from his ordinary ways of being and make him question these in relation to the novelty of 'non-home'. Instead, his reflections suggest that it is his life away from home that has become normal and ordinary for him:

> I have probably developed, I don't know if it is European identity. Being European means differentiating oneself from the rest of the world. It is not in the sense of differentiating, but in the sense of thinking and acting freely. I feel natural in this environment; it doesn't feel like going abroad. Or like, "I go abroad from Estonia, I go to Europe". It's not that, it's my environment. And I definitely want it to stay this way. And I am afraid that if I go there to Estonia, perhaps I'll get stuck there, and all this will somehow remain closed. Somehow I like this feeling of being able to take the train from London and go there and Berlin or the natural ease of doing these things. (Second interview, April 2007)

Although living abroad does not make Andres question his 'old' ways of being, the issue of moving between 'home' and 'non-home' is nevertheless explicit in his reflections. Andres, more than any other participant in this study, talks about the desire to settle down at some point in his life in order to build a home of his own. The dialectic of home and away is, in his case, not turned backwards but rather facing forward, emerging not so much as a longing for things that 'have been', but rather as longing for things that 'should' or 'could be' in the future. In considering his possible movement forward into the future, Andres creates two interconnected meaning fields—one about Estonia and the other about Europe—and imagines his future trajectories in relation to these. On the one hand, in these imaginary scenarios, he distances himself from Estonia that appears as a constraining place, where Andres can get stuck and where it is not necessarily easy for him to move and think freely:

My worldview is quite liberal and when I read some Estonian, read Estonian news […] well you can feel some sort of hostility towards strangers or a certain concern towards multicultural society, difference, open Europe. And that makes me upset and I can't understand it. (Second interview, April 2007)

Estonia thus emerges in opposition to Europe as a place where people can remain physically and mentally 'closed' and 'stuck'—an aspect that Andres does not want to be associated with and that makes him draw boundaries between himself and Estonia. In this sense, Estonia is not his place and Europe is 'his environment'. Yet, on the other hand, the meaning field of Estonia also emerges in Andres's imagination as 'home' and is thus connected to the different meanings that come with this concept (see also Chap. 4). In particular (and in a similar way to Nora), Estonia as home appears as a place where stability can be achieved and, therefore, long-lasting relationships can be created and can become to unfold. This semiotic move that reaffirms the connection between Estonia and 'home' allows Andres to manage the doubts and tensions that come with pursuing the life of a successful academician that every now and then makes him feel lonely and 'homesick':

The life of a PhD student […] leads to the situation where relationships are very difficult to maintain, so it is like some long-distance relationships […] So in that sense life is very unstable and irregular and then, of course, you think … Funny enough, lately I feel homesick, I don't know what exactly can cause this […] But lately I feel like, what if I go home instead. (First interview, September 2006)

Despite all his travels and ambitions, his doubts and worries about the constraints that Estonia poses on his freedom, he still sees that place as his home, a place to return to after his adventures. In the moments of feeling 'homesick', Andres thus imagines a scenario where he actually returns 'home' to Estonia and settles down there:

Why don't I go to Tartu University? Start to work! Teach! Stability! Start to enjoy the results of the work I've done until now. In that sense a kind of idealised picture of possible life in Tartu becomes created. (First interview, September 2006)

Andres's attempt to navigate between two competing life-goal orientations—pursuing a successful academic career and having a stable relationship—is thus accompanied by the creation of two related meaning fields of Estonia and Europe that connect the AS-IS world with his imaginary AS-IF world and create an imaginary space, where the two life-goal orientations are combined. This imaginary space of Estonia, and specifically Tartu, is idealised but still pulls Andres towards it strongly enough for him to visit Tartu in order to imagine actually living there. In our second interview, he tells me that during his last trip to Estonia, he took some time to visit Tartu to see how he 'feels there':

> Yes I do want to go there, do that, but I definitely think that I don't have to be there for 12 months. [...] And that is a kind of little thought that seems doable to me. To share my time between, let's say, Estonia and some other place somewhere in Europe. (Second interview, April 2007)

In this scenario, then, Andres is able to regulate the tension between the two competing life-goal orientations and, at the same time, also manage the tensions between 'constraining Estonia' and 'enabling Europe'. Continuing to see Estonia as 'home' thus makes sense to Andres, as it allows him to regulate these layered tensions by connecting the prospect of having a stable and rewarding private life to the return to Estonia while maintaining his connections with Europe.

These reflections that are focused on Andres's career plans and his struggles of finding his place between London and Estonia in a manner that is rewarding for him appear strongly in the first half of the study period. However, in the second part of the study, this focus shifts to Andres's new relationship and to the planning of future together with his partner, no longer only in relation to the possible return to Estonia. The event of meeting someone thus feeds into the way Andres sees his AS-IS world and creates plans for the AS-IF world. The semiotic constructions about home and away that would allow him to combine his life-goal orientations thus start to change as his focus from an imagined return to Estonia and having a stable relationship there, shifts to the reality of being in a relationship:

Going abroad has always meant that my academic career was more important than my private life. I have not prioritised my relationships and they
have ended. Now I think the private life [pause] is rather a priority. […]
Now I make my career decisions, I negotiate with my partner what to do
and how to do. To be with her is more important than other things. Or
other things are also important, but I try to make compromises that are
nice and reasonable. (Third and last interview, September 2007)

In a way then, starting a new relationship away from home opens up
another trajectory for Andres for imagining his future and combining his
two life-goal orientations. The focus on returning to Tartu loses its relevance in light of this new relationship that is also unfolding away from
home. It thus distances Andres from his homeland and his future connection with 'home' that he imagines and opens up possibilities of imagining
a future that is otherwise and unfolds elsewhere.

Living a Prolonged Childhood?

Andres's efforts to make sense of his movement between home and away
and his struggles to navigate between two competing life-goal orientations do not unfold in a vacuum but in a unique sociocultural context
with its collective affordances and meaning potentials that Andres needs
to consider in imagining his future trajectories. Andres's self-definition as
a young, ambitious and open-minded researcher who considers Europe
to be his environment allows him to function effectively in London, for
he is among people who share these ideals and values:

Here the freedom, being free from this pressure here in London. You feel,
you are not, all the others around you are the same. Or like, to have, to live
in a rented accommodation is completely normal, nothing special. You are
not an idiot if you don't get a mortgage. And in general, you can be a scientist and be relatively free from social obligations also in your age. Or at
least you don't feel that you are socially obliged to do something. This is a
positive aspect that I value a lot. (Second interview, April 2007)

The freedom of thinking and acting that Andres refers to in his reflections thus has a further dimension—to be free from social obligation to

conduct one's life in a particular way. According to Andres, there are multiple ways of living one's life in London, and the one that he has chosen is one of the many possible trajectories that is accepted by others as 'normal', as 'nothing special'. The social environment of London where 'the others around you are the same' thus affirms his choices and although his references to this social context are rather generic, he does talk about London as a social context to which he belongs and has close connections with. However, he also belongs to Estonia. His visits to his homeland and contacts with other Estonians make him question his choices and make him feel that his way of being in the world and his way of defining himself are not compatible with the ways of being in Estonian society:

> Some sort of freedom that you have here in London. You are over 30, but you don't feel this total social pressure that we have in Estonia. In that age you need to have achieved something and if you are just a PhD student, you are doing your research or something, you are just a nonsense bloke. You are just wasting your time, prolonging your childhood; this is precisely what I've been told in Estonia. That [pause] in Estonia, if you are away for a bit longer, you immediately feel … Others, who have returned from abroad have said this as well, someone I know who lives in Paris, says that he comes to Estonia, is there for a week and already feels that he should get a mortgage and buy a flat. This is the way you do it. (First interview, September 2006)

Being in-between home and away is thus visible in Andres's reflections. On the one hand, he gets affirmation of his way of life from the sociocultural environment where he lives and this allows him to feel good in his new environment. Yet, on the other hand, he is still embedded in the social and cultural networks of Estonia, unable to break free from these completely. Estonia as 'home' is still the place to return to one day and thus an important anchor in his self-definition. In these networks in Estonia, according to his own views, others position him as someone who is 'a nonsense bloke' that is 'prolonging his childhood'. This identity of a child, a 'non-responsible adult' thus clashes with his self-understanding of a 'liberal, open-minded young researcher' who is building a 'successful international academic career'. Andres not only feels the mismatch between his life and general way of being with the way things are in Estonia but he also feels that his life-trajectory is unfolding in a different way than those of his friends:

> My best friends became parents for the first time. Unexpectedly, it made me sad and made me once again question my life—how genuine is it in the end. Not that I have doubts about my choices, it's more that I have some sad moments when I think about the world I've lost and feel that I don't have this constant supportive closeness and other joys of that kind. (Questionnaire, November 2006)

The tension between his life-goal orientations returns here again, this time in relation to the social expectations surrounding the unfolding of his lifecourse. For Andres's decision to pursue the academic career and thus be on the move all the time, has made his trajectory different from those of his Estonian friends, who are having kids and settling down. At the age of 31, he is single, lives in rented accommodation and does not have kids and is, therefore, out of sync with his friends (Neugarten, 1979). When he turns towards home, instead of finding the support, familiarity, safety and security that comes from being an 'insider', he finds a difference that positions him 'outside' of the familiar and safe networks. 'Home' and the social network that come with it thus challenge some of his choices, decisions and self-understandings. At the same time, though, it reinforces the idea that Estonia really is the place to settle down and create stable relationships—in other words, to become a responsible adult:

> Perhaps there in Estonia I feel that if others are living their adult lives, I'm still prolonging my childhood and perhaps have not taken the full responsibility in life. (Questionnaire, October 2006)

For Andres, then, the oppositional meaning fields of 'Estonia' and 'London' also start to contain ideas about adulthood and what it means to be an adult in those places and semiotic spaces. On the one hand, in his meaning-making, the meaning field of Estonia emerges with its connection to 'responsible adulthood'. On the other hand, the meaning field of London emerges with its multiple trajectories and ways of being an adult. Andres finds himself in-between these two meaning fields, in a liminal space, a border zone, where the ideas from both fields come together with the potential to create a new meaning structure. Being in this space that is pregnant with potential, but does not yet provide a clear way forward, is difficult for Andres who feels that he has lost one world but has not yet been able to create another one.

In order to regulate these tensions and start to carve a way out from the liminal phase of this transition, Andres clings to his values, ideals and the self-image that he has created. In an attempt to find affirmation to these, he turns away from his Estonian friends and moves towards other 'in-betweeners': Londoners and other Estonians who live abroad and who are similar to him. Being away from home has thus torn down some of the semiotic structures that have so far helped him to build his life-trajectory, yet, simultaneously, it has also given him new resources and offered new social networks to support his movements, including his movement into adulthood:

> Those guys there are formalizing their lives fully, their responsibilities in life are changing radically etc. Instead, mine have either remained the same or have become altered to another direction. So there is less and less connection between us. Somehow we don't have common topics anymore. And perhaps I'm a bit ashamed of this difference. I feel that I'm clearly becoming estranged from my Estonian friends. (Questionnaire, February 2007)

All these semiotic auto-regulation efforts help to reduce the tension that comes from being and moving between home and away and the different semiotic structures and meanings of responsible adulthood that come with it. While the sense of being in-between these structures—having dismantled some of them, but not having yet built new and solid structures, is evident in my interactions with Andres throughout the study period; the developments in his relationship status make these tensions and struggles less pressing. It seems that being in a relationship and working towards a future together takes some of the pressure off and helps him to deal with the questions about the value of his life. As Andres starts to build a relationship with someone who has made similar choices to his and shares his values and ideals, he finds the affirmation he needs. He thus seems to be moving towards a more 'responsible' relationship with the world and that makes the difference between him and others less evident:

> But it has disappeared lately in the sense that I have experienced in my life, what suits me and what doesn't. And I know what suits me and what I like. And there is no point to go on about being here or there, in the sense that I know, what I want is somewhat different. I'm not envious of people's positions or achievements; the choices I have made have been different. (Third and final interview, September 2007)

Summary

In this chapter, my focus was mainly on the temporal dimension of human meaning-making and identity development. I examined how human conduct and meaning-making is always directed towards the future and guided by life-goal orientations that are constructed by human agents. I unpacked these ideas by discussing two case studies. Nora's experiences allowed examining how a young adult with an abundance of alternatives and possibilities constructs her life-goal orientations in the context of repeated mobility. Andres's case offered an opportunity to examine similar dilemmas but in the context where the imagined need to settle down and create one's own family creates further pressures and demands on one's short- and long-term movement into the future. Both cases together thus offer opportunities to examine how the movement between home and away and transition to adulthood can become interlaced and shapes the way plans are made and movement into the future is undertaken. They also allow examining how gender and age start to shape these processes.

On the one hand, the case studies evidence the abundance of choices available for young people today and the dilemmas this abundance creates for them. As Nora's and Andres's cases show, young adults do not necessarily have to follow a pre-set trajectory in building their adult lives, although as both cases indicate, the standard model of adulthood still strongly shapes the ways in which they imagine their futures and make sense of their own decisions (Blatterer, 2007). On the other hand, the experiences of Nora and Andres could also be seen as revealing the restricted choices some young adults have in contemporary societies, for both of them seem to view their mobile lifestyle not necessarily as a free choice, an opportunity and a luxury, but rather as a necessity to stay relevant and build a career in their chosen area (see also Säde's and Kersti's cases in Chap. 6). In line with existing research findings (Plöger & Kubiak, 2019; Salamońska & Czeranowska, 2019), their mobile lifestyles reveal the increased complexity that young adults have to deal with when making decisions and planning futures. For as Andres's and Nora's experiences indicate, experiencing repeated mobility and being constantly on the move suspends some of the possibilities to plan and make decisions—it is hard to plan if you don't know where or with whom you are going to be in the future. And this suspension creates tension and trouble, especially when encountering significant others who are not experiencing similar kinds of suspensions and are thus unable to provide support and guidance in the process of transition. As both case studies show, the social support and guidance for transitions are available, however, finding them may not be as straightforward and easy as it may seem.

The case studies discussed in this chapter also indicate that although young adults' life-goal construction might be made more difficult and/or temporarily suspended in the context of repeated mobility, their lives are nevertheless conducted in relation to imagined futures and plans for actualising these. The case of Nora, who cannot quite decide which direction within her chosen profession of law to pursue, however is drawn towards an image of herself as having a family and children in the future. The case studies also suggest that home and being away from home play an important role in the life-goal construction of mobile young adults. On the one hand, being away from home and on the move create tensions and suspend the planning. On the other hand, home and, in particular, return to home seems to also create a certain direction for future planning, providing a safe haven where one can finally settle down and use a base for family creation when all the moving is done. Home thus creates a thread from the past through the present into the future where significant encounters occur and in relation to which important decision and plans are made. It emerges as an anchor that holds the boat still while stormy weather passes and one can again see clearly enough to start navigating the sea towards a chosen destination.

References

Arnett, J. J. (2000). Emerging adulthood: A theory of development from late teens through the twenties. *American Psychologist, 55*(5), 469–480.

Baldry, S., Märtsin, M., & Eivers, A. (2018). Travelling without a destination? A dialogical analysis of professional identity construction among Australian psychology double degree students. *Identity: An International Journal of Theory and Research, 18*, 94–108. https://doi.org/10.1080/15283488.2018.1447483

Benson, J. (2014). Transition to adulthood. In A. Ben-Arieh, F. Casas, I. Frønes, & J. Korbin (Eds.), *Handbook of child well-being* (pp. 1763–1783). Dordrecht: Springer.

Blatterer, H. (2007). Contemporary adulthood. Reconceptualizing an uncontested category. *Current Sociology, 55*(6), 771–792.

Bühler, C., & Massarik, F. (Eds.). (1968). *The course of human life. A study of goals in the humanistic perspective.* New York: Springer.

du Bois-Reymond, M. (2009). Models of navigation and life management. In A. Furlong (Ed.), *Handbook of youth and young adulthood. New perspectives and agendas* (pp. 31–38). New York: Routledge.

Furlong, A. (Ed.). (2009). *Handbook of youth and young adulthood. New perspectives and agendas.* New York: Routledge.

Heinz, W. A. (2009). Youth transitions in an age of uncertainty. In A. Furlong (Ed.), *Handbook of youth and young adulthood. New perspectives and agendas* (pp. 3–13). New York: Routledge.

Henderson, S., Holland, J., McGrellis, S., Sharpe, S., & Thomson, R. (2007). *Inventing adulthoods: A biographical approach to youth transitions.* London: Sage.

Hviid, P., & Villadsen, J. W. (2018). The development of a person: Children's experience of being and becoming within the cultural life course. In A. Rosa & J. Valsiner (Eds.), *Handbook of sociocultural psychology* (pp. 556–574). Cambridge: Cambridge University Press.

Levinson, D. J. (1986). A conception of adult development. *American Psychologist, 41*, 3–13. https://doi.org/10.1037/0003-066X.41.1.3

Neugarten, B. L. (1979). Time, age, and the life cycle. *American Journal of Psychiatry, 136*, 887–894. https://doi.org/10.1176/ajp.136.7.887

Plöger, J., & Kubiak, S. (2019). Becoming 'the internationals'—How place shapes the sense of belonging and group formation of high-skilled migrants. *Journal of International Migration and Integration, 20,* 307–321. https://doi.org/10.1007/s12134-018-0608-7

Salamońska, J., & Czeranowska, O. (2019). Janus-faced mobilities: Motivations for migration among European youth in times of crisis. *Journal of Youth Studies, 0*(0), 1–17. https://doi.org/10.1080/13676261.2019.1569215

Thomson, R. (2011). *Unfolding lives: Youth, gender and change.* Bristol: The Policy Press.

Villadsen, J. W. (2019). Children's development—Between personal engagements and curriculum based pre-school practices. In P. Hviid & M. Märtsin (Eds.), *Culture in education and education in culture. Tensioned dialogues and creative constructions* (p. TBC). Cham: Springer.

8

Conclusion: Moving Forward

At the heart of this book were multifaceted stories of eight young adults who were on their journey into adulthood while being on the move between different cultural systems. Analysing their movements and changes—physical and developmental movements but also semiotic moves that involved their efforts to make sense of their experiences in the present and in the past and make plans for the future, while being embedded in cultural systems that were themselves undergoing transformations—were at the focus of my attention in this book. Offering a detailed account of the complex interlacing of these different kinds of movements—developmental transitions, mobility, meaning-making and cultural change—was one of the ways how this book sought to advance our understanding of human lifecourse development. On the one hand, it highlighted the variety of ways how early adulthood is experienced in our contemporary societies, thus challenging the traditional views about this developmental period (see, for example, Levinson, 1986). For example, some young adults struggled to make plans for the future in the face of their mobile lifestyle, while others resisted it and still others agonised about their inability to do so, while being confronted with the decisions and lifestyles of their peers. On the other hand, the case studies also

© The Author(s) 2019
M. Märtsin, *Identity Development in the Lifecourse*, Sociocultural Psychology of the Lifecourse, https://doi.org/10.1007/978-3-030-27753-6_8

revealed that the traditional views about adulthood with its focus on independence and need to settle down (see, for example, Blatterer, 2007) were still relevant for the study participants, creating challenges for them as their mobile lifestyle made the pursuit of some of these ideals impossible. The sociocultural and semiotic lens used in this book that brought to the fore the variety and complexity of young people's experiences, thus allowed moving away from understanding their experiences as 'typical' of the 'early adulthood stage' of development and, instead, enabled describing these as unique developmental trajectories unfolding through ruptures and transitions that are continuously made sense of. I will return to the issue of conceptualising development in early adulthood again below.

Yet, my aim in this book was not merely the description of eight unique developmental trajectories. Instead, my aim was to offer a novel conceptualisation of identity development that goes beyond the specifics of these cases and describes general processes and mechanisms of identity development that lie underneath their uniqueness. In this book, I suggested to view identity development not as a special kind of psychological process but rather as part of our ongoing process of meaning-making. From this suggestion followed the idea that identity can be seen as a by-product of the ongoing meaning-making, as a temporary stabilisation in the flow of interpretation and reinterpretation of signs, that over time becomes generalised and emerges as a field of hyper-generalised meta-signs about who we are, have been and are becoming. Identities are thus part of the semiotic architecture of the self and, at the highest level of this inner semiotic hierarchy, have the power to regulate and orchestrate the creation, modification, termination or maintenance of other signs. In short, identities guide the way we make sense of our experiences while at the same time also being constantly made and remade through our interactions with the environment, where ruptures trigger the processes of meaning-making, including identity development.

In this book, I considered four different contexts that created ruptures and triggered the process of meaning-making and identity development for the young adults: movement away from home, close relationships, educational achievements, and future planning. In all of these contexts, the young adults encountered experiences that blocked their movement into the future with the guidance of their existing ways of seeing themselves and posed the question: if I am not anymore this, then who am I? In all of the considered situations, the ruptures catapulted young people into an in-between, or a liminal, zone of transition (Stenner, 2017) where their old structures of meaning did not hold anymore, while the new ones had not yet been created. Their reflections revealed the challenges of being in these liminal zones; they revealed their efforts to construct new, often contrasting meaning fields about self and others and cross the borders between those meaning fields in order to figure out on which side of the border one sits and belongs. They thus evidenced the active meaning-making out of which new ways of seeing oneself—new identities—emerged. In many cases, the emergence of these 'new' ways entailed the return to the reconstructed 'old' ways, evidencing the idea that identities function as meta-signs that are, in their hyper-generalisability and nebulousness, not easily modifiable. In all of the contexts, the described dynamics of meaning-making revealed the importance of time in development. Time to make sense of the change and deal with the chaos that the rupture created. But also time in terms of future perspective—the need to make sense of the past in order to move forward into the future.

In concluding this book, it is appropriate to ask, what new has this conceptualisation offered to identity research? What new avenues for theory and research has it opened up? My answer to these questions is somewhat paradoxical, for I propose that moving forward, we do not necessarily need to develop theories and research that unpack the identity processes per se but, instead, need to focus on work that advances our understanding of human meaning-making in general. Based on the work presented in this book, human meaning-making can be seen as a border-making process that involves crossing and maintaining, creating and dismantling of borders across two dimensions: spatial borders between self and others and temporal borders between past and future (Zittoun et al., 2013). Identity development too can be viewed as a semiotic border-making process that works across these two dimensions. Outlining how these ideas could be advanced in future theorising and research will be the focus of the remainder of this concluding chapter.

Making and Crossing Spatial Borders

The idea that person and environment are inseparable and should not be studied in isolation from each other is not new and has been repeatedly discussed in psychological and sociological literature in recent decades. In this book, I considered the relationship between person and environment but, more broadly, I equated it with the relationship between self and other, where the environment contains multiple meanings and ideas from others, all offering alternative perspectives for the self that trigger and can be used in meaning-making. I conceptualised self and environment as interrelated parts of an open system that become constructed and function through the ongoing interaction and are thus mutually enabling and constraining. Building on semiotic cultural psychology, I proposed that they become inseparable through meaning-making that emerges as a process at the border between person and environment and links the two parts of the whole together. The other flows into the self as the meanings are internalised and the self feeds into the other through meanings that are externalised. The other is there when the meaning is created, by offering another perspective that the self can turn towards oneself, as, for example, in the case of Mari, whose journey between 'fake' and 'real' life was discussed in Chap. 4. It is also there when the personally created meanings are externalised and presented to the others who can either validate these or withhold their recognition, as in the case of Säde, discussed in Chap. 6, whose previous professional experiences were dismissed and silenced in her new educational environment. I thus argued that self and environment, with its multiplicity of meaning suggestions, do not stand in separation from one another but flow into each other, leaving traces of these mutual floodings behind. The self feeds into the collective and constrains the collective through this process, and the collective creates boundaries for the functioning of the self.

By taking this stance towards understanding the person and environment relationship, I suggested viewing identity development as a semiotic border-making process between self and environment that allows positioning self in relation to others and defining who one is, was and is becoming (Español, Marsico, & Tateo, 2018; Marsico, 2016; Marsico &

Tateo, 2017). I proposed to view it as a process through which borders are drawn and redrawn between different kinds of others, between self and others, and within self from the past through the present into the future. Importantly, the borders that are drawn are not fixed and impermeable but rather allow semiotic material to move through, redefining the borders in the process. Identity, as a highly generalised sign, becomes a semiotic regulator of this border-making process—a temporary stabilisation of the mutually transformative flow between person and environment, which temporarily stabilises and defines the person's position within and in relation to the environment. It says something about the person, but it says just as much about the environment. In other words, the individual makes the meanings, but the meanings are always made of something and in relation to something.

The conceptual tools developed in this book open up ways of exploring the dynamics of these mutual enabling and constraining processes. They offer opportunities for future research to shift the attention away from describing the two parts of the open system in isolation from each other and instead move towards exploring the semiotic moves at the border between self and environment. Put differently, the ideas presented in the book suggest that future work should not seek to reveal and describe the meanings that have already been created by self or other but, rather, should focus on exploring how the meanings that are created are taken up in the process of meaning-making in order to turn them into something else.

The case studies discussed in this book offered a complex sociocultural context for exploring these movements across the borders between self and other. On the one hand, the context of mobility presented the study participants with the need to simultaneously create and dismantle the borders between different cultures and societies and others embedded into these sociocultural environments. For many of them, this move across the country borders was not the first one and, in the imagination of several participants, it was also not the last one. Therefore, the developmentally interesting task for them was to find a way of encountering the other at the border and making sense of it and oneself in relation to it, while maintaining the readiness to move away again, reconstructing the borders once again (Levitan, 2019; Zittoun, Levitan, & Cangiá,

2018). Understanding how persons create semiotic tools that support them in the process of being constantly on the move and make sense of themselves as perpetual migrants is thus one of the future research directions revealed by the case studies discussed in this book.

On the other hand, the case studies were also embedded into the context of crossing borders between different periods in the lifecourse, namely adolescence and adulthood. As discussed in the introductory chapter, the changing nature of the transition to adulthood in contemporary societies has created various debates and discussions about this process. Some have suggested that in order to best capture these changes, we need to view the human lifecourse as including a new developmental stage—emerging adulthood (Arnett, 2000). The views put forward in this book offer an alternative view about this lifecourse transition. Viewed from the semiotic cultural perspective, the interesting question is not when and why this transition occurs and whether the identity explorations are fundamental in this phase of development or not. Rather, what is interesting from the perspective of development is the way in which young adults semiotically construct the border between adolescence and adulthood for themselves, define themselves in relation to that border and then move to cross it or not. As the case studies in this book evidenced, this border between adolescence and adulthood is flexible, can be created in many different ways and repeatedly, as well as crossed in a multitude of ways and times by different individuals or by the same person. Unpacking the dynamics of making and crossing borders between adolescence and adulthood, as well as exploring what is at stake in this process and what kind of future does this border-making and crossing enable the person to pursue, are thus the questions for future studies that are opened up by the case studies discussed in this book. These questions also bring us to the temporal dimension of human meaning-making.

Making and Crossing Temporal Borders

According to the views put forward in this book, human meaning-making, including identity development, does not occur only at the 'spatial border' between self and other but also at the temporal border between past and future. As Zittoun and others (2013) have written: "Time—irreversible, as it flows from the past infinity towards the future—is the key in any developmental investigation" (p. 379). In examining the experiences of the eight young adults in this book, I have sought to describe their journeys as always moving towards imagined and anticipated futures, made possible by the experiences they have had in the past. I have emphasised that in order to understand this movement, we need to consider the future-orientedness of human meaning-making. That is, we need to understand that as humans, we always make meanings, including meanings about the persons we are, want to be or become, ahead of time in order to pre-adapt to the unpredictable but anticipated future. In fact, we constantly construct goals and scenarios about the future and how we would like it to look like and then start to act in relation to those imagined scenarios. In conceptualising this future-orientedness, I built on Charlotte Bühler's theorising, proposing that our being in the world is guided by life-goal orientations that are part of the field of highly generalised meta-signs. These sign complexes thus help us to make sense of our experiences here and now but also allow us to revisit our pasts and imagine our futures. As life-goal orientations are interlaced with our identities, they allow us to imagine the kinds of people we are and would like to become and enable us to construct pathways for moving towards these AS-IF scenarios.

Imagination thus allows us to distance ourselves from the immediate experiences and create AS-IF scenarios about how things should or could be. And it is the imagination of a different future that often helps us to move out from a troubled situation, make sense of a rupture in our trajectory and continue our journey. Tania, whose case was discussed in Chap. 4, for example, returns home and to her parents' care in her imagination when life abroad becomes too difficult to handle, and this imagined safe haven gives her the break from the uneasy present and allows her to continue her independent life. But imagined futures can also create blockages and suspend our movements, make us feel stuck in the present, with no clear way out from a difficult situation. As Nora's and Andres's cases, discussed in Chap. 7, evidence, the experience of the repeated mobility from the past fed forward into the future in the form of an anticipated repeated mobility can suspend our movement towards our life-goals. It can create a liminal phase in a transition (Stenner, 2017) where old structures of meanings do not work anymore, but new ones are not yet available to allow escaping the uncertainty and ambivalence.

While theoretically rather well developed, this focus on time and becoming has been notoriously difficult to maintain in developmental research. In fact, most developmental psychology has abandoned this aim in favour of studying forms of functioning that have already emerged and thus become uninteresting from the point of view of development. In the research presented in this book, I used two different ways to maintain this focus on the future and on the forms that have not yet eventuated but are in the process of becoming. On the one hand, by choosing the semi-longitudinal design for the study and asking the participants to 'report' their experiences every month, I aimed to create conditions for exploring the emergence and disappearance of certain meanings, the oscillations between various intermediate forms out of which generalised and abstract signs that have the potential to guide the movement towards future can emerge. On the other hand, this focus on becoming was evident also in my interpretation, where I always tried to keep my attention on the orientation towards the future and on the purpose of meaning-making. What is at stake for this person when she makes sense of her experiences in this way? What future life-goal orientation or imaginary scenario for herself and for the others is she pursuing here?

In recent years, several fascinating attempts to develop methodologies that focus on the process of emergence have been proposed (Abbey & Surgan, 2012; Toomela & Valsiner, 2010; Valsiner, 2017). Yet, more work needs to be done here to ask research questions and develop methodologies that focus on the process of becoming and emergence and thus bring back development into the study of lifecourse transitions. This book can thus also be seen as an invitation for pursuing such future research agendas.

Weaving the Carpet of Life

In drawing this book to its close, I offer the reader a metaphor to think through some of the ideas presented in this book. In particular, I suggest viewing identity development through the metaphor of carpet weaving.

A carpet becomes woven by using parallel and multiple threads of yarn, which become tied together in knots. The threads or strands of meaning-making that differ according to their content are available for people to use for weaving their life-carpet. The personal experience of reacting to different life-events is accumulated in those threads. These threads have duration; they come from the past through the present and move towards the future. But these are loose threads, which can be taken up and tied together at any given moment of time in any given way. Joining a knot may become necessary when a rupture occurs and a person needs to temporarily find a balance in the flow of thoughts and ideas. Different signs, including identities, become created in those moments. A knot in the carpet—a new sign, is a temporary stabilisation of the ongoing flow of meaning-making. In the next moment of time, the attention wanders elsewhere and the previously tied knot becomes irrelevant and fades away. Or if the attention is drawn to that knot repeatedly, if it is tied again and again, becoming very strong in the process and thus starting to impact the way the entire carpet is shaped and looks like. In any case, the threads that were used to tie this knot can be used again to tie another knot somewhere else. What threads exactly are used to tie a specific knot is not known beforehand, nor is it clear how exactly the new knot will look like. The life-situations the person encounters shape what kinds of knots become created and the cultural environment in which the person lives gives her the tools and skills for knotting. The affordances of the weaving environment thus structure the way the carpet will look like. Nevertheless, the person who weaves the carpet also has an important role to play, for she is the one who does the knotting and she is the one who has an idea of the pattern she would like to achieve. So the knotting is not random but follows a design that can nevertheless change, as the weaver is free to change her mind. In this process of weaving, new threads become created over time and added to the carpet to be used again in later stages, while some of the previously used threads are left aside and not used anymore. Every thread can be seen as a sequence of little knots, as our meaning-making is filled with traces from the past and is pregnant with opportunities for creating imagined futures.

It is my hope that the conceptual threads developed in this book will be taken up by others and woven into their research carpets, creating new ways of imagining and researching development in adulthood and the role of identity development in it.

References

Abbey, E., & Surgan, S. (Eds.). (2012). *Developing methods in psychology*. New Brunswick, NJ: Transaction Publishers.

Arnett, J. J. (2000). Emerging adulthood: A theory of development from late teens through the twenties. *American Psychologist, 55*(5), 469–480.

Blatterer, H. (2007). Contemporary adulthood. Reconceptualizing an uncontested category. *Current Sociology, 55*(6), 771–792.

Español, A., Marsico, G., & Tateo, L. (2018). Maintaining borders: From border guards to diplomats. *Human Affairs: Postdisciplinary Humanities & Social Sciences Quarterly, 28*(4), 443–460. https://doi.org/10.1515/humaff-2018-0036

Levinson, D. J. (1986). A conception of adult development. *American Psychologist, 41*, 3–13. https://doi.org/10.1037/0003-066X.41.1.3

Levitan, D. (2019). The art of living in transitoriness: Strategies of families in repeated geographical mobility. *Integrative Psychological & Behavioral Science, 53*, 258–282. https://doi.org/10.1007/s12124-018-9448-4

Marsico, G. (2016). The borderland. *Culture & Psychology, 22*(2), 206–215. https://doi.org/10.1177/1354067X15601199

Marsico, G., & Tateo, L. (2017). Borders, tensegrity and development in dialogue. *Integrative Psychological & Behavioral Science, 51*(4), 536–556. https://doi.org/10.1007/s12124-017-9398-2

Stenner, P. (2017). *Liminality and experience. A transdisciplinary approach to the psychosocial*. London: Palgrave.

Toomela, A., & Valsiner, J. (Eds.). (2010). *Methodological thinking in psychology. Have 60 years gone astray?* Charlotte, NC: Information Age Publishing.

Valsiner, J. (2017). *From methodology to methods in human psychology*. Cham: Springer.

Zittoun, T., Levitan, D., & Cangiá, F. (2018). A sociocultural approach to mobile families: A case study. *Peace and Conflict: Journal of Peace Psychology, 24*(4), 424–432. https://doi.org/10.1037/pac0000313

Zittoun, T., Valsiner, J., Vedeler, D., Salgado, J., Gonçalves, M. M., & Ferring, D. (2013). *Human development in the life course. Melodies of living*. Cambridge: Cambridge University Press.

Correction to: Identity Development in the Lifecourse

Correction to:
M. Märtsin, *Identity Development in the Lifecourse*, Sociocultural Psychology of the Lifecourse, https://doi.org/10.1007/978-3-030-27753-6

The original version of this book has been revised,
An error in the production process caused the author's affiliation to be corrected into the series editor's affiliation by mistake. This has been corrected in the copyright page and the cover.

The updated version of the book can be found at
https://doi.org/10.1007/978-3-030-27753-6

References

Abbey, E. (2004). Circumventing ambivalence in identity: The importance of latent and overt aspects of symbolic meaning. *Culture & Psychology, 10*(3), 331–336.

Abbey, E. (2007a). At the boundary of me and you: Semiotic architecture of thinking and feeling the other. In L. M. Simão & J. Valsiner (Eds.), *Otherness in question. Labyrinths of the self* (pp. 73–92). Charlotte: Information Age Publishing.

Abbey, E. (2007b). Perpetual uncertainty of cultural life: Becoming reality. In J. Valsiner & A. Rosa (Eds.), *The Cambridge handbook of sociocultural psychology* (pp. 362–372). Cambridge: Cambridge University Press.

Abbey, E. (2012). Ambivalences and its transformations. In J. Valsiner (Ed.), *Oxford handbook of cultural psychology* (pp. 989–997). New York: Oxford University Press.

Abbey, E., & Surgan, S. (Eds.). (2012). *Developing methods in psychology*. New Brunswick, NJ: Transaction Publishers.

Abbey, E., & Valsiner, J. (2004). Emergence of meanings through ambivalence [58 paragraphs]. *Forum Qualitative Sozialforschung/Forum: Qualitative Social Research [Online Journal], 6*(1), Art 23.

Alvesson, M., & Sköldberg, K. (2000). *Reflexive methodology. New vistas for qualitative research*. London: Sage.

© The Author(s) 2019
M. Märtsin, *Identity Development in the Lifecourse*, Sociocultural Psychology of the Lifecourse, https://doi.org/10.1007/978-3-030-27753-6

Arnett, J. J. (2000). Emerging adulthood: A theory of development from late teens through the twenties. *American Psychologist, 55*(5), 469–480.

Arnett, J. J., Kloep, M., Hendry, L. B., & Tanner, J. L. (2011). *Debating emerging adulthood: Stage or process.* New York: Oxford University Press.

Aveling, E. L., & Gillespie, A. (2008). Negotiating multiplicity: Adaptive asymmetries within second-generation Turks' 'society of mind'. *Journal of Constructivist Psychology, 21*(3), 200–222.

Azmitia, M., Syed, M., & Radmacher, K. (2013). Finding your niche: Identity and emotional support in emerging adults' adjustment to the transition to college. *Journal of Research on Adolescence, 23*(4), 744–761. https://doi.org/10.1111/jora.12037

Bakhtin, M. M. (1986). *Speech genres and other late essays.* Austin: University of Texas Press.

Baldry, S., Märtsin, M., & Eivers, A. (2018). Travelling without a destination? A dialogical analysis of professional identity construction among Australian psychology double degree students. *Identity: An International Journal of Theory and Research, 18*, 94–108. https://doi.org/10.1080/15283488.2018.1447483

Bastos, A. C. (2017). Shadow trajectories: The poetic motion of motherhood meanings through the lens of lived temporality. *Culture & Psychology, 23*(3), 408–422. https://doi.org/10.1177/1354067X16655458

Beck, U., & Beck-Gernsheim, E. (2002). *Individualization: Institutionalized individualism and its social and political consequences.* London: Sage.

Benson, J. (2014). Transition to adulthood. In A. Ben-Arieh, F. Casas, I. Frønes, & J. Korbin (Eds.), *Handbook of child well-being* (pp. 1763–1783). Dordrecht: Springer.

Berger, R. (2015). Now I see it, now I don't: Researcher's position and reflexivity in qualitative research. *Qualitative Research, 15*(2), 219–234. https://doi.org/10.1177/1468794112468475

Bergson, H. (1907). *Loov evolutsioon [Creative evolution]* (M. Ott & H. Sahkai, Trans.). Tallinn: Imamaa.

Berry, J. W. (2009). A critique of critical acculturation. *International Journal of Intercultural Relations, 33*(5), 361–371.

Bertau, M.-C. (2007). Encountering objects and others as a means of passage. *Culture & Psychology, 13*(3), 335–352.

Bhatia, S., & Ram, A. (2001). Rethinking 'acculturation' in relation to diasporic cultures and postcolonial identities. *Human Development, 44*(1), 1–18.

Blatterer, H. (2007). Contemporary adulthood. Reconceptualizing an uncontested category. *Current Sociology, 55*(6), 771–792.

Boesch, E. E. (1991). *Symbolic action theory and cultural psychology*. Berlin: Springer-Verlag.

Bowles, A., Fisher, R., McPhail, R., Rosenstreich, D., & Dobson, A. (2014). Staying the distance: Students' perceptions of enablers of transition to higher education. *Higher Education Research & Development, 33*(2), 212–225. https://doi.org/10.1080/07294360.2013.832157

Briggs, A. R. J., Clark, J., & Hall, I. (2012). Building bridges: Understanding student transition to university. *Quality in Higher Education, 18*(1), 3–21. https://doi.org/10.1080/13538322.2011.614468

Brinkmann, S. (2010). Character, personality, and identity: On historical aspects of human subjectivity. *Nordic Psychology, 62*(1), 65–85.

Bühler, C., & Massarik, F. (Eds.). (1968). *The course of human life. A study of goals in the humanistic perspective*. New York: Springer.

Buote, V. M., Pancer, S. M., Pratt, M. W., Adams, G., Birnie-Lefcovitch, S., Polivy, J., et al. (2007). The importance of friends: Friendship and adjustment among 1st-year university students. *Journal of Adolescent Research, 22*(6), 665–689. https://doi.org/10.1177/0743558407306344

Büscher, M., Urry, J., & Witchger, K. (Eds.). (2010). *Mobile methods*. London: Routledge.

Bynner, J. (2005). Rethinking the youth phase of the life-course: The case for emerging adulthood? *Journal of Youth Studies, 8*(4), 367–384. https://doi.org/10.1080/13676260500431628

Cole, M. (1996). *Cultural psychology. A once and future discipline*. Cambridge, MA: Harvard University Press.

Collins, W. A., & van Dulmen, M. (2006). Friendships and romance in emerging adulthood: Assessing distinctiveness in close relationships. In J. J. Arnett & J. L. Tanner (Eds.), *Emerging adults in America: Coming of age in the 21st century* (pp. 219–234). Washington, DC: American Psychological Association.

Costall, A. (2007). The windowless room: 'Mediationism' and how to get over it. In J. Valsiner & A. Rosa (Eds.), *The Cambridge handbook of sociocultural psychology* (pp. 109–123). Cambridge: Cambridge University Press.

Côté, J. E. (2014). The dangerous myth of emerging adulthood: An evidence-based critique of a flawed developmental theory. *Applied Developmental Science, 18*(4), 177–188. https://doi.org/10.1080/10888691.2014.954451

Crafter, S., Maunder, R., & Soulsby, L. (2019). *Developmental transitions: Exploring stability and change through the lifespan*. London and New York: Routledge.

Cresswell, T. (2010). Towards a politics of mobility. *Environment and Planning D: Society and Space, 28,* 17–31. https://doi.org/10.1068/d11407

Dahinden, J. (2012). Transnational belonging, non-ethnic forms of identification and diverse mobilities: Rethinking migrant integration? In M. Messer, R. Schroeder, & R. Wodak (Eds.), *Migrations: Interdisciplinary perspectives* (pp. 117–128). Wien: Springer-Verlag.

Dahinden, J. (2013). Cities, migrant incorporation, and ethnicity: A network perspective on boundary work. *International Migration & Integration, 14,* 39–60. https://doi.org/10.1007/s12134-011-0224-2

Daniels, H. (2001). *Vygotsky and pedagogy*. London and New York: Routledge Falmer.

de Abreu, G., & Hale, H. (2011). Trajectories of cultural identity development of young immigrant people: The impact of family practices. *Psychological Studies, 56*(1), 53–61. https://doi.org/10.1007/s12646-011-0061-6

Després, C. (1991). The meaning of home: Literature review and directions for future research and theoretical development. *Journal of Architectural and Planning Research, 8*(2), 96–115.

Diriwächter, R. (2004). Ganzheitspsychologie: The doctrine. *From Past to Future. Clark Papers on the History of Psychology, 5*(1), 3–16.

Diriwächter, R., & Valsiner, J. (2005). Qualitative developmental research methods in their historical and epistemological contexts [53 paragraphs]. *Forum Qualitative Sozialforschung/Forum: Qualitative Social Research [Online Journal], 7*(1), Art 8.

Diriwächter, R., & Valsiner, J. (Eds.). (2008). *Striving for the whole. Creating theoretical syntheses*. New Brunswick, NJ: Transaction Publishers.

Dodds, A. E., Lawrence, J. A., & Valsiner, J. (1997). The personal and the social: Mead's theory of the 'generalized other'. *Theory & Psychology, 7*(4), 483–503.

Dovey, K. (1985). Home and homelessness. In I. Altman & C. M. Werner (Eds.), *Home environments* (pp. 33–64). New York: Plenum Press.

du Bois-Reymond, M. (2009). Models of navigation and life management. In A. Furlong (Ed.), *Handbook of youth and young adulthood. New perspectives and agendas* (pp. 31–38). New York: Routledge.

Eade, J. (2013). Crossing boundaries and identification processes. *Integrative Psychological & Behavioral Science, 47,* 509–515. https://doi.org/10.1007/s12124-013-9244-0

Edwards, A. (2005). Relational agency: Learning to be a resourceful practitioner. *International Journal of Educational Research, 43*(3), 168–182.

Eisenhardt, K. M. (1989). Building theories from case study research. *Academy of Management Review, 14*(4), 532–550.

Elliott, A., & Urry, J. (2010). *Mobile lives*. New York: Routledge.

Erikson, E. H. (1968). *Identity. Youth and crisis*. New York: W.W. Norton & Co.

Español, A., Marsico, G., & Tateo, L. (2018). Maintaining borders: From border guards to diplomats. *Human Affairs: Postdisciplinary Humanities & Social Sciences Quarterly, 28*(4), 443–460. https://doi.org/10.1515/humaff-2018-0036

Falmagne, R. J. (2004). On the constitution of 'self' and 'mind'. *Theory & Psychology, 14*(6), 822–845.

Flick, U. (2014). *An introduction to qualitative research* (5th ed.). London: Sage.

Flyvberg, B. (2001). *Making social science matter. Why social inquiry fails and how it can succeed again*. Cambridge: Cambridge University Press.

Fuhrer, U. (2004). *Cultivating minds. Identity as meaning-making practice*. London and New York: Routledge.

Furlong, A. (Ed.). (2009). *Handbook of youth and young adulthood. New perspectives and agendas*. New York: Routledge.

Gee, J. P. (2000). Identity as an analytic lens for research in education. *Review of Research in Education, 25*, 99–125. https://doi.org/10.2307/1167322

Gibson, J. J. (1986). *The ecological approach to visual perception*. London: Lawrence Erlbaum Associates Publishers.

Gillespie, A. (2005). GH Mead: Theorist of the social act. *Journal for the Theory of Social Behaviour, 35*(1), 19–39.

Gillespie, A., Kadianaki, I., & O'Sullivan-Lago, R. (2012). Encountering alterity: Geographic and semantic movements. In J. Valsiner (Ed.), *The Oxford handbook of culture and psychology* (pp. 695–709). Oxford: Oxford University Press.

Gomm, R., Hammersley, M., & Foster, P. (Eds.). (2009). *Case study method*. London: Sage.

Greco, M., & Stenner, P. (2017). From paradox to pattern shift: Conceptualising liminal hotspots and their affective dynamics. *Theory & Psychology, 27*(2), 147–166. https://doi.org/10.1177/0959354317693120

Hasan, R. (2002). Semiotic mediation and mental development in pluralistic societies: Some implications for tomorrow's schooling. In G. Wells & G. Claxton (Eds.), *Learning for life in the 21st century: Sociocultural perspectives on the future of education* (pp. 112–126). Oxford, UK: Blackwell.

Heinz, W. A. (2009). Youth transitions in an age of uncertainty. In A. Furlong (Ed.), *Handbook of youth and young adulthood. New perspectives and agendas* (pp. 3–13). New York: Routledge.

Henderson, S., Holland, J., McGrellis, S., Sharpe, S., & Thomson, R. (2007). *Inventing adulthoods: A biographical approach to youth transitions*. London: Sage.

Hendry, L. B., & Kloep, M. (2010). How universal is emerging adulthood? An empirical example. *Journal of Youth Studies, 13*(2), 169–179. https://doi.org/10.1080/13676260903295067

Hendry, L. B., & Kloep, M. (2011). Lifestyles in emerging adulthood: Who needs stages anyway? In J. J. Arnett, M. Kloep, L. B. Hendry, & J. L. Tanner (Eds.), *Debating emerging adulthood: Stage or process?* (pp. 77–104). Oxford: Oxford University Press.

Hermans, H. J. M. (2001). The dialogical self: Toward a theory of personal and cultural positioning. *Culture & Psychology, 7*(3), 243.

Hermans, H. J. M., Kempen, H. J., & van Loon, R. (1992). The dialogical self: Beyond individualism and rationalism. *American Psychologist, 47*(1), 23–33. https://doi.org/10.1037/0003-066X.47.1.23

Hermans, H. J. M., Konopka, A., Oosterwegel, A., & Zomer, P. (2016). Fields of tension in a boundary-crossing world: Towards a democratic organization of the self. *Integrative Psychological and Behavioral Science*, 1–31. https://doi.org/10.1007/s12124-016-9370-6

Hogg, M. A., Terry, D. J., & White, K. M. (1995). A tale of two stories: A critical comparison of identity theory with social identity theory. *Social Psychology Quarterly, 58*(4), 255–269.

Holland, D., Lachicotte, W., Skinner, D., & Cain, C. (2001). *Identity and agency in cultural worlds*. Cambridge: Harvard University Press.

Holland, D., & Lave, J. (Eds.). (2001). *History in person. Enduring struggles, contentious practice, intimate identities*. Santa Fe: School of American Research Press.

Hviid, P., & Märtsin, M. (Eds.). (2019). *Culture in education and education in cultures: Tensioned dialogues and creative constructions*. Cham: Springer.

Hviid, P., & Villadsen, J. W. (2018). The development of a person: Children's experience of being and becoming within the cultural life course. In A. Rosa & J. Valsiner (Eds.), *Handbook of sociocultural psychology* (pp. 556–574). Cambridge: Cambridge University Press.

Jones, G. (1995). *Leaving home*. Buckingham: Open University Press.

Jones, G. (2000). Experimenting with households and inventing 'home'. *International Social Science Journal, 52*(2), 183–194.

Josephs, I. E. (2002). 'The hopi in me': The construction of a voice in the dialogical self from a cultural psychological perspective. *Theory & Psychology, 12*, 161–173.

Kadianaki, I. (2009). Dramatic life courses: Migrants in the making. In *Dynamic process methodology in the social and developmental sciences* (pp. 477–492). Retrieved from https://doi.org/10.1007/978-0-387-95922-1_21

Kloep, M., & Hendry, L. B. (2011). A systemic approach to the transitions to adulthood. In J. J. Arnett, M. Kloep, L. B. Hendry, & J. L. Tanner (Eds.), *Debating emerging adulthood: Stage or process?* (pp. 53–76). Oxford: Oxford University Press.

Kompridis, N. (2007). Struggling over the meaning of recognition: A matter of identity, justice, or freedom? *European Journal of Political Theory, 6*(3), 277–289. https://doi.org/10.1177/1474885107077311

Koontz Anthony, A., & McCabe, J. (2015). Friendship talk as identity work: Defining the self through friend relationships. *Symbolic Interaction, 38*(1), 64–82. https://doi.org/10.1002/SYMB.138

Kress, G. R. (2010). *Multimodality: A social semiotic approach to contemporary communication.* London: Routledge.

Kylén, M., Löfqvist, C., Haak, M., & Iwarsson, S. (2019). Meaning of home and health dynamics among younger older people in Sweden. *European Journal of Ageing,* 1–11. https://doi.org/10.1007/s10433-019-00501-5

Lawrence, J. A., & Valsiner, J. (1993). Conceptual roots of internalization: From transmission to transformation. *Human Development, 36*(1), 150–167.

Lawrence, J. A., & Valsiner, J. (2003). Making personal sense. An account of basic internalization and externalization processes. *Theory & Psychology, 13*(6), 723–752.

Leese, M. (2010). Bridging the gap: Supporting student transitions into higher education. *Journal of Further and Higher Education, 34*(2), 239–251. https://doi.org/10.1080/03098771003695494

Levine, D. N. (Ed.). (1971). *Georg Simmel on individuality and social forms. Selected writings.* Chicago: The University of Chicago Press.

Levinson, D. J. (1986). A conception of adult development. *American Psychologist, 41*, 3–13. https://doi.org/10.1037/0003-066X.41.1.3

Levitan, D. (2019). The art of living in transitoriness: Strategies of families in repeated geographical mobility. *Integrative Psychological & Behavioral Science, 53*, 258–282. https://doi.org/10.1007/s12124-018-9448-4

Mallett, S. (2004). Understanding home: A critical review of the literature. *The Sociological Review, 52*(1), 62–89. https://doi.org/10.1111/j.1467-954X.2004.00442.x

Mannay, D. (2010). Making the familiar strange: Can visual research methods render the familiar setting more perceptible? *Qualitative Research, 10*(1), 91–111. https://doi.org/10.1177/1468794109348684

Manzo, L. C. (2005). For better or worse: Exploring multiple dimensions of place meaning. *Journal of Environmental Psychology, 25*(1), 67–86.

Manzo, L. C. (2014). On uncertain ground: Being at home in the context of public housing redevelopment. *Journal of Housing Policy, 14*(4), 389–410. https://doi.org/10.1080/14616718.2014.947125

Marcia, J. E. (2002). Identity and psychosocial development in adulthood. *Identity: An International Journal of Theory and Research, 2*(1), 7–28.

Marková, I. (2003). Constitution of the self: Intersubjectivity and dialogicality. *Culture & Psychology, 9*(3), 249–259.

Marsico, G. (2016). The borderland. *Culture & Psychology, 22*(2), 206–215. https://doi.org/10.1177/1354067X15601199

Marsico, G., & Tateo, L. (2017). Borders, tensegrity and development in dialogue. *Integrative Psychological & Behavioral Science, 51*(4), 536–556. https://doi.org/10.1007/s12124-017-9398-2

Märtsin, M. (2010). Identity in dialogue: Identity as hyper-generalized personal sense. *Theory & Psychology, 20*, 436–450. https://doi.org/10.1177/0959354310363513

Märtsin, M. (2012). A dismantled jigsaw: Making sense of the complex intertwinement of theory, phenomena and methods. In E. Abbey & S. Surgan (Eds.), *Emerging methods in psychology* (pp. 101–119). New Brunswick, NJ: Transaction Publishers.

Märtsin, M. (2017). Beyond verbal narratives: Using timeline images in the semiotic cultural study of meaning making. *Integrative Psychological and Behavioral Science.* https://doi.org/10.1007/s12124-017-9409-3

Märtsin, M. (2018). On the possibility of becoming otherwise. In B. Wagoner, I. Bresco, & S. Zadeh (Eds.), *Memory in the wild* (p. TBC). Charlotte, NC: Information Age.

Märtsin, M., Chang, I., & Obst, P. (2016). Using culture to manage the transition into university: Conceptualising the dynamics of withdrawal and engagement. *Culture & Psychology, 22*, 276–295. https://doi.org/10.1177/1354067X15621476

Märtsin, M., & Mahmoud, H. (2012). Never at home? Migrants between societies. In J. Valsiner (Ed.), *The Oxford handbook of culture and psychology* (pp. 730–745). Oxford: Oxford University Press.

Maunder, R. E., Cunliffe, M., Galvin, J., Mjali, S., & Rogers, J. (2013). Listening to student voices: Student researchers exploring undergraduate experiences of university transition. *Higher Education, 66*(2), 139–152. https://doi.org/10.1007/s10734-012-9595-3

McNamara Barry, C., Madsen, S. D., Nelson, L. J., Carroll, J. S., & Badger, S. (2009). Friendship and romantic relationship qualities in emerging adulthood: Differential associations with identity development and achieved adulthood criteria. *Journal of Adult Development, 16*, 209–222.

Mead, G. H. (1934). *Mind, self and society from the standpoint of a social behaviorist*. Chicago: The University of Chicago Press.

Molenaar, P. C. M. (2004). A manifesto on psychology as idiographic science: Brining the person back into scientific psychology, this time forever. *Measurement, 2*(4), 201–218.

Molenaar, P. C. M., Huizenga, H. M., & Nesselroade, J. R. (2002). The relationship between the structure of inter-individual and intra-individual variability. In U. Staudinger & U. Lindenberger (Eds.), *Understanding human development* (pp. 339–360). Dordrecht: Klüwer.

Molenaar, P. C. M., & Valsiner, J. (2005). How generalization works through the single case: A simple idiographic process analysis of an individual psychotherapy [40 paragraphs]. *International Journal of Idiographic Science* [Online Journal], Art. 1. Retrieved April 4, 2008, from http://www.valsiner.com/articles/molenvals.htm

Moore, J. (2000). Placing home in context. *Journal of Environmental Psychology, 20*, 207–217.

Motzkau, J. F., & Clinch, M. (2017). Managing suspended transition in medicine and law: Liminal hotspots as resources for change. *Theory & Psychology, 27*(2), 270–289. https://doi.org/10.1177/0959354317700517

Neugarten, B. L. (1979). Time, age, and the life cycle. *American Journal of Psychiatry, 136*, 887–894. https://doi.org/10.1176/ajp.136.7.887

Peirce, C. S. (1932). On sign. In C. Hartshorne & P. Weiss (Eds.), *Collected papers of Charles Sanders Peirce (Volume II)*. Cambridge, MA: Harvard University Press.

Phinney, J. S., Horenczyk, G., Liebkind, K., & Vedder, P. (2001). Ethnic identity, immigration, and well-being: An interactional perspective. *Journal of Social Issues, 57*(3), 493–510.

Phinney, J. S., & Ong, A. D. (2007). Conceptualization and measurement of ethnic identity: Current status and future directions. *Journal of Counseling Psychology, 54*(3), 271.

Piaget, J., & Inhelder, B. (1969). *The psychology of the child*. New York: Basic Books.

Plöger, J., & Kubiak, S. (2019). Becoming 'the internationals'—How place shapes the sense of belonging and group formation of high-skilled migrants. *Journal of International Migration and Integration, 20*, 307–321. https://doi.org/10.1007/s12134-018-0608-7

Rosa, A. (2007). Dramaturgical actuations and symbolic communication. Or how beliefs make up reality. In J. Valsiner & A. Rosa (Eds.), *The Cambridge handbook of sociocultural psychology* (pp. 293–317). Cambridge: Cambridge University Press.

Roth, W. M. (2007). The ethico-moral nature of identity: Prolegomena to the development of third-generation cultural-historical activity theory. *International Journal of Educational Research, 46*(1–2), 83–93.

Roy, N., Dubé, R., Després, C., Freitas, A., & Légaré, F. (2018). Choosing between staying at home or moving: A systematic review of factors influencing housing decisions among frail older adults. *PLoS ONE, 13*(1), e0189266. https://doi.org/10.1371/journal.pone.0189266

Rudmin, F. (2009). Constructs, measurements and models of acculturation and acculturative stress. *International Journal of Intercultural Relations, 33*(2), 106–123.

Salamońska, J., & Czeranowska, O. (2019). Janus-faced mobilities: Motivations for migration among European youth in times of crisis. *Journal of Youth Studies, 0*(0), 1–17. https://doi.org/10.1080/13676261.2019.1569215

Salvatore, S. (2015). *Psychology in black and white: The project of a theory-driven science*. Charlotte, NC: Information Age Publishing.

Salvatore, S. (2018). Culture as dynamics of sense-making. A semiotic and embodied framework for socio-cultural psychology. In J. Valsiner (Ed.), *Cambridge handbook of culture and psychology* (pp. 35–48). Cambridge: Cambridge University Press.

Sato, T., Yasuda, Y., Kido, A., Arakawa, A., Mizoguchi, H., & Valsiner, J. (2007). Sampling reconsidered: Idiographic science and the analysis of personal life trajectories. In J. Valsiner & A. Rosa (Eds.), *The Cambridge handbook of socio-cultural psychology* (pp. 82–106). Cambridge: Cambridge University Press.

Sawyer, R. K. (2002). Unresolved tensions in sociocultural theory: Analogies with contemporary sociological debates. *Culture & Psychology, 8*(3), 283–305.

Shi-xu. (2006). Mind, self and consciousness as discourse. *New Ideas in Psychology, 24*(1), 63–81.

Shotter, J. (2003). 'Real presences': Meaning as living movement in a participatory world. *Theory & Psychology, 13*, 435–468.

Shotter, J. (2008). *Conversational realities revisited: Life, language, body and world*. Chagrin Falls, OH: Taos Institute.

Shotter, J., & Gergen, K. J. (1989). *Texts of identity*. London: Sage Publications.

Singh, P., Brown, R., & Märtsin, M. (2012). Negotiating pedagogic dilemmas in non-traditional educational contexts. An Australian case study of teachers' work. In H. Daniels (Ed.), *Vygotsky & sociology* (pp. 93–113). London: Routledge.

Sonesson, G. (2010). Here comes the semiotic species: Reflections on the semiotic turn in the cognitive sciences. In B. Wagoner (Ed.), *Symbolic transformation. The mind in movement through culture and society* (pp. 38–58). London and New York: Routledge.

Stein, C. H., Petrowski, C. E., Gonzales, S. M., Mattei, G. M., Hratl Majcher, J., Froemming, M. W., et al. (2018). A matter of life and death: Understanding continuing bonds and post-traumatic growth when young adults experience the loss of a close friend. *Journal of Child and Family Studies, 27*(3), 725–738. https://doi.org/10.1007/s10826-017-0943-x

Stenner, P. (2017). *Liminality and experience. A transdisciplinary approach to the psychosocial.* London: Palgrave.

Stets, J. E., & Burke, P. J. (2000). Identity theory and social identity theory. *Social Psychology Quarterly, 63*(3), 224–237.

Stetsenko, A. (2005). Activity as object-related: Resolving the dichotomy of individual and collective planes of activity. *Mind, Culture and Activity, 12*(1), 70–88.

Stetsenko, A., & Arievitch, I. M. (2004). The self in cultural-historical activity theory. *Theory & Psychology, 14*(4), 475–503.

Stryker, S., & Burke, P. J. (2000). The past, present, and future of an identity theory. *Social Psychology Quarterly, 63*(4), 284–297.

Swenson, L. M., Nordstrom, A., & Hiester, M. (2008). The role of peer relationships in adjustment to college. *Journal of College Student Development, 49*(6), 551–567.

Symonds, J. (2015). *Understanding school transition: What happens to children and how to help them.* London: Routledge.

Szakolczai, A. (2015). Liminality and experience. Structuring transitory situations and transformative events. In A. Horvath, B. Thomassen, & H. Wydra (Eds.), *Breaking boundaries: Varieties of liminality* (pp. 11–38). New York: Berghahn Books.

Szakolczai, Á. (2017). Permanent (trickster) liminality: The reasons of the heart and of the mind. *Theory & Psychology, 27*(2), 231–248. https://doi.org/10.1177/0959354317694095

Tanner, J. L., & Arnett, J. J. (2009). The emergence of 'emerging adulthood'. The new life stage between adolescence and young adulthood. In A. Furlong (Ed.), *Handbook of youth and young adulthood. New perspectives and agendas* (pp. 39–45). London and New York: Routledge.

Tanner, J. L., & Arnett, J. J. (2011). Presenting 'emerging adulthood': What makes it developmentally distinctive? In J. J. Arnett, M. Kloep, L. B. Hendry, & J. L. Tanner (Eds.), *Debating emerging adulthood: Stage or process?* (pp. 13–30). Oxford: Oxford University Press.

Tateo, L., & Marsico, G. (2013). The self as tension of wholeness and emptiness. *Interaccoes, 9*(24), 1–19.

Thomson, R. (2011). *Unfolding lives: Youth, gender and change.* Bristol: The Policy Press.

Thomson, R., Bell, R., Holland, J., Henderson, S., McGrellis, S., & Sharpe, S. (2002). Critical moments: Choice, chance and opportunity in young people's narratives of transition. *Sociology, 36*(2), 335–354.

Toomela, A. (2007). Culture of science: Strange history of the methodological thinking in psychology. *Integrative Psychological and Behavioral Science, 41*, 6–20.

Toomela, A., & Valsiner, J. (Eds.). (2010). *Methodological thinking in psychology. Have 60 years gone astray?* Charlotte, NC: Information Age Publishing.

Urry, J., & Grieco, M. (Eds.). (2012). *Mobilities: New perspectives on transport and society*. London: Routledge.

Valsiner, J. (1998). *The guided mind. A sociogenetic approach to personality*. Cambridge: Harvard University Press.

Valsiner, J. (2000). Data as representations: Contextualizing qualitative and quantitative research strategies. *Social Science Information, 39*(1), 99–113.

Valsiner, J. (2001). Process structure of semiotic mediation in human development. *Human Development, 44*, 84–97.

Valsiner, J. (2002). Forms of dialogical relations and semiotic autoregulation within the self. *Theory & Psychology, 12*(2), 251–265.

Valsiner, J. (2005). Scaffolding within the structure of dialogical self: Hierarchical dynamics of semiotic mediation. *New Ideas in Psychology, 23*(3), 197–206.

Valsiner, J. (2007a). *Culture in minds and societies: Foundations of cultural psychology*. New Delhi: Sage Publications.

Valsiner, J. (2007b). Human development as migration: Striving toward the unknown. In *Otherness in question: Labyrinths of the self* (pp. 349–378). Charlotte: Information Age Publishing.

Valsiner, J. (2007c). Semiotic autoregulation: Dynamic sign hierarchies constraining the stream of consciousness. *Sign System Studies, 35*(1/2).

Valsiner, J. (2014). *An invitation to cultural psychology*. London: Sage.

Valsiner, J. (2017). *From methodology to methods in human psychology*. Cham: Springer.

Valsiner, J., & Diriwächter, R. (2008). Conclusion: Returning to the whole—A new theoretical synthesis in the social sciences. In *Striving for the whole: Creating theoretical synthesis* (pp. 211–237). New Brunswick: Transaction Publishers.

Valsiner, J., & Van der Veer, R. (2000). *The social mind: Construction of the idea*. Cambridge: Cambridge University Press.

Van der Veer, R. (1994). Pierre Janet's relevance for a socio-cultural approach. In A. Rosa & J. Valsiner (Eds.), *Explorations in socio-cultural studies. Vol. 1. Historical and theoretical discourse* (pp. 205–209). Madrid: Fundación Infancia y Aprendizaje.

Van der Veer, R., & Valsiner, J. (1991). *Understanding Vygotsky: A quest for synthesis*. Cambridge: Blackwell.

Villadsen, J. W. (2019). Children's development—Between personal engagements and curriculum based pre-school practices. In P. Hviid & M. Märtsin (Eds.), *Culture in education and education in culture. Tensioned dialogues and creative constructions* (p. TBC). Cham: Springer.

Vygotsky, L. S. (1978). *Mind in society. The development of higher psychological processes*. Cambridge: Harvard University Press.

Vygotsky, L. S. (1987). *The collected works of L. S. Vygotsky, volume I. Problems of general psychology*. New York: Plenum Press.

Vygotsky, L. S. (1989). Concrete human psychology. *Soviet Psychology, 27*(2), 53–77.

Wagoner, B. (2009). The experimental methodology of constructive microgenesis. In J. Valsiner, P. Molenaar, N. Chaudhary, & M. Lyra (Eds.), *Handbook of dynamic process methodology in the social and developmental sciences* (pp. 99–121). New York: Springer.

Wardhaugh, J. (1999). The unaccommodated woman: Home, homelessness and identity. *The Sociological Review, 47*(1), 91–109.

Wartofsky, M. (1979). *Models—Representations and the scientific understanding*. Dodrecht and Boston: Reidel.

Wertsch, J. V. (2007). Mediation. In H. Daniels, M. Cole, & J. V. Wertsch (Eds.), *The Cambridge companion to Vygotsky* (pp. 178–192). New York: Cambridge University Press.

Wilcox, P., Winn, S., & Fyvie-Gauld, M. (2005). 'It was nothing to do with the university, it was just the people': The role of social support in the first-year experience of higher education. *Studies in Higher Education, 30*(6), 707–722. https://doi.org/10.1080/03075070500340036

Woodhall-Melnik, J., Hamilton-Wright, S., Daoud, N., Matheson, F. I., Dunn, J. R., & O'Campo, P. (2017). Establishing stability: Exploring the meaning of 'home' for women who have experienced intimate partner violence. *Journal of Housing and the Built Environment, 32*(2), 253–268. https://doi.org/10.1007/s10901-016-9511-8

Yin, R. K. (2003). *Case study research: Design and methods* (3rd ed.). Newbury Park: Sage Publications.

Zittoun, T. (2004). Symbolic competencies for developmental transitions: The case of the choice of first names. *Culture & Psychology, 10*(2), 131.

Zittoun, T. (2007a). Dynamics of interiority. Ruptures and transitions in the self development. In L. M. Simão & J. Valsiner (Eds.), *Otherness in question. Labyrinths of the self* (pp. 187–214). Charlotte: Information Age Publishing.

Zittoun, T. (2007b). Symbolic resources in dialogue, dialogical symbolic resources. *Culture & Psychology, 13*(3), 365–377.

Zittoun, T. (2007c). The role of symbolic resources in human lives. In J. Valsiner & A. Rosa (Eds.), *The Cambridge handbook of sociocultural psychology* (pp. 343–361). Cambridge: Cambridge University Press.

Zittoun, T. (2012). Life-course: A socio-cultural perspective. In J. Valsiner (Ed.), *The Oxford handbook of culture and psychology* (pp. 513–535). New York: Oxford University Press.

Zittoun, T. (2017). Modalities of generalization through single case studies. *Integrative Psychological and Behavioral Science, 51*(2), 171–194. https://doi.org/10.1007/s12124-016-9367-1

Zittoun, T., Duveen, G., Gillespie, A., Ivinson, G., & Psaltis, C. (2003). The use of symbolic resources in developmental transitions. *Culture & Psychology, 9*(4), 415.

Zittoun, T., Levitan, D., & Cangiá, F. (2018). A sociocultural approach to mobile families: A case study. *Peace and Conflict: Journal of Peace Psychology, 24*(4), 424–432. https://doi.org/10.1037/pac0000313

Zittoun, T., Valsiner, J., Vedeler, D., Salgado, J., Gonçalves, M. M., & Ferring, D. (2013). *Human development in the life course. Melodies of living.* Cambridge: Cambridge University Press.

Index[1]

A

Abstractive generalisation, 35
Adulthood, 1–18, 46, 76, 86, 94, 95,
 99, 100, 105, 106, 125,
 145–147, 152, 155, 161–163,
 167, 168, 172, 176
Adventure, 11, 13, 16, 73, 83–102,
 157
Affirmation, 119, 127, 128, 141,
 160, 162, 163
Affordance, 12, 30, 159, 175
Ambiguity, 35, 57, 93, 101
Ambivalence, 35, 36, 39, 43–45,
 101, 110, 118, 174
Anticipated future, 13, 14, 35, 39,
 41, 42, 56, 173
Artefact, 26
Auto-regulation, 35, 72, 162

B

Becoming, 1, 8, 15, 24, 38–42, 45,
 46, 53, 56, 60, 62–65, 78, 86,
 92–99, 109, 116, 118, 120,
 122, 126, 127, 134–135, 139,
 147, 151, 162, 168, 170, 174,
 175
Being in-between, 93, 100, 115,
 160, 162
Being on the move, 1, 11–13, 17,
 101–102, 106, 167
Belonging, 13, 14, 16, 27, 46,
 73, 83–102, 129, 139,
 142
Border-crossing, 65, 88, 106
Border-making, 16, 18, 44, 55, 86,
 87, 89, 92, 106, 107, 121,
 122, 169–172

---

[1] Note: Page numbers followed by 'n' refer to notes.

© The Author(s) 2019
M. Märtsin, *Identity Development in the Lifecourse*, Sociocultural Psychology of the
Lifecourse, https://doi.org/10.1007/978-3-030-27753-6

Borders, 5, 17, 18, 26, 27, 33, 34,
    44, 54, 55, 89–92, 97–99,
    106, 107, 109, 122, 169–174
  semiotic, 107
Border zone, 89, 91, 97, 98, 109,
    111, 162

C

Case study, 11–18, 23, 46, 60–62,
    65, 73, 86, 87, 93, 100, 101,
    107, 116, 117, 121, 122, 126,
    128, 134, 140–142, 147, 148,
    163, 164, 167, 171, 172
Change, 3, 4, 6, 7, 9, 29, 30, 39, 43,
    45, 46, 57, 59, 62, 70–72, 86,
    95–97, 101, 108, 113, 118,
    126, 158, 167, 169, 172, 175
Competence, 17, 73, 125–142
Conduct, 6, 7, 13, 17, 24, 38–41,
    54, 56, 60, 66, 76, 101, 128,
    147, 160, 163
Constraining, 29, 31, 33, 85, 98,
    156, 158, 170, 171
Constraint, 9, 12, 86, 157
Continuity, 3, 8, 13, 23, 35, 43, 45,
    84, 86, 99, 131, 134, 141, 148
Cultural system, 12, 76, 85, 167
Culture
  collective, 26–31, 73, 110
  personal, 26–28

D

Data, 16, 53, 54, 58, 60, 61, 63–66,
    69–72, 75–78
Development, 1–18, 23–46, 53–78,
    85, 87, 96, 98–101, 106, 119,
    121, 125–127, 146, 147, 162,
    163, 167–170, 172, 174, 176
Dialectics, 16, 85, 100, 156
Dialogue, 2, 4, 31, 34–38, 40, 43,
    72, 75, 92, 98, 101, 140, 149
Dilemma, 4, 114, 116, 118, 146,
    147, 152, 154, 155, 163
Distancing, 17, 36, 121, 153
Duration, 5, 175
Dynamic system, 56

E

Early adulthood, 10, 105, 167, 168
Educational transition, 17, 125, 142
Emergence, 1, 24, 54–58, 61, 64,
    87, 169, 174
Emerging adulthood, 8–10, 15, 149,
    150, 172
Enabling, 7, 29, 85, 89, 98, 150,
    158, 170, 171
Environment, 2, 5, 6, 12, 15–17,
    25–28, 30, 32, 37, 55–58, 74,
    88, 90–95, 99–101, 107, 108,
    113, 117, 119–121, 125,
    127–129, 132, 133, 135–141,
    147, 152, 156, 157, 159, 160,
    168, 170, 171, 175
Experience, 3, 4, 6, 7, 10, 12–14,
    16, 17, 24, 27, 36, 38–46,
    53–58, 60, 64–67, 69–74,
    76–78, 83–87, 89–91, 93, 94,
    97–102, 106–121, 125–136,
    138, 141, 142, 146, 150,
    152–156, 163, 164, 167–170,
    173–175
Externalisation, 27, 28, 30, 35, 55,
    65

F

Feed-forward, 37, 39, 40
Flow of being, 6, 12, 42, 43, 65,
    106, 109, 156
Friendships, 17, 105, 106, 113–115,
    118–120, 122, 127
Future, 3, 7, 12–14, 17, 18, 27,
    38–46, 54–58, 60, 61, 66, 72,
    83, 86, 87, 95, 96, 102, 107,
    110–113, 119, 120, 126–130,
    132–136, 138, 141, 142,
    145–147, 149–152, 154, 156,
    158, 159, 162–164, 167–169,
    171–175
Future-orientation, 16, 44, 111,
    148

G

Generalisation, 10, 13, 38, 53, 58,
    59, 61, 62
Goal orientation, 148
Guidance
    cultural, 40
    semiotic, 110

H

Home, 10, 12–14, 16, 61, 73,
    83–102, 106–108, 112–114,
    118–120, 125, 129, 134, 137,
    140, 142, 147, 148, 151–164,
    168, 173
Hyper-generalisation, 36,
    38
Hyper-generalised meta-signs, 16,
    36–38, 42, 43, 46, 131, 136,
    148, 168

I

Identity, 1–18, 23–46, 53–78, 84,
    85, 87, 92, 95, 96, 98–100,
    106, 107, 113–115, 119, 121,
    122, 125, 127–130, 132–135,
    140, 141, 147, 148, 150, 154,
    156, 160, 163, 168–176
Identity development, 1–18, 23–46,
    53–78, 85, 96, 98, 99, 99,
    106, 119, 121, 127, 147, 163,
    168, 169, 170, 172, 174, 176
Idiographic, 59–62
Idiosyncratic, 8, 26, 29, 42, 53, 58,
    60, 62, 126
Imagination, 6, 55, 96, 100, 151,
    157, 171, 173
Imagined future, 41, 57, 147, 148,
    151, 152, 154, 164, 173, 175
Inseparability, 16, 25
Internalisation, 24, 27–30, 55
Intertwinement, 5, 16, 30, 53
Intra-psychological system, 31, 33,
    37, 55, 57, 147
Irreversible time, 40, 55, 56, 61

J

Journey/journeying, 7, 13, 15, 16,
    31, 84–88, 92, 100, 125, 126,
    133, 135, 138, 141, 149, 167,
    170, 173

L

Laminal model, 33, 34, 42
Lifecourse, 3, 5–7, 14, 18, 41–46,
    86, 105, 116, 134, 146, 147,
    161, 167, 172, 174

Life-goal, 13, 41, 42, 45, 56, 72, 98,
101, 107, 115–119, 121, 122,
128, 131, 140, 146, 147, 152,
158, 159, 161, 163, 164, 173
Life-goal orientation, 118, 119, 139,
153–155, 174
Liminal, 44, 45, 98, 101, 109, 110,
162, 169, 173
Liminality, 37, 44, 45, 101

M
Making plans, 18, 73, 145–165
Meaning, 1, 3, 4, 11, 12, 16, 24,
26–35, 37–46, 55, 57, 64–72,
83–87, 95, 98, 100, 109–111,
113, 115, 117, 120, 128, 130,
131, 136–138, 142, 150, 152,
154, 157, 159, 162, 169–171,
173, 174
Meaning field, 35, 43, 57, 72, 76,
85, 89, 92, 96, 108, 109,
111–113, 115, 117, 120, 121,
130, 138, 151, 152, 154,
156–158, 161, 162, 169
Meaning-making, 1–4, 10, 12–18,
23, 25, 30, 32–42, 46, 55–57,
65, 69, 71–73, 71n1, 77, 90,
91, 96, 98, 100, 108, 110,
114, 118, 121, 147, 151, 154,
161, 163, 167–175
Meta-signs, 16, 34–38, 40–43, 46,
64, 111, 117, 131, 136,
147–148, 154, 168, 169, 173
Methodology, 16, 54, 78, 174
Methodology cycle, 16, 53, 58, 62,
63, 70, 75–78
Methods, 16, 24, 53–78

Migration, 11, 12, 43, 121
Mobile life, 101, 148
Mobility, 1–18, 76, 85, 87, 93, 100,
105, 106, 121, 125, 126, 140,
167, 171
Moving, 3, 9, 12–16, 23, 37, 41, 43,
45, 53, 56, 63, 70, 77, 85, 86,
93, 94, 99, 100, 107, 108,
110–113, 116, 119, 127–129,
132–134, 140, 149–153, 156,
162–164, 167–176
Multi-furcation point, 57, 134, 149
Multiple-case study, 60–63
Mutual transformation, 6, 25, 171

N
Nomothetic research, 61

O
Open system, 25, 27, 170, 171
Oppositional, 89, 96, 109, 111, 112,
117, 151, 152, 154, 161
Otherness, 12, 43, 97, 98, 100
Others, 2–4, 17, 18, 27, 28, 31, 37,
38, 42, 44, 55, 67, 76, 77,
83–85, 87, 89–94, 97, 99,
101, 107, 114, 167–175

P
Pathway, 5, 7–10, 17, 29, 127, 133,
134, 141, 145, 150, 151, 173
Person and environment
intertwinement, 5
Person and environment relationship,
170

Pre-adaptation, 42, 55, 56, 173
Process, 2–6, 10, 13–18, 23–30,
    32, 33, 35–46, 53, 55–57,
    59–66, 70, 73–78, 84–89, 92,
    96–98, 101, 106, 107, 111,
    115, 119, 122, 127, 136, 140,
    147, 163, 164, 168–172, 174,
    175
Promoter sign, 40, 41

R

Recognition, 13, 17, 46, 73, 75,
    122, 125–142, 170
Relationships, 5, 9, 11–15, 17,
    28–30, 36, 46, 54–56, 58, 65,
    66, 73, 76–78, 83, 87, 90, 98,
    99, 102, 105–122, 126, 127,
    134, 152–155, 157–159,
    161–163, 168, 170
  intimate, 9, 14, 148, 155
Repeated mobility, 12, 13, 18, 107,
    108, 121, 147, 156, 163, 164,
    173
Rupture, 3, 6, 12, 13, 15, 16, 42–46,
    57, 73, 77, 88, 96, 99,
    106–108, 113, 116, 118,
    127–129, 135, 140, 141, 156,
    168, 169, 173, 175

S

Self, 1–4, 6, 17, 18, 24, 27, 36–38,
    43–46, 84, 85, 87, 92, 97,
    106, 107, 113, 122, 125, 127,
    128, 131, 140, 153, 168–172
Self-confidence, 15, 17, 73, 90, 99,
    125–142

Semi-longitudinal, 13, 62, 64, 174
Semiosis, 37, 38, 55
Semiotic architecture, 36, 38, 43,
    168
Semiotic cultural psychology, 3, 5,
    12, 16, 170
Semiotic hierarchy, 168
Semiotic mediation, 16, 24, 27–31,
    36, 55
Semiotic move, 90, 91, 93, 107, 111,
    115, 117, 121, 122, 157, 167,
    171
Semiotic organisation
Semiotic regulator, 42, 56, 171
Semiotic tool, 172
Sign, 3, 4, 15, 25, 27, 32–40, 42, 43,
    55, 56, 58, 64, 111, 136, 151,
    168, 171, 173–175
Sign construction, 34–36, 39–42,
    55
Sociocultural environment, 17, 30,
    37, 55–57, 94, 101, 128, 132,
    138, 139, 152, 160, 171
Sociocultural life-course studies, 3, 5,
    18
Sociocultural perspective, 25
Space, 1–3, 5, 13, 23, 26, 27, 29–31,
    42, 55, 57, 69, 70, 73, 83, 84,
    91, 93, 98, 101, 109, 111,
    158, 161, 162
System, 11, 12, 25–28, 38–40, 42,
    43, 55, 56, 59, 61, 76, 85, 137

T

Temporal, 18, 120, 163, 169,
    172–174
Tensegrity, 39, 43, 56

Tension, 14, 18, 29, 31, 35, 39, 40, 43–45, 55–57, 65, 69, 70, 72, 73, 85, 94–96, 100, 101, 106, 110, 112, 113, 116, 118, 120, 126, 130, 131, 137, 138, 147, 152, 153, 155, 157, 158, 161, 162, 164

Time, 1, 3–6, 8, 10, 12–14, 16, 23, 27, 33, 39–43, 54, 56, 59, 60, 62–64, 67–69, 71, 74, 76, 84, 89, 90, 95, 96, 106, 108, 110–112, 114, 117, 118, 129–132, 134–137, 145, 146, 149, 150, 153, 158, 160, 161, 168, 169, 172–175

Timeline, 67–69, 72

Trajectory, 7, 40, 42, 44, 53, 57, 58, 60–62, 66, 72, 85, 87, 99, 110, 119, 120, 122, 128, 132–134, 139, 141, 142, 145, 146, 150, 152, 154, 156, 159–163, 168, 173

Transitional experience, 6, 7, 43, 110

Transitions, 1–18, 33, 42–46, 56, 72, 95, 98–101, 105, 106, 110, 112, 113, 115, 116, 119–122, 126, 127, 129, 135, 140–142, 155, 162, 164, 167–169, 172–174

Transition to adulthood, 1–18, 86, 125, 145, 147, 163, 172

Transition to university, 126, 140, 141

Trouble, 6, 31, 96, 98, 164

U

Uncertainty, 6, 36, 43, 57, 95, 110, 145, 147, 150, 152, 174

V

Voice, 1, 31, 35, 72, 114

W

Ways of being, 6, 16, 44, 45, 85, 86, 94, 97–101, 110, 127, 129, 133, 156, 160, 162

Y

Young adulthood, 8, 10, 105

Printed by Printforce, the Netherlands